Confronting the Nation

GERHARD L. WEINBERG
World in the Balance: Behind the Scenes of World War II   1

RICHARD COBB
French and Germans, Germans and French: A Personal Interpretation of France under Two Occupations, 1914–1918/1940–1944   2

EBERHARD JÄCKEL
Hitler in History   3

FRANCES MALINO and BERNARD WASSERSTEIN, editors
The Jews in Modern France   4

JACOB KATZ
The Darker Side of Genius: Richard Wagner's Anti-Semitism   5

JEHUDA REINHARZ, editor
Living with Antisemitism: Modern Jewish Responses   6

MICHAEL R. MARRUS
The Holocaust in History   7

PAUL MENDES-FLOHR, editor
The Philosophy of Franz Rosenzweig   8

JOAN G. ROLAND
Jews in British India: Identity in a Colonial Era   9

YISRAEL GUTMAN, EZRA MENDEL-SOHN, JEHUDA REINHARZ, and

CHONE SHMERUK, editors
The Jews of Poland Between Two World Wars   10

AVRAHAM BARKAI
From Boycott to Annihilation: The Economic Struggle of German Jews, 1933–1943   11

ALEXANDER ALTMANN
The Meaning of Jewish Existence: Theological Essays 1930–1939   12

MAGDALENA OPALSKI and ISRAEL BARTAL
Poles and Jews: A Failed Brotherhood   13

RICHARD BREITMAN
The Architect of Genocide: Himmler and the Final Solution   14

JEHUDA REINHARZ and WALTER SCHATZBERG, editors
The Jewish Response to German Culture: From the Enlightenment to the Second World War   15

GEORGE L. MOSSE
Confronting the Nation: Jewish and Western Nationalism   16

DANIEL CARPI
Between Mussolini and Hitler: The Jews and the Italian Authorities in France and Tunisia   17

George L. Mosse

Confronting the Nation

Jewish and Western
Nationalism

Brandeis University Press
Published by University Press of New England
Hanover & London

Brandeis University Press

Published by University Press of New England, Hanover, NH 03755

© 1993 by Trustees of Brandeis University

Printed in the United States of America   5   4   3   2   1

UNIVERSITY PRESS OF NEW ENGLAND publishes books under its own imprint and is the publisher for Brandeis University Press, Brown University Press, University of Connecticut, Dartmouth College, Middlebury College Press, University of New Hampshire, University of Rhode Island, Tufts University, University of Vermont, and Wesleyan University Press.

LIBRARY OF CONGRESS CATALOGING-IN-PUBLICATION DATA

Mosse, George L. (George Lachmann), 1918–
    Confronting the nation : Jewish and Western nationalism / George L. Mosse.
        p.   cm. — (The Tauber Institute for the Study of European Jewry series : 16)
    Includes bibliographical references and index.
    ISBN 0–87451–635–8. — ISBN 0–87451–636–6 (pbk.)
    1. Nationalism—Philosophy. 2. Fascism. 3. Jews—Germany—Identity. 4. Zionism—Philosophy. 5. Germany—Ethnic relations. I. Title. II. Series.
JC311.M666   1993
320.5'4—dc20   93–17227

For Yehoshua Arieli

Contents

Confronting the Nation

Introduction:
Confronting the Nation

This book concerns modern nationalism and the Jews who have so often been among its victims. Yet this is not a book about antisemitism or about the persecution of the Jews, but about the changing concept of the nation and how the Jews confronted this change. Our world, even late in the twentieth century, is still a world of nation states, and nationalism still determines to a large extent the collective identity of European men and women. But nationalism was not static; it evolved over a period of time. At first, from the beginning of modern nationalism until the end of the nineteenth century, the quest for political self-determination tended to predominate, and here nationalism retained a flexibility that embraced a variety of political, social, and religious attitudes. Toward the end of the nineteenth century, however, the supposed supremacy and cultural autonomy of the nation challenged this flexibility, as many people came to perceive the nation as a civic religion that determined how people saw the world and their place in it. Thus, for example, "integral nationalism" in France or völkish nationalism in Germany, gained an important foothold from which, after the First World War, they could accelerate their quest for power. Nationalism as a civic religion is the common theme that informs the chapters that follow. Though the book is divided into two parts, one dealing with the nation and the other addressing what the Jews made of it, the identical concern with a heightened and irrational nationalism links both of them.

The self-representation of the nation also engages our particular attention, for it is an important ingredient of all nationalism and vital for the creation of a civic religion. National flags, anthems, festivals, and monuments, among other myths and symbols, helped the nation penetrate the daily life of its people. Nationalism as a civic religion attempted to create a fully worked-out liturgy that, with its symbols and mass actions, would come to direct people's thoughts and deeds. The existence of such a civic religion does not brush aside the social, economic, or political reality, for it was the nation as a living organism that determined the perception of these realities for many people, that attempted to mediate, so to speak, between men and women and the world in which they found themselves. How a nation displayed itself was of crucial importance to the way in which it was perceived; it summed up its ideals and its claims to power.

The book, then, starts with a discussion of how the nation displayed itself to its people. Nations had always represented themselves through their rituals and ceremonies, during which, for example, the singing of a national anthem took place; such anthems, discussed in the next chapter, were perhaps, together with flags, the most widespread means of national self-representation. The nation has displayed itself in many ways, as the first section of this book demonstrates, but in modern times such self-representation has been more often visual and oral than solely through the written word. This, in turn, served to give a new dynamic to the nation. During the last two centuries the masses of the population were emerging as a political force and had to be integrated into the national community. Ritual, songs, and national symbols were used to shape the crowd into a disciplined mass in order to give it direction and maintain control; they nationalized the masses.[1]

The nation at the beginning of modern times aestheticized politics through its self-representation by using visual symbols; not only did it use flags or national monuments, but it left its imprint on official buildings as well, largely through the imposition a national style, such as the Gothic in Germany. Moreover, a national stereotype was created; men (not women) who through their posture and appearance symbolized the nation's strength and discipline—for example, the "new German" or, as we shall see, the "new Jew." It was no coincidence that the aestheticization of politics took place during the nineteenth century when the arts were becoming an integral part of middle-class life. Paintings, music, theater, as well as museums, served to transfigure the real world: art reconciled and comforted a Europe newly transformed by the quickening pace of economic and urban life. The hold of traditional religion was weakening to permit the coexistence of several gods.[2] The nation appealed to the identical need for "the beautiful, true, good, and holy," and in a more democratic age used its display to integrate people and nation. This process, already underway at the beginning of the nineteenth century, truly came into its own at its end. Gustav Le Bon, the influential father of crowd psychology, wrote in 1889 that crowds think in images and that the language they could understand must reflect this fact.[3] His theory was applied with some success by those who wanted to nationalize the masses, to integrate them into the nation, whether before the First World War or in the Europe of the dictators.

Political style became as important as traditional political theory. Through such a style, with its festivals and rituals, its plastic language, the masses were given a feeling of political participation. The chapter on "Political Style and Political Theory" discusses the origins of this political style that was at the center of national self-representation. Its roots have been traced back to the French Revolution, and indeed that revolution has been accused of originating modern populist dictatorships. While it cannot be said to have inspired modern totalitarianism directly, it created a political style that was essential to the self-representation of nations. Two essays below address the relationship of the French Revolution to the heightened nationalism of our times: one, "Political Style and Political Theory," discusses the contribution of the Revolution itself, and the other, "Fascism and the French Revolution," analyzes what fascists at the climax of the civic religion of nationalism thought they owed to its example.

However dictatorial the civic religion of nationalism proved to be in the end, many other definitions of nationhood continued to exist. Nations could present themselves as parliamentary democracies (and the second chapter contains such an example), or they could make more comprehensive claims as a living faith. Here, and throughout the book, other forms of nationhood will be discussed from time to time as alternatives to a nationalism that tended to deprive the individual of any space he could call his own. However, eventually the Jews had to come to terms with nationalism as a civic religion, either toward the end of the nineteenth century, exemplified by the rise of a radical right, or, eventually, through the fascist and national socialist regimes in Europe.

The Jews in the process of assimilation faced social and political obstacles that have found their historians and are of key importance for understanding modern Jewish history. But the Jews also confronted the nation itself as image and reality, and, increasingly, as an all-encompassing ideal. The nation, after all, fulfilled the quest for community at a time when traditional bonds were dissolving, and as the pressures of modernity increased many saw this community exemplified through fascism or the radical right. I have devoted a chapter to an analysis of the radical right's idea of community, which seems to maintain something of its fascination into our time.

While the relationship between the Jews and nationalist movements like fascism and national socialism has been analyzed many times, the confrontation between Jews and the changing concept of the nation has received relatively little attention. We can only give some limited indications of this confrontation here, proceeding by example, as the chapter headings indicate, in order to open up a subject that seems vitally important in an age when so much depended, as it does still today, upon people's perceptions of reality—how it presents itself—rather than on reality itself.

The link between "The Nation Displays Itself" and "The Jew and the Modern Nation"—the two sections of the book—needs emphasis. The first section seeks to throw light upon the self-representation of the nation through various examples, as well as upon its ideal of community, so important to an understanding of the purposes the nation sought to fulfill. The second part of the book deals with the Jews themselves, who for the most part were ill-prepared to confront the new civic religion. Here the scope of the book will contract to focus upon specific German examples. Germany and German Jews become central to our argument. The nation's turn to greater exclusiveness can be clearly demonstrated through this example, while the German Jews themselves, through their strongly articulated liberalism, invoked the coexistence of liberal ideals with modern nationalism.

Jews were essentially liberals, a worldview that, through the Enlightenment, had been instrumental in their emancipation, and that seemed to guarantee the tolerance they needed to exist as Jews in modern society. And indeed, most nations at the time of Jewish emancipation saw no contradiction between liberalism and allegiance to national ideals. We hear from Germany at the beginning of the nineteenth century, for example, that fatherland and mankind are the two ideas that must inform every noble soul; that the man who acts as if he were both a patriot and a citizen of the world is protected against any immoral behavior.[4]

Throughout modern times, as we have mentioned already, one strain of nationhood attempted to follow that tradition and continued to provide room for the Jews to assimilate. But here our concern is with nationalism as it became ever more all-inclusive and in the end made such tolerance impossible. Yet most Jews continued as liberals, and Zionists like Max Nordau and Gershom Scholem, discussed here, though they engaged themselves fully in the Jewish national cause, did not discard their allegiance to liberal principles. There were, of course, exceptions: for example, those right-wing Zionists whose nationalism took on the appearance of a civic religion, and who will be mentioned in our discussion as well; or that third of the Italian Jewish community that was committed to fascist ideology.[5] Nevertheless, liberalism found shelter among the Jews when everywhere else it seemed in decline.

The essay "The Jews and the Civic Religion of Nationalism" deals with the dilemma presented to Jews by a nationalism that rejected liberal traditions, and thus sets the tone for what is to follow in the section on "The Jews and the Modern Nation." However, even the more benign nationalism at the time of German-Jewish emancipation, which could accommodate liberal concerns, contained the seeds of a greater exclusivity. This is worth emphasizing in order not to underestimate the danger inherent in all nationalism. Thus, for example, Johann Gottlieb Fichte turned away from the nationalism and cosmopolitanism of his youth, and in his famous "Speeches to the German Nation" (1808) proclaimed that the German Volk itself was an instrument of divine revelation, the equal of revealed religion. To be sure, its task was different from that of religion. The German Volk was not concerned with eternal life, but instead with how life should be lived on earth. This gave the nation an immediate legitimacy that excluded those who were different. Fichte changed under the influence of Prussia's defeat by Napoleon I and the subsequent French occupation. A century later the First World War, defeat, and the subsequent French occupation once again propelled German nationalism forward. It took on the trappings of a civic religion, and this time its dominance became grim reality. Nationalism varied in strength with the pressure of events, whether war, defeat, economic crises, or simply the strains and stresses of modernity that always lay readily at hand, and that it promised to overcome.

The Jews in Germany faced the increasing strength of this civic religion, but in France, for example, by the end of the nineteenth century, it also held sway among influential political circles as "integral nationalism." And yet, the contrast between Germany and France is illuminating, for while in

France a radical right demanded the exclusion of Jews from the nation, liberalism and a strongly unified concept of nationality could coexist. The most popular and semiofficial history text in French schools in use from before the First through the Second World War, for example, presupposed the existence of a cohesive French nation from the Middle Ages to the present. This France provided no place for any minority, be they Protestants, Jews, or Bretons; the textbook simply ignored their existence.[6] Yet throughout the Third Republic the status of French Jews was validated through their public service, while in Germany such service was largely closed to Jews. The French state was identified with the Third Republic, and its officials claimed to watch over the public good regardless of cultural and religious differences.[7] The nation, in all its singularity, was preeminent in Germany, and its public service protected itself against cultural and religious diversity. But in addition France possessed, through the tradition of the Enlightenment and the French Revolution, an effective therapy against the exclusion of Jews. Here, in spite of one of the most effective antisemitic movements of the radical right in Europe, Jews continued in high government positions until the defeat of France in the Second World War. Germany lacked such an antidote and a strong tradition of republican statehood that might have diminished the claims of the nation.

A ready-made historical past was essential in order to provide the nation with its roots; it informed most of its myths, symbols, and rituals. The Jews as newcomers did not share this past even if, as in the France of the Third Republic, or even in Germany, this fact did not for a long time markedly interfere with their assimilation. Jews were patriots from the very beginning, volunteering, for example, in the wars of national liberation against Napoleon I. Yet, the stronger the civic religion of nationalism, the greater was the worship of the national past as an obstacle to acceptance of Jews living in the present. Many of the essays that follow reflect this fact. Yet even here there were exceptions, documenting further the many varieties of nationalism. Not all versions of the civic religion of nationalism proved inhospitable to Jews. Italian fascism, for example, accepted Jews during the first fifteen years or so of its rule, though undertones of hostility and suspicion could be detected long before the 1938 racial laws were introduced.

Above all, the aesthetics that determined so much of the self-representation of nations did not have to be antisemitic; on the contrary, if freed from the undue burden of history, it was indifferent or even friendly toward the assimilation of Jews. The French Revolution, which had, after all, largely initiated the new political style, by and large rejected appeals to history and even used the ancients, which were often invoked, not as models but as a source of utopian inspiration.[8] Nevertheless, the Revolution demanded unquestioning allegiance to the nation. Here the nation was an idea—liberty, fraternity, equality—and history merely its disembodied image, a memory different from that serviceable national past whose acts supposedly gave the nation its character and power. While as a rule the nation needed the appeal to history in order to strengthen its image of security and restfulness—of eternity—in a chaotic world, there were exceptions as well that made a difference as far as the Jews were concerned.

Through the aestheticization of politics—with its ceremonies and songs and the beauty of its symbols—the artistic avant-garde at the beginning of this century played its role in the construction of a national faith. This avant-garde did not look to the past but accepted chaotic modernity with its rush of time, while simultaneously advocating the civic religion of nationalism. The chapter on "The Political Culture of Italian Futurism" seeks to explain this phenomenon. The linkage of avant-garde and nationalism took place most prominently in Italy, introducing a certain revolutionary élan into Italian fascism that was missing in national socialism, which lacked this antihistorical dimension. For example, while Mussolini's ill-defined "new fascist man" created the fascist future (influenced by the new man of the futurists described in chapter 6), Hitler's "new German" was solidly rooted in history, modeled directly on Germanic heroes or upon warriors of the far or recent past who had fought successfully against Germany's enemies. Typically enough, where belief in the power of the national past was absent or muted, hostility against the Jews was either absent, as with the futurists, or much toned down.

The evolution of the nation had proved first merely a latent and then a growing threat to Jewish citizenship. Jews, by comparison, found it relatively easy to integrate into middle-class society, with its manners, morals, and educational ideals. Here there was no demand for allegiance to an exclusive civic faith; no conflict arose between liberal values and an ideology that tended to define community through a shared past. But even so, adjustments were necessary, for Jews in the Middle Ages and early modern times had possessed their own distinctive society with its own rules of conduct. "Jewish Emancipation: Between *Bildung* and Respectability" addresses this kind of assimilation in Germany. Little attention has been paid

to matters of habits and comportment in discussions about Jewish emancipation, and yet the entry of Jews into middle-class respectability was of
great importance in determining how Jews were viewed by their new surroundings, whether they were acceptable as members of the national community. The antisemites made much of the accusation that Jews had never
acquired proper manners and morals and could never learn to become respectable citizens. Here, once more, outward appearance and behavior
mattered, just as the nation was present through human stereotypes as well
as symbols and rituals of allegiance. Middle-class respectability and nationalism were linked by a certain aesthetic that informed the national
stereotype—the "clean-cut Englishman," the "new German," or the "new
Jew"—as well as documenting the accepted norms of society.[9]

Neither the past nor an exclusive nationalism provided the model for
the standards of education, character-formation, and respectability the
German middle class had set for itself. Here the ideas of the Enlightenment
had a strong impact, and Jews who met such standards were readily ad-
mitted.[10] But as time went on, the standards were progressively narrowed
as a more exclusive nationalism made its mark. The chapter on "Bookburning and Betrayal by the German Intellectuals" belongs to the construction of the civic religion of nationalism, but it also demonstrates how a
process that had once helped assimilate German Jews reached its end.

The extent to which Jews had internalized middle-class ideals is illustrated by the chapter on Max Nordau (1849–1923) and his attempt to
create a new Jew. As the second most important leader in early Zionism
after Theodor Herzl he presented middle-class values in Jewish national
dress. Gershom Scholem (1897–1982), to whom we devote another chapter, is today considered to have been one of the intellectual leaders of Zionism, and his writings on ancient and modern Jewish history, as well as
his towering personality, exercise a continuing influence on Israel and
abroad. There can be no doubt of his commitment to Jewish nationhood
(he emigrated to Palestine in 1923 when such an act was regarded among
German Jews as eccentric at best). Yet he, too, embraced liberal and progressive values, as the essay devoted to him in this book demonstrates.
Scholem's nationalism was unique and promising. Less conventional than
that of Max Nordau, it rejected ideal types, was open-ended, and denied
that the nation was based upon organic growth. It is a fitting alternative
to the more normative confrontation between Jews and the nation with
which to end this book.

Clearly, assimilation had been a success, in that Jews, even those who were Zionists, had internalized the values and much of the ideology of the society into which they had been emancipated, and which had been important in their emancipation. Many like Gershom Scholem or Max Nordau brought some of these values to their own Jewish nationalism, while others became patriots in their own nations provided that these left them space to exist as Jews. As it turned out, whether they were Zionists or German patriots, their relationship to nationalism was never easy or free from contradictions, largely owing to their liberalism, and perhaps to the realization that those who differed from the norm, even through no fault of their own, were potential outsiders in all nations.

This introduction, then, attempts to place the essays into their proper environment. Throughout this book I have attempted to preserve unity in diversity—not a bad political or scholarly principle, and one that provides food for thought without falsifying the complexity of history.

The civic religion of nationalism seems no longer to hold sway in the nations of its erstwhile triumphs. A different, more benign, nationalism still seems the rule in Western and Central Europe as well as in Italy, one similar to that patriotism that had stood at the beginning of modern nationhood. The Jews seem no longer truly endangered; the liberalism for which so many of them stood has largely become official ideology. Such a happy end and belated justification could not have been foreseen before the Second World War. Yet appearance may once again disguise reality—the danger inherent in all nationalism—for the civic religion of nationalism is not dead; it has, for example, found renewed expression in those nations that reconstituted themselves after the collapse of the Soviet Union. Moreover, in all of Europe, West or East, political parties exist that are ready to use the civic religion today as it had been used in the past, to exploit people's search for a firm faith, for community, and for easily recognized enemies in an ever more secular, confusing, and dangerous age. The end of the twentieth century has seen in Western nations a rapid increase in the numbers of men and women who are without any real function in industrial society, who consider themselves unwanted, and, as a new underclass, are ready to use the civic religion of nationalism once more against liberalism and the establishment.

Historians in recent years have not paid much attention to the concept of the nation, even apart from the Jew's place in it, either because they have taken its existence for granted or because it seemed relatively uninteresting compared to the social and technological changes that brought about the disorientation of so many people over the last centuries. But it was the nation and its nationalism that tried to blunt the edge of that change, serving in large part to shape people's perceptions of their place in the world. Jews have a special urgency in exploring diverse aspects of the history of nationalism, and while, for some, founding their own nation presented a solution to their latent or real outsiderdom, for others, still the vast majority, it continues to be an ever-present danger. Yet the nation is here to stay; nationalism has proved enduring, surviving murderous wars as well as the forty-five years of postwar Bolshevik rule in Eastern Europe. Even within their own state, once it was founded, Jews had to cope with a variety of nationalisms. The hope is to return the nation to a nationalism whose essence is solidarity rather than exclusiveness. This book is a reminder that such an alternative existed and, at the same time, of the constant danger that the nation might once again develop into a civic religion.

PART ONE

The Nation
Displays Itself

CHAPTER ONE

National Anthems:
The Nation Militant

"It is time we passed a law reinstating orders and decorations," one high official of the German Federal Republic is reported to have said in 1955, "otherwise during official occasions one can hardly distinguish between the honored guests and the headwaiter."[1] While today, in most of the world, orders and decorations would not be regarded as prerequisites of national sovereignty, every nation must possess a flag and a national anthem. While all newly independent states speedily adopted such anthems after the Second World War (and, once more, after the collapse of Bolshevism in Eastern Europe), the Federal Republic in 1945 found itself without a national anthem. The "Deutschland-lied," at first glance, seemed to have a spotless past; after all, it was adopted as the national anthem by President Friedrich Ebert in 1922. But it had been kept in use during the Third Reich and was now said to have been introduced by President Hindenburg.[2] A new flag was also needed, as the Third Reich had used the black, white, and red flag of Imperial Germany. But here the black, red, and gold flag of the Weimar Republic lay readily at hand, though in the Bundestag debate on the adoption of a flag in 1949 some deputies expressed a certain nostalgia for the older flag under which Germans had fought and died in two world wars. Yet the debate was concluded almost at once, and the new flag became part of the law of the land, for, as one deputy put it, national symbols were all that was left to devastated Germany.[3]

It took another three years to settle upon a national anthem. The first verse of the "Deutschland-lied," which had given most offense with its "Deutschland, Deutschland über alles, über alles in der Welt," was dropped, and only the third verse, which called for "Einigkeit und Recht und Freiheit" ("unity, justice, and freedom"), was kept. The attempt to do without a national anthem altogether had led to constant embarrassment; indeed, the effort to abolish all national anthems at the European Field and Track Contest of 1954, and to substitute fanfares of trumpets instead, was never repeated.[4] Some kind of anthem was needed, and the first Bundestag had opened its session in 1949 by singing "Brüder reicht mir die Hand zum Bunde" ("brothers, give me your hands in friendship").[5] However, tradition could not be ignored. President Theodor Heuss attempted to introduce a new national anthem that he had commissioned after the Second World War, but, like "Brüder reicht mir die Hand zum Bunde," it fell an easy victim to a return of the "Deutschland-lied," even though a poll taken in 1986 found that three-fourths of the German population did not know its third verse. But, if anything, they remembered the first verse, and lately, in 1986, the whole song has been revived and taught as the national anthem— in, of all places, Theodor Heuss's Swabia.[6] The modern nation that had always presented itself as rooted in history could not suddenly acquire new symbols.

Yet such had not been the case at the turn of the eighteenth century. National anthems grew up, together with a new national consciousness, in the age of the French Revolution. Even if some songs, like "God Save the King," reached back far into the eighteenth century, they became national anthems only at this time. Most national anthems were shaped by, or read in the light of, the wars of the French Revolution and Napoleon—wars that presented a clear break with history. The modern nation at its birth was a nation in arms. The citizens' armies of volunteers and conscripts in France, Prussia, and even England mobilized masses of men for the first time; these armies gave them a feeling of participation in the fate of the nation, and disciplined them as well. The national anthem was part and parcel of a whole network of symbols through which the new nation sought to present itself to its people and engage their undivided allegiance.[7] The flag, the anthem, and most national festivals always retained something of the nation-in-arms about them, even in times of peace. Within all of these national symbols, but especially in national anthems, waging war was an essential ingredient of national self-representation. Studying national anthems means examining how war was built into most nationalisms, which, in turn, formed a bridge through which the acceptance of war as an instrument of national politics became a factor almost taken for granted in modern life.

The change in the status of the soldier was crucial here. From the lot of mercenaries or of those forced into the army—taken from the dregs of society or driven by economic necessity—the soldierly life turned into a demanding but attainable ideal. Thus, in practically all of the festivals of the French Revolution, soldiers and their glorious death in war played a part.[8] The volunteers who had rushed to the colors in the French Revolution and the so-called Wars of Liberation—a new phenomenon in military life—manufactured their own national myths, which, especially in Germany, gained great influence. Theirs was a crusade, a holy war; this was a German Easter, and those who died were assured of resurrection. Concern with death, sacrifice, and total commitment runs throughout the poetry of these wars, not only in Germany, but in France as well, and so does the elation of having finally found meaning in life. In Germany, whether they were poets of the Wars of Liberation or those who belonged to the famed "generation of 1914," the volunteers were the mythmakers of modern wars, the heralds of nationalism.[9]

The national anthems that grew up at this time reflected many of the themes of the new national consciousness, themes derived in large measure from nations engaged in the Revolutionary and Napoleonic wars: French conquest and English defense, Prussia's trauma of occupation and her elation when it finally came to battle. Some reference to war and death in war was part of most national anthems, though there are exceptions, as we shall see. The theme of brotherhood or camaraderie was also strong: most volunteers, but many conscripts as well, had experienced a new kind of community held together by common danger and a common goal. Youth and manliness played an important role as national ideals; these mythmakers were young, exuberant, and had taken to heart the lines from Schiller's "Reiterlied" ("Cavalry Song") according to which only the soldier is free, because he has looked death in the eye and has discarded life's anxieties. Indeed, the elation of youth was bound up with the theme of personal and national regeneration, with the longing for the exceptional that came alive when, both in Germany and France, volunteers and their flags were blessed in church before joining the war. The nation as provider of hope for the future was implied in all of these themes, but never spelled out—except perhaps, in the "Deutschland-lied," which paints a happy and healthy world of wine, women, and song.

There is no need to dwell at length on the theme of camaraderie. It is found as a dominant theme in the "Marseillaise," and in the "Deutschland-lied" as a reference to a Germany "das brüderlich zusammenhält" ("which lives in fraternal unity"). Referring to men as brothers was part of the national myth; the nation made possible a true community of comrades not only through war, but also because, in contrast with the older ideal of friendship, the comrades were united in the service of a higher cause.[10] References to youth are rarely found in the texts of the anthems themselves, as opposed to popular nationalist poetry. But youth was present, either indirectly or by association, in the occasional mention of virility as well as in the rhythm of the music. We shall soon see how the "Deutschland-lied," as a future national anthem that did not mention youth, or even imply youthfulness, became closely associated with the death of youth in battle.

The concept of manliness grew up in the late eighteenth century and struck root through the Wars of Liberation. It was conjured up in almost ecstatic terms by the poets of these wars as we hear of the *Männerstreit,* the *Männerschlacht,* the *Männerehre*—as, for example, in Max von Schenkendorf's poem called "Freiheit" ("Freedom"): "Wo sich Männer finden, / die für Ehr und Recht / mutig sich verbinden / weilt ein frei Geschlecht," ("Where there are men who courageously unite on behalf of honor and their rights, there we find a free race").[11] Surely the same ideal is implied in the references to the "valiant and brave" sons of Sweden or in "Lithuania land of heroes," to take just two national anthems. Manly youth was part of the warrior image, of the nation besieged by its enemies. The themes of youth and camaraderie were not part of those anthems which centered upon a ruler: neither "God Save the King" nor the Austrian "Heil Dir im Siegerkranz, / Retter des Vaterlands," contains such sentiments. They would have been quite unsuitable to their subject even before "God Save the King" became "God Save the Queen" with the ascension of Queen Victoria. But even royal anthems at times contained the dominant theme of national anthems: picturing the nation at war, even if personal sacrifice was not demanded.

The wars that saw the rise of modern national consciousness also distinguished between private death and death for the nation. Mercenary troops had taken their death for granted and done their best to avoid being killed and wounded. "Ich bin noch nicht bereit / zu jener Ewigkeit . . . Meine

Lebenszeit is aus, / ich muss ins Totenhaus" ("I am not yet ready for eternity . . . but my life span is finished, and I must go to my grave"): so ran one of their songs.[12] But the "Marseillaise" told proudly that when its young heroes fall the sacred soil of France will reproduce them all. The soldier was part of an unending chain of being that reached beyond death to his resurrection. In many of the songs of the French Revolution, patriotic death was described in analogy to Christian ideals, as an armed martyrdom,[13] and attention was paid to the soldiers' last resting place even though the military cemetery as a shrine of national worship had to wait until after the First World War. C. Cambry, in his officially sanctioned but never-executed design for a new cemetery in the revolutionary Paris of 1792, suggested that the ashes of fallen soldiers be mixed with those of France's great men, and placed in a pyramid at the very center of the cemetery.[14] More significantly, the so-called *Hessendenkmal* of 1793, which commemorated the defense of Frankfurt against the French, listed for the first time a great number of the fallen by name, without paying attention to their military ranks. This memorial has been called the first German answer to the French ideal of human equality;[15] rather, it documents the radically changed status of the common soldier as symbolic of the heroism of the nation.

This change was also reflected in the poetry of the time, where death in war became the fulfillment of life: the individual melts into the nation and comes to partake of its immutability. In Germany, the poet and patriot Friedrich Gottlieb Klopstock had praised such a death already by the mid-eighteenth century, but few had then followed, in contrast with the cacophony of voices which joined in during the Prussian Wars of Liberation against Napoleon. Theodor Körner's famous "Reiterlied" of 1813 highlights the new relationship between soldier, nation, and death: "Die Ehre ist der Hochzeitsgast, / das Vaterland die Braut. / Wer sie recht brünstiglich umfasst, / den hat der Tod getraut" ("Honor is the wedding guest, the fatherland, the bride, and whoever holds her in fervent embrace has been married by death").[16] Such puffed-up language would have destroyed the national anthems, whose simplicity served to make them comprehensible, and encouraged people to join in song. Körner's "Nur in dem Opfertod reift uns das Glück" ("We shall gain happiness only through sacrificial death")[17] was a more suitable summary of what the nation thought it required in order to dominate men's allegiances. Many examples of national anthems that express such a demand come to mind: the Belgians, in their

"Brabanconne" of 1830, give their arms, hearts, and blood to the father-land; the Italians, in their "Inno de Mameli" of 1847, are ready to die; the Mexicans—to pass to another continent—will fight to the last breath (1850); the Swedes are willing to live and die for their country (1844); while the Swiss have two national anthems, one adopted in 1843, peaceful and pastoral, the other dating from 1811, during the turbulence of the Napoleonic Wars, echoing Schiller's verse that only those who die for the fatherland are free.

The "Star-Spangled Banner" largely, but not entirely, fits this pattern. Composed in 1814 after a night of fighting in the Anglo-American War, it is directed against the foes' "haughty host" and paints a picture of war. It does not explicitly mention death in war, though ideas of heroism are present in the "home of the brave." But in its fourth stanza it also refers to "war's desolation," a phrase that would be out of place in the other anthems discussed, which seek to exalt war and its sacrifice.

We shall return to the more peaceful, pastoral anthems later. They are, by and large, confined to the smaller nations, while the more powerful states combine the glorification of death in war with a defensive or offen-sive posture directed at putative enemies. In its refrain, the "Marseillaise," originating as a song in war, calls for the impure blood of the enemy to flow in the wake of the revolution's fierce heroes. The "Deutschland-lied" has none of Theodor Körner's "Kampfes kühne Wollust" ("the bold vo-luptuousness of battle"),[18] but, more typical for many national anthems, takes a defensive posture: "Wenn es stets zum Schutz und Trutze brüderlich zusammenhält" ("[Germany] unites in brotherly love for protection and defense"—though the latter could be translated as "defiance"). Moreover, it contains no reference to death in war and emphasizes the positive: that is, a united Germany as it should be, rather than the struggle for unification.

The "Deutschland-lied" lacks the linkage between death and the nation which gives most anthems their warlike cast. But here the myth based upon the first two lines, with their "Deutschland, Deutschland über alles, über alles in der Welt," proved to be of greater importance than reality. For even these lines were originally directed against German rulers who stood in the way of unification, and not against any foreign power, not even against the French. Yet the single-minded focus on things German, their unqualified praise, made it relatively easy to seek an aggressive interpretation of the song. Its author's, Hoffmann von Fallersleben's, own "Nur in Deutschland will ich ewig leben" ("Only in Germany will I live forever")[19] points to a commitment which threatened to liquidate what had remained of the cosmopolitanism of the Enlightenment. Ernst Moritz Arndt had still defined the freedom he wished to obtain for Germany in the Wars of Liberation as the freedom for all mankind; indeed, in a practical expression of this sentiment, the Polish flag accompanied the German flag to the Hambach Castle in 1832, as part of the celebration of Germany's first national festival.[20] But already Theodor Körner and Max von Schenkendorf, the most popular poets of the Wars of Liberation, who left their imprint upon future nationalism as well, restricted their idea of freedom to Germany itself. National anthems, by and large, reflected such a restricted vision, though the "Marseillaise" at first—and in spite of its specific references to the French—could be taken in its general language to apply to all peoples. The "Deutschland-lied" exemplified a narrower national vision, and that made it easier for German nationalists, despite its actual text, to link the first verse to sacrificial death in war.

Already in the Wilhelminian Empire the "Deutschland-lied" had been reinterpreted by conservatives in a more aggressive direction, read in the light of the ever-present poetry of the Wars of Liberation. For example, a book published in 1896 by the antisemitic and volkish Verein Deutscher Studenten (Association of German Students) reinterpreted the rather harmless lines about "Deutsche Frauen, deutsche Treue" ("German women, German fidelity") as referring to the Valkyrie who floats above the heroes in battle and gives them encouragement.[21] But of decisive importance in the association of the future national anthem with death in war was the famous German Army Bulletin of 11 November 1914, which stated: "Westlich von Langemarck brachen junge Regimenter unter dem Gesang 'Deutschland, Deutschland über alles' gegen die erste Linie der feindlichen Stellung vor und nahmen sie." ("West of Langemarck, youthful regiments took by storm the first line of the enemy's trenches, singing "Deutschland, Deutschland über alles.") This battle was the baptism by fire of regiments allegedly made up of thousands of students and many former members of the German Youth Movement, bringing to life, in the euphoria of the very first months of the war, the image of youth volunteering and sacrificing itself joyously (in reality, only 18 percent of the regiments at Langemarck were students; most were older conscripts).[22]

The battle of Langemarck became symbolic of the triumph of heroic youth; it would be correct to speak of the cult of Langemarck in defeated Germany after the First World War. In 1932, Josef Magnus Wehner, a right-wing war novelist, summarized the myth of Langemarck that made the "Deutschland-lied" such an integral part of Germany's regeneration through war, and he did this in a speech given at the request of the major German student organization (the Deutsche Studentenschaft), and read in public at all German universities.

Ehe das Reich sich verhüllte, sangen die von Langemarck. Sterbende sangen! Stürmende sangen, sie sangen in Reihen, die Kugel im Herzen, sie sangen im Lauf, die jungen Studenten, sangen in die eigene Vernichtung hinein, vor dem übermächtigen, aus tausend Geschützen brüllenden Feinde . . . Aber mit dem Lied, mit dem sie starben, sind sie wiederauferstanden. . . . (Before the Reich covered its face in shame and defeat, those at Langemarck sang. The dying sang! They sang running, in serried ranks, a bullet in their heart, young students running to their own destruction in face of the overwhelming forces and the roaring of thousands of enemy guns. They died with the "Deutschland-lied" on their lips . . . and through the song with which they died, they are resurrected).[23]

Certainly, this was powerful imagery, coopting a song that President Ebert had thought peaceful enough to adopt as the national anthem of the Weimar Republic.

The changes in the way in which national anthems were perceived as they worked themselves out through history must not be forgotten in reading the text. Not only the "Deutschland-lied," but the "Marseillaise" itself went through a similar change of perceptions. In 1879, when the "Marseillaise" became once again the French national anthem, it was seen as a song of national reconciliation in expectation of a future victory over the Germans. Certainly, neither the restored Bourbons nor Napoleon III had seen the "Marseillaise" in this light. They had banned it as a revolutionary anthem. Defeat, and its use during the Paris Commune, had brought about this change.[24] But, as a consequence, militant workers felt they could no longer sing the "Marseillaise," and therefore asked a socialist worker, Pierre de Geyter, to write a new song to lines by Eugène Pottier, a member of the First International. The "International" was born as a reaction against the abuse of the "Marseillaise," and was tested in 1896 when workers clashed with nationalists in Lille—but now it was the nationalists who sang the "Marseillaise," and the workers the new "International."

The "Marseillaise," like the "Deutschland-lied," was eventually coopted by the political Right. Whatever havoc this may have played with their original intentions, the nation militant remained the major theme of national anthems despite the changes in perception with the passage of time. The overriding concern with war and defense in the vast majority of national anthems—after all, the "Deutschland-lied" was concerned with defense as well—remained the same, along with the restricted vision and the new concept of death, regardless of whether the music was festive or military.

The Italian fascists and the national socialists brought the implications inherent in the nature of national anthems to their climax. They instituted what might be called a veritable cult of anthems as part of their cult of the Nation. Fascist Italy did this in a formal, national socialist Germany in a more informal manner. Perhaps Italy's operatic tradition encouraged every fascist organization to have its own official anthem: even though they were subordinate to "La Giovinezza," the main fascist hymn. Pietro Mascagni, better known for his *Cavalleria rusticana,* wrote the anthems for labor and for the elite corps of fascist youth; Guiseppe Blanc, the composer of "La Giovinezza," had written operettas; indeed, the melody of the "Giovinezza" had been used in his "Festival of Flowers."[26] But originally, at the beginning of this century, the "Giovinezza" had been a popular student song created by Blanc and the young poet Nino Oxilia, who was killed in the First World War.[27] As such, it was a salute to youth and beauty, a backward look at a life of study and lovemaking that had given way to the harshness of life—a banal student song such as those that existed in most countries at that time.

Seeing how the "Giovinezza" passed from being a lighthearted student song to the official Fascist party anthem played side by side with the traditional anthem on all occasions, returns us to the main theme of our analysis. First of all, the Alpini, the Italian mountain troops, took the song with them into the Libyan war before it became the official song of the Arditi, the Italian storm troopers in the First World War. This elite of front-line soldiers added one extra verse to the "Giovinezza," asserting that youth does not fear death but prefers it to dishonor and will die smiling when confronting the enemy.[28] This new verse of the Arditi made the song fit to become the fascist anthem: youth, beauty, and death were basic themes of fascist mythology, associated with sacrifice, and it should not surprise us that the "Hymn of the Ballila," the fascist youth, sends them to their death as well.[29] Just so, the citizen-soldiers of the French Revolution were said to have fought singing the "Marseillaise,"[30] and the flower of German youth, as we saw, died with the "Deutschland-lied" on their lips. Within the mythology of nationalism, such national anthems not only praised death in war in their texts, but themselves were tested in battle.

The national socialist "Horst-Wessel-Lied," used as a national anthem and the equal of the "Deutschland-lied," was not in need of transformation. The relevant themes were present from the beginning; the fallen who march in the ranks of the living, the ideal of camaraderie symbolized by the serried ranks, the destruction of the enemy, and even youthfulness, which, though it is not expressed in the text, is implied in the rhythm. Significantly, the song ranked next in importance by the *SA Liederbuch,* "Wenn alle untreu werden" ("When all men break their faith"), written by Max von Schenkendorf, dates from the Wars of Liberation and emphasizes youth and manly virtue consecrated to die for the love of the fatherland: a *Liebestod* (death in an ecstasy of love), as it was called, not unlike that image of death conjured up by Theodor Körner in his "Reiterlied." Such themes had made the battle of Langemarck the most symbolic battle of the First World War. The Nazis brought the Langemarck cult to its climax,[31] and that may well be one reason why the "Deutschland-lied," which Adolf Hitler himself disliked, could not be so easily discarded.

The élan produced by the dawn of the Nazi Revolution, as it was officially called (*Revolutonärer Aufbruch*), gave many songs the form of national anthems as it placed them in the liturgy of individual Nazi organizations. The "Deutschland-lied" was now only one of the many anthems which gave the "Horst-Wessel-Lied" pride of place. The liturgy of nationalism as the self-representation of the nation now penetrated all organized forms of social and political life, and with it came a variety of anthems which could be called, according to their themes and liturgical functions, national anthems in miniature.

These fascist and national socialist anthems used the same musical forms as most other national anthems which we have discussed. When Alfred Rosenberg told the National Choir Festival (*Sängertag*) of 1935 that such national socialist music must not be sentimental—the expression of a weak and underdeveloped masculinity, as he put it—but simple, plain and heroic,[32] he merely repeated ideals that were followed by the music of most national anthems. To be sure, the Italian anthem, and many Latin American anthems of Italian inspiration, showed operatic influence, but others were close to marches or to church music. Whatever musical forms were used, all national anthems depend upon a clear and expressive rhythm as the unifying factor of their music. The nature of this rhythm depended upon whether the anthem was supposed to be primarily sung while marching or standing;[33] in either case, people had to be able to join in the singing. The "Marseillaise" was the first anthem to use a militant marching rhythm, as opposed to older anthems like "God Save the King" that took Christian hymns as their model.[34]

The age of nationalism was also the first age of mass politics, and this fact led to the introduction of rhythm into all ceremonies—marches, parades, and festivals—in order to transform the undisciplined masses into a disciplined crowd. At the beginning of the nineteenth century, when the revolutionary festivals were in place, and the "Marseillaise" had begun its own triumphal march through Europe, Goethe wrote that rhythm had a magic about it which makes us believe that we are part of the sublime.[35] Almost prophetically, Goethe linked rhythm with the need felt by many men and women in the age of the French and Industrial revolutions to find firm ground under their feet, to pull a piece of eternity down into their lives. Joining in the national liturgy, singing national anthems, they did just that, sublimating themselves to the greater national community. After the birth of the "Marseillaise," most national anthems were played *allegretto con fuoco*, whether or not they supported the French Revolution: for example, the "Preussen-Lied" was played in this manner.

The national anthems discussed up to now were written and composed during or after the French Revolution. They were essentially anthems of national self-representation even if they did, at times, mention a ruler. But some influential anthems originated prior to the French Revolution, though they were adopted as national anthems only during the age of awakening national consciousness. They were meant to be sung standing rather than in movement, and bore the imprint of prayers or church hymns. "God Save the King" was the most influential of these anthems, surpassing the "Marseillaise" in popularity as the model for other national anthems: Austria, Sweden, and Switzerland are only some of the nations that adopted its style and its music. Unlike the "Marseillaise," it was not sung first on the way to do battle, but in 1715 in the Drury Lane Theatre in honor of King George II.[37]

And yet "God Save the King" also became popular through war: namely, when the king distinguished himself against the French and when, in 1746, he repelled the invasion of the Stuart Pretender.[38] While the first verse of the anthem is prayerful, the second asks God to scatter the king's enemies: ". . . and make them fall; confound their politics—frustrate their knavish tricks." The music that accompanies the words, and that proved so popular throughout Europe as a hymn to the ruler, becomes livelier whenever the king is called to defeat his enemies or when he is depicted as a sovereign.

Moreover, in such anthems, as opposed to those that glorify the nation rather than the ruler, there is often a gap between aggressive words and hymnlike music. King Christian of Denmark, for example, in the Danish national anthem of around 1780, hammers so effectively with his sword that it passes through Gothic helm and brain, and this to the slightly changed tune of "God Save the King." In England, however, "God Save the King" did not satisfy the growing militancy during the crisis of the Napoleonic Wars. "Rule Brittania, Rule the Waves" had been published by James Thomson in 1729 in order to arouse public feeling against a sup-posed "peace-at-any-price policy" toward Spain.[39] But it now became a second national anthem, militant and triumphant. At the same time, the figure of John Bull was used to symbolize the British people in their struggle against France. The hunger for symbols that represented the spirit of the entire nation, rather than the nation through a single ruler, made inroads even into that nation whose ruler proved to be secure. But, as we have seen, such symbolism was usually, though not always, combined with a warlike spirit.

Were there, then, no national anthems that represented a nation wholly at peace? The anthems of the smaller powers were apt to concentrate upon an analogy between the nation and nature, instead of upon defensive or aggressive wars. The "Swiss Psalm," for example, is such an anthem, men-tioned before, while Liechtenstein's national anthem pictures a country of quiet happiness. The "Swiss Psalm" asked the Swiss to pray as dawn rises above the Alps, and other pastoral anthems, like those of the Czechs, Finns, and Norwegians, also concentrated upon the native landscape. This was the tradition to which some nations turned after the Second World War in order to purge their past. Austria's new national anthem, sung to music derived from one of Mozart's "Masonic Cantatas," begins with the words "Land of Mountains, Land of Streams, Land of Fields." Theodor Heuss's proposed new national anthem described the Germans as belonging to a land of faith, hope, and love, united in peace. Such anthems, then, had nothing warlike about them, and did not even mention the necessity of defending the fatherland against aggressors.

Songs directed toward the future, and containing an important utopian element, went one step further: they praised peace rather than war. However, these were not, properly speaking, national anthems but the songs of the labor movement. Yet they fulfilled a function identical to that of national anthems, giving the workers a sense of corporate identity. To be sure, the texts of many of these songs, including the "International," had a thrust similar to that of national anthems. Vernon Lidke, in his analysis of German workers' songs, comes to the conclusion that their fundamental structure was directed against an enemy such as the rich—the exploiters and oppressors. Moreover, many of these songs were sung to patriotic melodies.[40] And yet, for all the real and potential aggressiveness of many workers' songs, their tone was fundamentally different from that of most national anthems.

For example, the most popular German workers' song, the "Workers' Marseillaise"—the national anthem of the German workers' movement—first calls for engaging the workers' countless enemies in a hazardous struggle, but then goes on to assert that it is not calling for hatred against the rich, but for equal rights for all. The "International," which appealed to the workers to attain their rights by force, ends by saying that when this has been accomplished the sun will shine forever. Such appeals to a better world, a world at peace, are missing from most national anthems. The nation looked backward, not forward: history, and not a utopian vision, gave it the immutability it needed in order to tame the accelerating speed of time. When, for example, in the "Deutschland-lied," German women, German faithfulness, and German song are conjured up as future ideals, they are immediately linked to history: "Sollen in der Welt erhalten / Ihren alten schönen Klang" ("They shall retain their traditional and noble repute"). The theme of regeneration was part of both workers' songs and national anthems. In the former, however, the analogy was usually to spring, to an awakening into a better world; in the latter, it came with the immutable landscape or the heroic in war. After the Second World War, as far as I know, only the anthem of the German Democratic Republic took up the form and themes of these workers' songs.

Yet none of the newly adopted post-World War II anthems in Europe, including those of the Soviet Union, continued to link national consciousness and war in the by-now-traditional manner. Surely this change has little to do with actual politics, which would have made the traditional self-representation of the nation perhaps even more appropriate after 1945 than before. Instead, it seemed the result of changed attitudes toward death in war: fear of death had replaced thoughts of glory or resurrection in a vision of Armageddon conjured up by a war that knew no distinction between civilians and soldiers, as well as by the use of the atomic bomb. Western and Central Europe brought home no unknown warrior with great ceremony to keep the older hero company, and no new war memorials were built to take their place beside the Menin Gate at Ypres or the Tannenberg Monument. Instead, wartime ruins were left standing as a warning to future generations. Yet power politics would go on as usual, and the warlike stances of nations continued unbroken. The function of national symbols was no longer to arouse men to march to war and to sacrifice their lives, but instead to calm the fear of death and to project a healthy, happy, and peaceful world. War was no longer glorified as part of national self-representation, but masked through keeping it at the greatest possible distance from individual lives.[41]

The most important and widespread national anthems never lost their origins in a nation-at-arms; as we saw, even a national anthem from a different tradition, like "God Save the King," contained warlike passages. It remains to be determined to what extent this self-representation of the nation, which remained so consistent over a long period of time, influenced general attitudes toward death and war. It is certain that for over a century generations took for granted that the nation demanded the sacrifice of its youth accompanied by poetry and song.

CHAPTER TWO

National Self-Representation During the 1930s in Europe and the United States

During the Second World War most nations claimed that this was the "age of the common man," that the war was "a people's war." This emphasis upon the people as shaping their own destiny can be traced back to the French Revolution. It played its part during the nineteenth century, but it came truly into its own with the First World War and its aftermath: the beginning of the age of mass politics. Politics was now perceived as an extension of the general will of the people, and almost all statesmen, whether in parliamentary democracies or in dictatorships, saw themselves as an instrument of this general will. Abraham Lincoln, the hero of Carl Sandburg's monumental biography, which played an important role in the new American nationalism of the 1930s, voiced this exaltation of the people when he claimed that he knew no greater hero than the people themselves, and that he was merely their instrument.[1]

The general will of the people was mediated by the nation, and it was through the nation that the people were thought to express themselves. National self-representation became crucial in engaging the people's allegiance, giving them a political faith with which they could identify. The nation symbolized what a people had in common: their language, history, and the landscape in which they lived. It transcended reality by turning facts into myth, and by speaking through symbols which people could understand and with which they could readily identify. The nation became a civic religion, a development that, once more, originated in the French Revolution, and that proved ready-made for the age of mass politics.

Parliamentary democracies were obviously at a disadvantage here, though after the First World War they, too, gave new thought to the staging of national festivals and built new national monuments, which were meant to represent a nation transcending party and factional politics. Here, for example, the cult of the fallen soldier after the First World War played a large role, and this cult varied only in the elaborateness of its ceremonial, not in its essence, whatever the form of government, whether it was a parliamentary democracy like France or Weimar Germany, a fascist dictatorship, or the Soviet Union. Discussing the self-representation of each separate nation, weighing its differences and similarities from other nations, is obviously impossible here, especially as this topic has not yet been investigated either for the 1930s or, indeed, with reference to most nations. Therefore, we must generalize in order to make a beginning of such a comparative study.

The Great Depression created new pressures and a new urgency to transform politics into a civic religion that would give men and women security and shelter. This wish for certainty was focused upon the nation as the expression of the general will; it took the form, more often than not, of a demand for national regeneration. Such a demand in the Europe of the 1930s gave the advantage to the fascist states. Their regime was based upon a well-worked-out political liturgy, which people could join, worshiping the nation through the personality of their leader.[2] For example, in France many leading politicians from the left and the right were drawn into the "magnetic field of fascism" over the debate, throughout the 1930s, of how French parliamentary democracy might best regenerate itself. Bertrand de Jouvenel, a well-known writer and public figure comparing France unfavorably to Nazi Germany, wrote in 1936 that France lacked self-confidence because it had not yet found a new form of politics which might galvanize the collective energy of the nation.[3] It was clear that what the old politics lacked, the new politics might provide. "Government [in fascist states] had become a kind of grandiose spectacle," wrote Bertrand de Jouvenel, "where even the humblest can play their part; somewhat like the mystery plays of the Middle Ages. How could it be otherwise," he continues, "when industrial and urban civilization has depersonalized man."[4]

France did not stand alone. In the same year in which de Jouvenel called for a new politics, the Rexists in Belgium became a major political force even as the wave of fascist movements reached new heights. The demand for a new politics based on national self-representation through the liturgy of a civic religion rather than parliament drew many people to fascism. For example, young Frenchmen of the right, like Robert Brasillach or Drieu la Rochelle, were attracted to fascism by—among other factors—their admiration for the national socialist Nuremberg rallies as exemplifying the new politics through the beauty of its liturgy—that aesthetics of politics which was so effective as an integral part of the self-representation of the nation.[5]

The nation had always claimed to provide stability in a restless world. Through its ideal of a national community it sought to restore personal relationships. National unity meant a community of affinity, now strengthened by that camaraderie which millions had experienced in the trenches. The nation represented itself through timeless symbols and ancient myths. Because it saw itself as a civic religion with a claim to timelessness, the nation was bound to represent itself through preindustrial symbols. Nature, the soil, villages, and farms spoke of rootedness and made the time stand still. The political liturgy that nationalism provided for modern mass politics, with some exceptions, centered upon these symbols.

Within this framework some basic national symbols were shared by the European nations and the United States. For both, the decade after the Great Depression was a time of national renewal. Nationalism seemed in the ascendant over more cosmopolitan definitions of politics based upon the traditions of the Enlightenment. The "native landscape" itself became a national symbol: the mountains and fields. This was reflected, for example, in the wave of so-called mountain films in defeated Germany— where men and women climbed peaks and conquered glaciers as an act of personal and national purification—or in the special status of the Italian Alpini in the First World War. The regional landscapes of the American painters Grant Wood, Hart Benton, or Stewart Curry reflected a similar feeling.[6] Nature was defined as the native landscape exemplifying national values, peculiar and familiar to one nation and alien to all others. In the case of the American painters, confronting the problem of a vast continent with many different landscapes, national expression, to use Grant Wood's formulation, was to arise from a regional point of view,[7] and yet his own "farmers' utopias" were as national symbols not very different from the meaning held by the German landscape with its peasants—an image long predating the national socialists—or, for that matter, the photographs of Mussolini harvesting.

All these nations confronted modernity, a modernity that had gone badly wrong as demonstrated by the Great Depression, while the fusion of nature and nation promised a stable and healthy society. Modernity was condemned as it intruded upon the landscape and uprooted the peasant. Thus, in Germany, before and during the Third Reich, novels had the Jews build factories on the land in order to destroy the roots of the nation.[8] Grant Wood, living in the American Midwest, in "Death on Ridge Road" (1934) showed wildly speeding motor cars about to crash as they invade the rural landscape, while the telephone poles on the side of the road perform a wild dance.[9] Yet modernity in the shape of technology could not be ignored but had to be accepted as part of national self-representation. The rural image of the nation was not meant to extol an underdeveloped state, useless in the quest for power. For all the centrality of this image, modern technology had to be given its due in the self-representation of the nation—if indirectly—not only in the fascist nations arming for war, but in the parliamentary democracies as well.

National socialism saw itself as reconciling technology and *Innerlichkeit* (inwardness).[10] The nation was considered strong enough to absorb modern technology into its preindustrial symbols. This pattern still has to be properly disentangled. The "Machine in the Garden," which was said to characterize the absorption of modern technology into the rural ideal of the United States,[11] had its forerunner in the German picture postcard that, during the First World War, showed a machine gun in a bed of roses.

The nation as a civic religion had to combine immutability with the ideal of an industrialized modern state. The phrase "magical realism" best described the relationship between modernity and the national myth in the 1930s. It was used in one form or another in Germany, Italy, and the United States, and, even when the phrase itself was absent, its spirit was not. Modern reality was perceived as the framework for deeper truths that lay behind it. The German writer Ernst Jünger defined "Magical Realism" as a concept in which reality was transparent like a mirror which separates the surface— the merely mechanical—from the deep "moving power" beneath it: the national mystique.[12] In Italy the movement Novocento was composed of artists and writers who wanted to create a native style which was both natural and neoclassical, and they used the formula "Magic Realism," created for them by the writer Massimo Bontempelli, to describe this style.[13] Here strictness of design, symbolizing modernity, was combined with a romanticized content. The classical and clean-cut lines were supposed to project modernity, just as in fascist mass meetings the disciplined masses were to symbolize modern force and power and not some medieval chivalry. Grant Wood's modernized version of the agrarian myth must be put in the identical context: his sleek landscapes and streamlined woods framed his agrarian utopia. A historian has called these paintings "romantic realist midwestern landscapes"[14] without being aware of the implications contained in this phrase. These are examples of how the problem of accepting modernity and at the same time rejecting it on behalf of the immutability of the nation was overcome as part of national self-representation.

The "poetically transformed realism" which influenced the political liturgy of national socialism had a similar thrust. Here also a romantic mood was combined with modernity of design, a clear and almost mathematical simplicity.[15] Nazi mass meetings attempted to put such poetically transformed realism into practice, but it existed in the public ceremonies of Italian fascism as well. This is partly what Francesco Sapori meant when he wrote that fascists should live romantically and according to the classical ideal.[16] The nation represented itself as both up-to-date in modern design and advanced technology and at the very same time symbolic of the poetry of life.

We can no longer take the rural image of the nation as it was projected in art and literature or the film as pure coin. Nazi films showed a world devoid of modern technology or cities. The Italian popular novel at the beginning of the 1930s was written from a rural perspective.[17] The search for America which occupied so many United States writers in the 1930s ended for many of them in the discovery of rural America as symbolic of the true nation. The writers and artists in the Italian movement called Strapaese wanted to project Italy's rural roots. But neither in fascist Italy nor in the United States did the rural image of the nation, even if framed by modernity, win a complete victory over its rival which accepted the city and the new speed of time as national characteristics. The Italian futurists (to be discussed in a later chapter) remained on the scene, and in the United States many painters and writers continued to see city life as integral part of the American dream. Nevertheless, the alliance of nation and nature predominated. It was the core of that "moving power" that informed the romantic or magical realism.

Much of the art through which nations presented themselves to their people was close to the socialist realism that, after 1934, became the only style available for Soviet artistic and literary expression. Andrei Zhdanov called this "revolutionary romanticism," a phrase closely related to "magical realism."[18] Realism was combined with a certain sentimentalization, and the idea, put forward by Zhdanov, that artistic representation must take account of ideological transformation,[19] seems, at first glance, similar to the poetic transformation of reality that we have mentioned. Yet in the 1930s the emphasis upon the revolutionary in "revolutionary romanticism"—that art and literature must provide a glimpse of the future, which in turn meant accepting modern industrialism—gave socialist realism a dynamic absent from the largely static magical or romantic realism. But to the degree that nationalism came to dominate socialist realism it moved ever closer to the mainstream of national representation, a development encouraged by the war and the cult of Stalin.

All modern nationalism worked within limited confines: though a revolutionary nationalism did exist at one time, this was not to be normative. The task of twentieth-century nationalism was to provide shelter and continuity, roots for an ever more rootless world. Any forward-looking dynamic, indeed any sudden change, was bound to endanger the mission and success of the nation. After all, modernity could only provide a frame for the civic faith.

National symbols looked backward rather than forward: Germania in medieval dress, Britannia in ancient armor, Marianne often surrounded by symbols of the past, a chaste and respectable young lady.[21] National monuments also pointed backward in time, usually to the glory of Greece or Rome, and even the memorials to the soldiers fallen in the First World War often pictured them as ancient heroes. The historic nature of national symbols is mostly taken for granted, though Germany experimented with modern forms of national symbols during the Weimar Republic. For example, the sculptor Ernst Barlach stood the usual notion of the heroic upon its head, his war monument in the Cathedral of Magdeburg symbolized the will to sacrifice in war through figures expressing anguish, death, and despair.[22] Neither this monument nor Bruno Taut's proposed huge crystal ball was well received as a war memorial, and Barlach's memorial was eventually taken from the cathedral by the Nazis. Innovation failed and tradition triumphed. Here precedent counted, the identification with a usable past. National self-representation left no real margin for experimentation; it had to project images of continuity; it looked backward rather than forward.

American romantic realism differed from its European counterpart. The Great Depression led to a search for the true nation—just as in Europe—but here the search did not end in the confirmation of a national mystique, a civic religion, but instead was informed by the rediscovery of a wide variety of men and women as symbolic of America. The hitherto unimagined existence of workers, minorities, the rural, and the poor excited the American artistic and literary imagination.[23] The 1930s "romantic realist" school of New York painters studied the shop girl, the passengers on the elevated railway, the failed small-town financier, among others, as documenting the American scene. More famous writers and artists found their America on the land: the sharecropper and his family stood for the face of the nation. This was a search for roots, for the Volk, but not on the European model. The self-representation of the United States came to differ from the common ground on which most nations stood.

The questioning of urbanism, the sense of historical continuity, and the needs it addressed were shared by most of Europe and the United States. John Dos Passos wrote in *The Ground We Stand On* (1940) that ". . . a sense of continuity with generations gone before can stretch like a lifeline across a scary present."[24] This did lead to the mythologizing of the past, of the founding fathers, and of Abraham Lincoln, as well as to the idealization of a rural America as exemplified by the regional painters. Moreover, the Ancients were annexed as well, as central symbols of national self-identification. The Capitol in Washington and most state capitols identified the United States with the glory of Greece and Rome. Just so, classical motifs informed war memorials and national monuments. The combination of past national heroes and classical ideals of power and beauty was traditional in European national self-representation, and the United States did not differ from Europe in this respect.

However, many Americans who had embarked on a search for the true face of the nation did not discover distant heroes or sentimentalized peasants, but real people, victims of the Great Depression. To be sure, there was a measure of heroism in the sharecropper living in dire poverty, as shown by Margaret Bourke-White and Erskine Caldwell's *You Have Seen*

Their Faces (1937), which, like many other books of this kind, was at one and the same time a protest against the Great Depression and the rediscovery of America. America in the 1930s was the only nation where books of photographs and text, stark documentaries, were central to the attempt at a national regeneration. Nowhere else did photographs wishing to be true to life create national symbols. To be sure, photographs had been used long before in order to awaken national consciousness, but these were, for the most part "photographs which falsify history,"[25] often staged (as during the American Civil War and the First World War) or used to present idealized pictures of poets and statesmen, focusing on their strength and resolve. Photography was highly malleable, and its truthful use as a medium that projected the national character as symbolic of the nation was unique.

Even here such truthfulness was easily corrupted in spite of the best intentions. The photographs of Margaret Bourke-White that accompanied Caldwell's text tended to sentimentalize poverty. Even so, she pictures a singularly inglorious America in contrast to the usual glorification of the nation. Such realism was not supposed to be an exercise in debunking, which had been popular in the United States at the turn of the century.[26] Instead, here was an inventory of America suffused with a sense of discovery, even self-celebration. And yet this enthusiasm for America did not end up in the arms of an abstraction like the Volk, or in a homogenized view of the nation, but was centered instead upon individuals with all their failings and the ugliness of their lives. John Steinbeck's *The Grapes of Wrath* (1939), another good example of the documentary, combined its strong social message based upon the tribulations of the Joad family of sharecroppers—individualists one and all—with folk wisdom, the worship of the people, and agrarian mysticism. Why, then, this difference in national symbolism between Europe and the United States, existing side by side with those similarities we have stressed already?

To be sure, the great variety of peoples in the United States who did not share a common history presented a problem for its nationalism that was absent among the more cohesive populations of Europe. The hunger for self-scrutiny that followed the Great Depression[27] was meant to stress the differences between Europe and America. The documentaries were accompanied by a revival of American folk music and a new interest in folk art.

The New Deal played an important role in the direction this national revival took and served as its inspiration. Behind the photographs of the ravages of the Depression lurked the hope that once seen it would be put right. President Roosevelt's own curiosity about what went on in America, his way of keeping in direct touch with public opinion, encouraged imitation.[28] But it was the WPA (Works Projects Administration), and especially its project to write a complete Baedecker of the United States, that encouraged the documentary approach to nationhood. The American Guide Series—378 books and pamphlets—was a unique national monument. This was no mere road map or tourist guide, but an analysis in depth, including the history, social life, and culture of every state, city, and village of the United States; the series has been called a repository as well as a symbol of the reawakened American sense of its own history.[29] But this was history emphasizing the variety of men, women, races, and classes.

Here nationalism, with its attempt at documentation and its pride in the many regions and peoples which made up the nation, had a different thrust from the nationalisms of Europe: this was no romantic realism, which the American regional painters represented, where the present framed a national mystique, but a realism based upon the individual. The very structure of American society that we have mentioned so often, its multiethnic composition and its regional loyalties, required the maintenance of a national consciousness based upon universal values and an individualism inspired by Enlightenment thought. According to the language of the Enlightenment, freedom and individual self-determination alone guarantee justice and progress.[30]

The individualism so obvious in the photographs and text of the documentaries of the 1930s was deeply embedded in the consciousness of the nation. But it is important to remember as well that the United States was founded during the period of the Enlightenment and that its ideals persisted in the New World at a time when nationalism had helped to liquidate the Enlightenment in almost all European nations.[31] "Unity in diversity" was a slogan not unknown to European nationalism, but in America it was near to reality in the absence of a dominating national mystique. To be sure, there was an attempt to reinforce a sense of shared history through ambitious biographies, historical romances, and identification with the past. Franklin D. Roosevelt was apt to invoke the spirit of Lincoln. Moreover, it is no coincidence that in 1934 the National Archives were opened, or that in 1936 Colonial Williamsburg was inaugurated. But even so, for all the appeals to past history, history never truly dominated the national faith.

The photograph as a means of national self-representation was unique to the way in which it was used to document the American national character in the 1930s, and so were the Americans it portrayed as over against the ideal types of European nationalism. Yet this specific development of American nationalism of the 1930s, and its continuation of the Enlightenment, must not obscure the fact that American nationalism also operated within the framework of national stereotypes. The Enlightenment's love for classifying animals and men could have a result opposite from the individualism and tolerance usually associated with its ideals. This love of classification proved congenial to nationalism in Europe and the United States in helping to draw the line between the insider and the outsider, those considered members of the Nation and those who must be excluded.

The basic requirements of nationalism were identical in all nations, coexisting uneasily with particular perceptions of nationality, just as the agrarian utopia of the American regional painters, so close to traditional European models of nationalism, coexisted with modern photography as a means of national self-identification. The United States was no different from other nations in discriminating against those who had been the traditional foils of modern nationalism, and whose imagined or potential nonconformity seemed to menace the stability of society: the blacks, the Jews, and those who did not conform to the established social norms. Here racial classification proved advantageous, though its use was relative rather than absolute; some nations, such as the United States, gave white nonconformity more room than other nations, such as Germany. Nevertheless, liberality was always limited in the world of nationalism; like Proust's Swan in *À la recherche du temps perdu*, nonconformity was tolerated as long as it did not seem to menace the social or national consensus.

Stereotyping was an integral part of all national self-representation, and, though stereotypes of insider and outsider differed in detail among diverse nations, they had basic characteristics in common.[32] Both men and women as national stereotypes were young, and indeed the cult of youth was shared by all nations; it was central to the dynamic that nationalism tried to project despite its concern with historical continuity. The cult of youth went hand in hand with the perceived necessity for clear-cut gender divisions that society thought essential for its existence. Women, as we mentioned earlier, represented the nation as passive symbols, looking backward rather than forward, preserving historical continuity. Young men imitated Greek or Roman youth, evoking the image of ancient warriors, as, for example, at the Forum Mussolini in Rome or in many German war memorials after the First World War. Such youth were muscular and lithe, modeled upon statues of Greek youth, which, for a long time past, had provided the masculine ideal.

Young masculinity symbolized the national dynamic: fascist movements represented themselves as youth movements in contrast to the supposedly old and tired parliamentary democracies. When Bertrand de Jouvenel in the 1930s wrote about Germany ruled by its youth confronting France ruled by the aged,[33] he was echoing an opinion prevalent at the time, adding one more reason why so many were drawn to fascism. Here also, as in its political liturgy, fascism seemed to have gone further in developing its means of national self-representation than other systems of government. There was common ground among all nations in the important symbols they sought to transmit: not only rural ideals of the claim to immutability, but also the idealization of male youth as exemplifying the dynamic of an eternally youthful nation. National symbols that exalted the wisdom of old age were rare, if they existed at all. The nation was old, but eternally young.

The First World War strengthened the ideal type of virile and disciplined youth. Moreover, it legitimized the warrior image of youth through the cult of the fallen soldier.[34] For example, in the fascist states the Ballila or the Hitler Youth played an important role in the commemorative ceremonies for the fallen soldiers, and these rites, in turn, were part of their premilitary training. Even in parliamentary democracies war monuments kept such youth in the public eye, while every effort was made to organize youth, usually by political parties. But here the image of youth was not focused so successfully or, seemingly, put into the foreground of national self-representation. The self-representation of the nation as virile and youthful held true for the United States as well as for Europe. Its emphasis upon the new nation was not so different from the image of the young, as over against the old, nations, which in Europe itself was turned by the nationalist right against parliamentary democracies.

However, though the basic image was shared on both sides of the Atlantic, the same differences confront us here as in our discussion of that magical realism in which Europeans were apt to clothe their national symbols; once again, this was due to the specific geographical situation of the United States and its individualistic tradition. The United States, just as Europe, had fought its wars, but even after the First World War the symbol of the warrior youth was never in the ascendant. The conquest of nature, and the war against the Indians, both irrelevant to Europe, determined the image of the ideal American youth. The myth of youth was linked to the subduing of a continent and not to foreign war. Thus, the free-roaming, self-reliant young man was the quintessential symbol of the new nation.[35] Cowboy heroes fighting nature and the Indians were young, virile, courageous, but not disciplined. Images of unspoilt nature were joined to individual courage and daring. At the end of the 1920s another symbol joined the traditional image of American youth, that of the "lone eagle," who by his flight across the Atlantic had performed a national act of purification. Charles E. Lindbergh was not the first to fly across the Atlantic, but he was the first to do so alone in a small light plane; he thus expressed the ideal type of the self-sufficient individual, after a decade of supposed social and political corruption.[36] The frontiersman or the "lone eagle" did not vanish into the mass like the fascist warrior youth, and, unlike that youth, he was engaged in an ongoing battle rather than training for future wars.

In order to symbolize the nation, youth had to demonstrate their moral concerns through their outward appearance. Classical models were, once again, essential here: youths as national symbols in Roman armor or as nude Greek warriors. The frontiersman or cowboy was no ancient youth (though these also existed as symbols in the United States), nevertheless he shared his stereotyped looks with the idealized youth of Europe: he was white, muscular, thin, and clear-eyed. The ideal youth of national self-representation still needs detailed analysis, but his contours can be readily discerned. Such a stereotype, once more, constituted one of the basics of modern nationalism, found in most European nations and the United States. His foil was the "outsider," characterized by his ugliness and lack of virility, morality, and courage. Indeed, the supposed enemies of society and the nation were never young: the Jew usually was an old man and feeble (there are in nineteenth-century German literature no Jews who climb mountains or ride horses); the sexual deviant was weak, emaciated, and near death, old before his time. Blacks were seen as strong and virile, but theirs was a manhood that, through its perceived ugliness, lacked all external signs of manly beauty and morality.[37] Thus, most nations took youth as their stereotype and transformed their supposed enemies into the counter-type of this ideal.

To be sure, bygone national heroes were not necessarily young or thought of in terms of their youth. Past heroes were not classified by age. Men like Bismarck, Mazzini, or Lincoln transcended the cult of youth. Present leaders were not so lucky: the images of age and youth used against parliamentary democracies were also projected upon their leadership, or rather their presumed lack of it. Fascism, once again, seemed to transform national myth into reality. Its leaders were actually young men, certainly by contrast to the prime ministers or heads of state who preceded them. When transposed upon the present leadership, youth meant, above all, acting out the dynamic of national renewal. The fascist dictators were always in motion, driving, flying, speaking.

Leadership in parliamentary democracies did not lend itself to such an image, a fact that was of importance in times of crisis such as the 1930s, after the shock of the Great Depression. Mass politics required not only a political liturgy, the construction of a civic religion, but also the focus upon a leader as symbolic of the nation. Yet in the 1930s few images of strong leadership existed within a parliamentary framework, such as those projected, for example, by Paul Van Zeeland in Belgium, Édouard Daladier in France, and Franklin D. Roosevelt in the United States. However, popularity was never solely dependent upon fulfilling the liturgical demands of mass politics. During times of continual crisis like the 1930s, popular reforms energetically pursued, peace made or maintained against great odds, were certainly actions that focused attention upon the leader without threatening parliamentary democracy.

The Second World War, like all wars, encouraged the traditional self-representation of the nation. This self-representation had always been marked by national wars, and now both the Soviet Union and the United States drew closer to those basic images of national self-representation we have mentioned so often. The flexibility of national symbols and national myths was never great: immutability, the ideal of youth, magical or romantic realism, informed the self-representation of most nations. During war the basic traditions of nationalism renewed their appeal: whatever debates took place about the modernization of some symbols, like military cemeteries, tradition won out in the end. The nature of modern nationalism as a civic religion was reaffirmed; for all religious liturgy resists change.

The fascination which the liturgy of nationalism exercised in the interwar years was not to be repeated after the Second World War. The nature of total war may well be responsible for that fact. The Soviet Union was the exception. There the political liturgy continued with renewed strength as the means of self-representation: national symbols such as national monuments or political ceremonies did not lose their force. The reasons for this continuity cannot occupy us here, but the unprecedented dimensions of the Russian war experience may offer one explanation. Moreover, the Second

World War played the same role in Russia that the First World War had played in Europe: the Soviet Union could not acknowledge the "imperialist war" as legitimate.

A comparative history of national self-representation in the 1930s must take account of the basics of nationalism, which tend to be alike in Europe and the United States, as well as the differences in the perceptions of national identity. Here the United States provided an important example of a nation where a traditional nationalism existed side by side with a novel, individualistic nationalism. All nations faced the need to integrate modernism into their essentially immutable view of the nation, and they did this, for the most part, by using modernism as a framework for so-called "deeper forces" expressive of national identity and allegiance. The use of photography in America led to a realism which accepted modernity more wholeheartedly than the other devices we have discussed. The fundamental contrast in matters of national self-representation after the Great Depression existed between the parliamentary democracies and regimes that used political liturgy to help enforce a consensus. Everywhere men and women wanted to be part of a community, desired integration into the nation as giving new meaning to their individual lives and providing security and shelter. The difficulties parliamentary democracies encountered in meeting such needs after the First World War account in some measure for their weakened position, and for their ever present temptation to look to those nations that provided a more coherent civic religion.

CHAPTER THREE

Community in the Thought of Nationalism, Fascism, and the Radical Right

The longing for community has been one of the driving forces of the modern nation. The more the world was demythologized, the more men longed for shelter. The greater the belief in man as all-powerful, using reason to dominate the universe, the greater the longing for a community based upon shared emotions and camaraderie. Modern ideals of community derived from the deprivations implicit in the eighteenth-century Enlightenment: they were a reaction to a universe where men's superiority lay in their knowledge, and where knowledge led to man's domination over nature and politics but left him naked and unprotected. Unending vistas stretched before the human mind; the prospect of infinity left man frightened and lonely. Even before the eighteenth century had begun, Saint Évremonde had told the French Academy that the idea of vastness was always defective: "we are frightened of being alone."

At the same time, as government and society became increasingly complex, life itself was taking on an ever more abstract quality. New moral values appeared to constrict man's passions and behavior. Just as bureaucracy was growing, and as abstract ideas such as "the people" and "the nation" were taking the place of older, more personal dynastic and social relationships, "good behavior" was coming to mean personal restraint. The reliance upon classical authorities by the eighteenth-century Enlightenment, evangelism, and pietism, as well as the ethos of a dynamic middle class, led to a new ideal type. At a time of increasing economic and social opportunity, life was becoming ever more structured. To be sure, romanticism provided an outlet for the emotions that was to prove of enduring popularity, but the romantic chaos of feeling had to be tamed through emphasis on order. Men's passions were to be controlled without recourse to cold reason. The presupposition that men wanted the romantic poetry of life without abandoning the ordered society, that they wanted to express their individuality and yet live among comrades, is basic to an understanding of the rightist ideal of community.

For the European right, the framework for a solution of such contradictory hopes and longings was readily at hand. Nationalism could reconcile the need for emotion and order, for individualism and community. Dreams and longings were channeled toward national goals, led by a dedicated leadership. This community was not abstract but personalized through camaraderie, through its liturgy and its symbols. Personal interrelationships were given a new meaning through shared goals and emotions, while national flags, anthems, and monuments helped to make concrete the abstract ideas of the nation or people. Modern nationalism grew to maturity in the age of the French Revolution; it was the first effective movement in the nineteenth century to posit a comprehensive ideal of community. Such, then, was the background to the strength and development of this rightist ideal, which rested upon the national mystique.

The dynamic of nationalism dominated most of the nineteenth century, infiltrating both politics and social life. Nationalism allied itself, from time to time, with most political and social movements, but toward the end of the century, such alliances were wearing thin. Differences among their various theories and ideals of community played their part in straining the alliance. Conservatives were often nationalists, but their ideal of the Christian state was static, based upon traditional hierarchies. When conservative movements, like the Action Française, advocated an integral nationalism, whose closeness to the civic religion of nationalism we mentioned at the start of this book, they collided with a nationalist dynamic devoted to greater social and political equality. In that dynamic, the ordered society was not abandoned, but it was based upon a hierarchy of function, not of status. Thus, from the last decades of the nineteenth century, these two nationalisms coexisted. The first was based upon nostalgia for the *ancien régime,* with its nobility, kings, and estates; the second arose out of the dilemmas of modernity, and saw in the ideal of a cross-class community of comrades the solution to men's contradictory needs and longings. Germans used the term "Volk" to describe such a community, while in France it was called national socialist long before Hitler annexed this term. Conservatism itself, as it sought a popular base after World War I, moved ever closer to this nationalism. It was forced to confront the modern age with weapons other than the reconstruction of ancient regimes that were long past and dead. Not conservatism, however, but the liberalism supported by so many Jews was the principal enemy of such nationalism, for it seemed to continue the rationalism, individuality, and depersonalization of the Enlightenment. ˙

Fact supported theory. Conservatives supported the establishments which many thought hostile to the aims and purposes of the national ideal. The reality of a united Germany or Italy seemed to betray the hopes of those who had struggled to bring about national unification. Sober reality refused to bend to the ideal community. The Third French Republic, born in defeat, was condemned as feeble and corrupt. Middle-class complacency and struggle for wealth, symbolized by the corruption of parliamentary government, seemed to exemplify the victory of materialism over the nation. The materialism of the establishment confronted the materialism of socialists. The struggle for ever greater wealth threatened to divide the nation. In order to counter the menace from above and below, the ideal of the national community was transformed into a third force, supposedly transcending both capitalist and socialist materialism.

The nationalist ideal of community was developed fully during the last decades of the nineteenth century, when the radical right took it over. The radical right sought to revive, or continue, at the close of the century, the enthusiasm that characterized the wars of the French Revolution at the beginning of the century. It mattered little whether men had fought for the glory of France or for German national liberation. They had, so the myth ran, committed themselves selflessly to patriotic acts, and been indifferent to the power of gold or the whims of political parties. Before World War I the radical right was strongest in France. French national socialists advocated the right to work, workers' insurance schemes, and even trade unionism against capitalist exploitation. However, they opposed only finance capitalism, supposedly controlled by the Jews, advocating a society composed of small property holders. The worker was regarded either as a potential property holder, who should be paid well enough to move up in the social scale or even share in the profits of his employer, or as an artisan who owned his own means of production. While such supposedly socialist ideas became paternalistic in fascist Italy or Nazi Germany, in pre-World War I France they continued a Jacobin tradition and never lost their hostility toward the establishment. Social aims were coupled with political demands: rule by a strong leader, regardless of social background, would be based on plebiscites which allowed the people to express their ideas directly, without the distortions injected by political parties or elected officials.

General Georges Ernest Boulanger, in his quest for power in France from 1886 to 1889, demonstrated the popularity of charismatic leadership and the appeal of plebiscitary democracy. He united behind him men and women of all classes and of every political orientation, from royalists to socialists. Certainly, his call for revenge against Germany and his strongman image were necessary ingredients for his temporary success. But, above all, Boulangism demonstrated the fateful ability of the radical right to adjust to the age of mass politics. Though Boulangism was a failure, largely because the strong man proved weak in the face of adversity, its lessons were transmitted to a later generation by Gustav Le Bon through his book *The Crowd* (1889). As we wrote earlier in our introduction to this book, Hitler and Mussolini both read the book and absorbed its lessons. Le Bon had been impressed with the conservatism of Boulangist crowds and the importance that inherited ideas seemed to have for them. National socialists also believed that common origin, shared language, and geography formed the emotional unity of the nation—that national mystique which Maurice Barrès summed up as *la terre et les morts* (the land and the dead). The myths of the native soil and the unbroken chain of ancestors were symbolized by the liturgy of nationalism, by its festivals, folk dances, folk tales, and national monuments. The national community expressed itself through a shared culture, not through economic programs. Thus eventually the political right could emphasize unity while adopting any economic policy that might serve its ends. Such flexibility was one of the chief reasons for Hitler's and Mussolini's economic success, and this, in turn, strengthened the rightist ideal of community.

The national community allegedly fought for its existence against enemies surrounding it on all sides. Indeed, putative adversaries were vital to this ideal, representing both hope and resistance, because the very act of overcoming them would give the community power of will and an outlet for action. Liberalism, conservatism, and socialism were the enemies. Just as the right and its nationalism transformed its own myths into concrete symbols, so the enemy was not left abstract: he was embodied in Jews and parliamentarians. The external enemy—German, French, or English—was further removed, but he was made immediately present by a conspiratorial link with the internal enemy.

The enemy within the nation proved more important than the enemy without; he was more immediately present and simpler to identify. The Jews as the only sizeable minority in Europe were cast in this role, the more easily because of the different language and dress they maintained in the ghettos of Eastern and Central Europe. As a people without a nation, Jews were incapable of forming or creating any kind of community, so we are repeatedly told in France and Germany, and in consequence they tried to destroy all existing communities. This accusation was one of the most portentous leveled against the Jews, given the importance of community in defining personal and political relationships. Moreover, assimilated Jews were, for the most part, liberals, prominently involved in the economic crises of the turn of the nineteenth and twentieth centuries. Especially in France, the Jews as bankers and financiers seemed to symbolize the power of unproductive capital confronting the producers who unjustly lived in misery and want. Édouard Drumont, one of the most prominent national socialists, believed that Jewish wealth was so enormous that its redistribution would abolish poverty in France.

The ancient image of the Jew as usurer was revived and presented as a living symbol of the enemy. Such national socialists turned to the past, not only to find common national roots but also to contrast the strains of modern capitalism with a time when money had been earned by individual labor, not by speculation and investment. The Jew symbolized the hostile world of capitalist domination, while the true community was based upon so-called productive labor. Both in France and in Germany this archaic idea of productivity became a slogan to be used against the supposedly unproductive enemy. In practice this meant advocating a society of modest property holders, small businessmen, and artisans. This idea at times received considerable working-class support in a France plagued with financial scandals. The Jew as a parasite was an image spread throughout Europe, in rapidly industrializing Germany and France as well as in rural Eastern Europe where Jew and middle class were often identical. Italy was the exception here. In a country without any antisemitic tradition, the nationalists concentrated on calling for the overthrow not of so-called outsiders but of the establishment itself. Men like Giovanni Papini and Gabriele

D'Annunzio reveled in the rhetoric of violence. Within the deeply divided, and yet on the whole stable, European society, nationalists were united in building their ideal community upon the utter defeat of the putative enemy. There was to be no compromise between Satan and the religion of nationalism.

Through its opposition to a supposedly weak and degenerate establishment, this nationalism encouraged that struggle between generations that was an integral part of the *fin de siècle.* The young wanted to break through their parents' code of behavior, their materialism and complacency. Youth longed for self-expression, asserting the need for free development against adult tutelage and repression. The German Youth Movement, founded in 1901, was a hiking association for schoolboys without adult supervision, and soon became symbolic of the revolt of youth against their elders. As it expanded throughout the nation, many of these roamers (*Wandervögel*) proclaimed their allegiance to a Germanic faith based upon tradition, nature-lore, and the beauty of Nordic man. They attempted to found a community, a so-called *Bund,* that would be a paradigm for national renewal. The German woods and dales, the small towns that nestled within them, and the songs of old, made for a union of the individual with the Volk. Through an understanding of this landscape and of the customs and history of their country, the youth of Germany would be carried toward the formation of a true spiritual community, in contrast with the sabre-rattling patriotism and conservatism of their elders.

This ideal of the *Bund* was German, deeply embedded in the Youth Movement, but the radical right everywhere shared its emphasis upon the close-knit male community. The *Bund* was a natural outgrowth of the desire for male camaraderie, of the example provided by the Free Corps and the volunteers who had fought in the revolutionary wars at the beginning of the nineteenth century. The emphasis upon masculinity as the pillar upon which the nation rested was shared by all nations, but in Germany it gathered strength as a full-blown political theory that regarded the nation itself as a *Bund* of males. The movement for women's rights, active, above all, in Protestant nations, prompted a reaction by men keen to preserve their dominance in the public realm. But even in France the fascist *équipes* of the 1920s and 1930s were *Bünde,* intellectuals rejoicing in male comradeship and vitality. Italian fascism also glorified masculinity in its exaltation of war and struggle. Mussolini, bare-chested and hairy, became the symbol of a masculine and energetic nation, while the Nazis initially presented themselves as a *Bund* of men.

The idealization of the masculine as symbolic of vigor and beauty went hand in hand with a strong concept of leadership. The leader led because, as the German Youth Movement proclaimed, he did everything better than anyone else. This was a democratic ideal of leadership: leaders and followers shared common roots and myths. Personality and Eros were decisive in this charismatic leadership ideal. The community, so the theory ran, instinctively recognized and followed the "natural leader" (who in the Youth Movement often recruited his followers directly). Political parties and factions were considered divisive; the *Bund* merely needed a leader and a liturgy through which all could participate in its myths and symbols. In the Youth Movement, this liturgy took rudimentary forms such as singing together and dressing alike; it became more complex as practiced on a national scale. The nation had from the beginning expressed itself through myths and symbols, but now popular participation became ever more important. The small *Bund,* as a youth movement, was always in danger of isolation, but the *Bund* as expressing the national community became part and parcel of the fascist ideal. It facilitated the formation of coherent elites within the fascist nation.

Clearly, the ideals of leadership and popular participation in the *Bund* helped to accommodate the rightist ideal of community to the mass age. Gustav Le Bon, watching Boulangism in action, had already asserted that the crowd was subject to the "magic of leadership," provided the leader shared its myths and longings, and acknowledged the conservatism of crowds. Nationalism provided the integrating element of this community, while the leader and the liturgy jointly gave it goals and dynamic. The rightist ideal of community and the strategy of modern mass politics coincided.

This ideal of the national community was full-grown by the turn of the century, yet it had failed politically. Leaders like Édouard Drumont or Maurice Barrès and those of the German Youth Movement had not been able to break through into national politics. Not until after World War I was this nationalist community to present a viable alternative to existing governments. To be sure, the radical right had already shown itself capable of adjusting to mass politics; especially in France, it had even found occasional mass support. But, by and large, this ideal of community existed within specific groups or *Bünde,* for the most part led or reinforced by intellectuals and their journals. From the very beginning this nationalist mystique had based its ideal upon a shared culture: the myths and symbols of the national past. Political frustration led to an emphasis upon culture that enabled intellectuals, writers, publicists, and artists to extend such ideals of community into the mythical past, to posit the existence of a collective unconscious that would serve to strengthen the ties binding the individual to the nation.

Everywhere the national community was supposed to follow cultural models, put forward, for example, in Italy by journals like the *Regno,* the *Leonardo,* or *La Voce* and in France by men like Charles Maurras and Maurice Barrès, who inspired an enthusiastic following. They were Pied Pipers leading youth toward the ideal society. Germany was a special case until after the First World War; instead of several strong personalities dominating the radical right in the name of cultural renewal, it possessed in the Wagner circle a close-knit intellectual coterie. For most right-wing Germans Bayreuth meant culture pure and simple; Adolf Hitler was not the only rightist leader to make regular pilgrimages to this shrine.

Richard Wagner wanted to bring the mythical past to the people—the Germans, he held, were characterized by an inner substance which had never changed. The ancient sagas which he staged expressed both past and present. Such a view of history was common to all of the radical right, the very essence of the national mystique: *la terre et les morts.* Wagner's Nibelungen fought against both feudal oppression and the power of gold. *Lohengrin* and *Parsifal* presented the German Volk as guardians of Christian morality: sin, repentance, and salvation were integrated into the German heritage. Stress upon innocence could justify any and all political manipulation. The dominant middle-class morality was annexed to Germanic symbols and myths; here there was no battle to liberate the younger generation from the older. Revolt against the establishment was absorbed and nullified by a sentimental and moralistic Christianity. Moreover, the Jewish origins of Christianity were rudely rejected: Christ had revealed himself to the Germans, and they monopolized all spirituality, exemplifying the virtues of chastity, hard work, honesty, and good behavior. The values that Wilhelminian Germany prized so much were integrated into the ideal community. Both Richard and Cosima Wagner, as well as their son-in-law Houston Stewart Chamberlain, were racists who blamed the Jews for all their misfortunes. When Houston Stewart Chamberlain, in his *Foun-*

dations of the Nineteenth Century (1899), reintroduced a dynamic into the ideal of the Volk, he did not emphasize the revolt of the young against the old, but instead proclaimed a race war of Aryans against Jews. This was a dynamic that, unlike that of the revolt of youth, did not threaten social and political life or established moral standards.

The Bayreuth circle illustrates the ease with which racism could become a part of the ideal rightist community: Drumont in France can serve as an additional illustration. But this was not inevitable. The German Youth Movement accepted Jews provided they met its standards of beauty and comradeship. It was to be the strength of the rightist community that it absorbed so many different ideals of the nineteenth century: racism, middle-class morality, the vigor and protest of youth, ideas of law and order, as well as concepts of democratic leadership. Yet all of these were in the final resort based upon nationalism, on the appeal to the emotions rather than reason, on the longing for camaraderie, and on an activism that took up ideas of masculine beauty and vigor.

As such, this rightist ideal stood in the midst of a German society that consisted of a network of associations, running from professional organizations to religious congregations, from charitable societies to workers' sports clubs. All these by the turn of the century tended to form veritable subcultures with their amateur players, their choirs, and their sport and reading societies. The socialists were perhaps the most complete subculture; their network of workers' organizations covered almost every aspect of work and leisure. The radical right also attempted to capture the whole man and to give direction and meaning to his life. Here the radical right confronted the radical left: they were mortal enemies because of the difference in ideology, but also because each presented a total concept of community. Most people fell in between, desiring only partial commitment to community, content with membership in their particular associations but focusing some loyalty outside this specific framework.

World War I served as a funnel for the ideals of community of the radical left and the radical right. The nation at war seemed to provide the feeling of community lacking in peacetime. However, in the end, the war benefited the right rather than the left, for it was the ideal of the nation that informed the war experience and that, in one way or another, was present nonetheless among those who lacked all enthusiasm for the conflict. Even after the initial enthusiasm had declined, millions experienced for the first time the concrete meaning of community through front-line camaraderie. An opponent of the war, Henri Barbusse in his novel *Under Fire* (1916) exalted such comradeship and sought to continue wartime camaraderie into peace. His antiwar movement, which eventually joined the Communist party, was open only to front-line veterans. Indeed, camaraderie in the trenches became an integral part of that war experience which for so many was the highlight and the sole meaningful episode of their life. Yet, in analyzing the vital part the war played in deepening this sense of community, we must distinguish between the reality of war and the myths of the postwar world.

We do not really know what, in practice, camaraderie meant to the front-line soldier. Most of the time it was probably not built upon a well-developed sense of community or patriotic fervor, but existed as a simple fact of life, vital for survival in the trenches. Moreover, loyalty to the immediate squad, which Barbusse describes so well, was certainly more important than single-minded allegiance to a national ideal. Yet, for all that, the fact that camaraderie was a fact of life before it became a myth in the postwar world gave it a special dimension. The recollection that under battle conditions "equality established itself naturally," as one French observer put it, meant that in the future the ideal of camaraderie was firmly joined to equality of status.

The ideal of democratic leadership no longer depended on groups like the German Youth Movement, but was demonstrated in practice by sergeants and officers, whose leadership soldiers accepted. To be sure, many officers were despised by their men, but there existed sufficient numbers of charismatic leaders to fuel the myth of leadership as it was perpetuated by many articulate and literate officers after the war. For example, Lieutenant Ernst Wurche, the German hero of Walter Flex's immensely popular *Wanderer Between Two Worlds* (1917), was said to have won the hearts of his men through his honesty, purity, and beauty, and his concern for their personal welfare. To an Italian soldier his captain, "young, tall and good," symbolized all national virtues. An English officer was said to be the epitome of charity: ". . . there was something religious about his care for our feet. It seemed to have a touch of the Christ about it." Authoritarian leadership was part of the myth of wartime camaraderie as it was projected into the postwar world.

Youth was prized, and the battle between generations was continued in the enmity felt by the front-line soldier for the general staff. All warring nations saw in the young soldiers their ideal type: sun-drenched like England's Rupert Brooke or blond, handsome, and shy like Flex's Ernst

Wurche. Everywhere this was youth supposedly hardened in battle, young Greeks come alive, a new race of men, as Ernst Jünger proclaimed, with "supple, thin, muscular bodies," men of steel. Such a stereotype was not confined to Germany. Gabriele D'Annunzio proclaimed it in Italy and Mussolini took up the refrain. The French right joined, but in a more relaxed manner, for a victorious nation had no need to project such a militant stereotype. The memorials to the fallen are, through their representation of youth, visible tributes to this ideal type. Such ideal types were thought to be born comrades and leaders. They alone could rebuild the defeated nation and lead it to victory. Eventually, fascism presented itself as a movement of youth, camaraderie, and leadership. The First World War did not create, but lent a new vitality to, a stereotype that had been evolving since the eighteenth century. Before and after the war it emphasized "sunniness," classical beauty, and harmonious proportion. The ideal type was joined to the ideal community.

No doubt, this worship of youth was enhanced by the atmosphere of exceptionality which surrounded these warriors. At first the custom of blessing regiments in church before they left for battle was kept intact: "now we are made sacred." Even when such formal blessings were abandoned because of the press of numbers, the sense of exceptionality, of having a sacred mission, was kept alive. The often repeated phrase that death on the battlefront made life worthwhile throws light on how many must have perceived the quality of their peacetime lives. The ideas of camaraderie, leadership, youth, and masculinity which I have discussed were surrounded with an aura of sacredness and sacrifice: ordinary men were lifted to a new level of excitement and purpose. The fact that this ideal of community came to be associated with exceptionality gave it a thrust that eventually made it all the more essential to find and conquer a peacetime enemy. The fight against communists by the fascist squadristas or the Nazi storm troopers was viewed as a continuation of the sacred mission begun in the war. Mussolini, so one follower exclaimed, promised an "*apoteosi di grandezza*," a combat leading to victory or death.

Camaraderie, youth, vigor, exceptionality: these were all factors in deepening the sense of community, propelling it into a hostile postwar world. Moreover, the urge toward the "authentic" in a complex society seemed to find fulfillment through such a community. This feeling was probably stronger in Germany than elsewhere, as Germans were said to experience in battle that vitality and spontaneity which Herder had insisted on seeing at the roots of national history. Such experiences were myth rather than reality, manufactured by writers like Ernst Jünger with his glorification of men's primitive instincts. Here the genuine and the primitive became identified: genuine man as the noble savage, or rather as one of those barbarians who, according to Oswald Spengler, would eventually triumph over civilization. Barbaric strength was pitted against modern decadence, a contrast to be fully exploited by Nazi rhetoric.

The rightist ideal of community was aggressive. Battle was exalted, not only because it directed man to his roots, but also because it symbolized a world of unambiguous relationships. Battle, it was asserted, knows no compromise; there can be no confusion of enemy and friend. During the war the poet Richard Dehmel exclaimed that "decisiveness brings light into the dust and smoke of battle." Earlier, before the war, Georges Sorel had written that French proletarians, like their ancestors in the French Revolution, stood for struggle and conquest, and that a successful workers' strike has to be dressed up in the patriotic myth of battle. Later, after the war, Adolf Hitler wrote that the masses do not understand handshakes. Hitler and his predecessors saw in the myth of battle, because of its decisiveness, a means to mobilize the masses. Such emphasis upon clarity was to attract many intellectuals, who confused decisiveness in battle with strictness of literary form. Ezra Pound, typically enough, contrasted the supposed honesty of fascism with the "indefinite wobble" of parliamentary government. Decisiveness and primitive strength were confused with the struggle of honesty against hypocrisy. Gabriele D'Annunzio delighted in describing the shiftless look and fat stomachs of Italian parliamentary deputies, the very opposite of the admired storm troopers in war, daring and flaming youths.

The rightist idea of community annexed these myths and stereotypes that the war had encouraged: the beauty of youth supported the nation in joyfully identifying and crushing the enemy. Such were the comrades idealized by the myth of the war experience—certainly a far cry from the squad of Barbusse. Though this camaraderie became a powerful myth above all in the defeated or dissatisfied nations, everywhere youthful sacrifice symbolized the strength of the nation. Mass death in war not only gave the national community stereotypes and martyrs for the faith, but also ways in which the ideal could be worshiped and remembered when there was no battle to feed the myth.

Mass death in war was integrated into the national community made sacred through the blood of the martyrs. Death did not remove a fallen comrade from his squad: he became a spiritual rather than a bodily presence. "Camaraderie is stronger than dying," a Nazi poet tells us; "comradeship is stronger than death—camaraderie is divine—within it glows the spark of eternity." After the war, for example, in Italy and Germany, the fallen were said not to have died at all, but to live on, exhorting survivors to resurrect the fatherland. Christian themes of death and resurrection were annexed by the national community. Typically enough, when Mussolini built the huge military cemetery of Redepuglia, he crowned it with the three crosses of Calvary. The fallen were martyrs, their blood sealed the community of comrades, symbolized after the war by the flag of the martyrs, the "blood flag" as the Nazis called it, the flag that D'Annunzio kissed so often when calling on Italians to satisfy their territorial claims.

Military cemeteries became the new shrines of worship, symbolizing the sacrifice for the nation on the part of those who "lived on for evermore." The national mystique was made concrete through such places of worship where, as for the British dead, rows of graves were placed underneath the cross of sacrifice and in front of the chapel of resurrection. Moreover, the native landscape was incorporated into these cemeteries symbolizing the eternal, sacred national force that stood outside the ravages of time. Siting military cemeteries in natural surroundings assumed great importance. "Heroes' groves" in Germany, Italy, and France placed the graves within a wood where the contemplation of nature disguised the reality of death.

Typically enough, soldiers' graves were always separated from civilian tombs, given their own space in which the nation could worship itself through its martyrs. The graves were standardized, but never mass-produced (which would dishonor the fallen); all countries required identical gravestones and plots, symbolizing in death the camaraderie of the living, and every gravestone must be artisan work. Thus the antimodernism that had always been part and parcel of this ideal of community was reinforced. The memory of the fallen was invoked against mass production and mass society. The latter represented that depersonalization which, ever since the eighteenth century, had led to a retreat into the shelter of the national community.

The war furthered the liturgy of nationalism, enriched it by adding to flags, anthems, and monuments the cult of the fallen. The experience of camaraderie left its mark on left- as well as right-wing solidarity, but the cult of the fallen was bound in the end to benefit the nationalist right. This holds less true for the victorious nations which passed from war to peace without undue disturbance or challenge from new forms of government. The cult of the fallen in England and France sometimes even included a reminder never to go to war again, and veterans' organizations in these nations supported the parliamentary establishment. But in the defeated nations, or those like Italy that thought their victory betrayed, the war experience was all too easily turned against supposedly weak and hostile governments. Indeed the radical right, through confrontation politics in Italy and Germany, sought to continue the war at home before once again carrying it to the enemy abroad.

The war experience came into the postwar world as a myth propagated by writers, artists, political leaders, and veterans' organizations. But this myth had some basis in reality as men sought to confront the horror of war and to cope with their own sacrifice. Sacrifice for the fatherland, by means of the cult of the fallen, became an ideal for the living to emulate.

Through postwar fascism the radical right moved from the periphery to the centre of the political arena. The community ideal was activated but without significant modification. However, once self-styled revolutionaries had become the establishment, the ideal had to compromise with reality. The embourgeoisement of fascism proceeded apace, as Mussolini put a tight rein on his *fasci di combattimento* and as Hitler curbed his storm troopers. What, then, about young against old, about the camaraderie of the chosen against a bourgeoisie that was finished, as Hitler and Mussolini so often proclaimed? Albert Speer, the stage-manager of the Third Reich, through the use of light at mass meetings, could blot out the fat stomachs of the Nazi *Gauleiters*, so different from the stereotype—but the politics of compromise remained.

What, then, about decisiveness? The enemy had to be overcome, and this fact was used as an excuse for compromise with the establishment, which was still needed, for example, in the German struggle against Jews, Communists, or the French. Moreover, the mixture of practicality and rhetoric, of the dynamic political liturgy with its mass participation and the reality of law and order, was highly popular. From the very beginning this ideal of community had promised both restfulness and movement. The promise of fascism would be realized when the enemies were crushed and prosperity established. The Italian fascists talked about the man of the future who would bring out the true potential of the new community: a human being formed by the fascist experience. The Nazis saw the SS as assuring the final domination of Aryan rule. This ideal—coupled with the absence of any concrete economic or social policy—facilitated a flexible posture even while proclaiming that utopia was at hand. After all, Hitler had condemned those of the radical right who wanted to maintain ideological purity at all costs. What good, he asked in *Mein Kampf,* was any ideology if it could not be translated into practice through political action? Moreover, bourgeois morals and manners had always been an integral part of this ideal. Nationalist emphasis on respectability undoubtedly facilitated the integration of the establishment into the fascist state.

Despite all compromise, victory brought into sharp relief the threatening aspects of this community ideal. It had always served to capture and channel men's activism and their search for a purpose in life. Now this dynamic became aggression against the enemy within, and the street battles that had preceded the seizure of power gave place to systematic persecution. However, the need for respectability meant proceeding slowly and cautiously, keeping the dynamic alive for the elite of followers, but at the same time preserving a front of law and order for the general public. Thus Mussolini took his time before banning all left-wing and center opposition parties in his crusade against bolshevism and socialism. Hitler was able to suppress Communists and socialists in short order, followed by all other political parties. But his anti-Jewish policy unfolded only slowly, taking four years after the seizure of power to drive the Jews into complete isolation. Moreover, unity, at least at the beginning, did not require the exercise of mass terror. After the chaos of the postwar years, there was an exhilaration at the restoration of law and order, at the new sense of purpose and direction.

At the same time the feeling of camaraderie was maintained through constant mass meetings with their political liturgy, but above all through the formation of countless subgroups and squads, within which it was easier to communicate and feel a sense of purpose. Fascism took over the whole network of existing organizations, giving them new purpose and direction for its own gain. But fascist organization also built upon the rightist tradition, for the radical right had always sought to advance its cause through a multitude of *Bünde,* "orders of knighthood," which in Germany often took names from the far-distant past (such as the *Arta-manen,* to which the young Himmler belonged) or from the Wars of Liberation, like the *Fichte Bund,* which played some role during and after the war. But the Free Corps who, refusing to demobilize after the war, continued to fight the Poles in the east, were also *Bünde*: officers and men held together by a shared patriotism and charismatic leadership.

Not only in Germany, but also elsewhere, young veterans formed small groups, partly to continue the intimate camaraderie they had known at the front, and partly as an instrument of national revival. Thus Henry de Montherlant in France formed such a short-lived "order" before he and others like Jean Prévost found camaraderie and a purpose in the glorification of sports and the healthy and beautiful body. The sports stadium continued the camaraderie of the war. The German right also stressed sports, just like these young Frenchmen who equated the beautiful body and the beautiful nation. After the war, sport—symbolizing vigor, beauty, and action—further cemented the community. Fascism made use of such precedents as well as of the older love for association.

What was called "equalization" (*Gleichschaltung*) in Nazi Germany meant the integration of all groups into the community as microcosms within the macrocosm. The same process took place in Italy, and indeed within every European fascist movement; even those that never achieved power attempted to implement a network of groupings, if only on a partial scale. These went beyond the professional or social aims of the traditional organizations, taking in all aspects of life—infusing them with a new purpose and a more limited and tangible camaraderie than that experienced through mass rites, which, in any case, tended eventually to lose much of their effectiveness through overuse.

Within this network of subgroups some were designed as elite organizations whose membership was selective, not open to the general public. The SS in Germany provided an obvious example, an "order of knighthood" representing a racial elite destined to rule conquered Europe. Racism in Germany strengthened elite ideas and pushed them to their ultimate limit. Italy also knew elite fascist formations, but the absence of racism and of ideas of selectivity never gave any of them the importance of Himmler's SS. The Hitler Youth and the Ballila were not exclusive; indeed, every effort was made to extend their membership to all German and Italian youth.

Fascism subdivided the ideal community into smaller and more congenial groups, most of which competed for ideological and physical fitness. However, principles of leadership were more important than any elitism: a hierarchy of leaders connected the national party with the various subgroups which made up the national community. Leaders were not elected but appointed from above—charismatic personalities, it was hoped, who could command instinctive allegiance. The reality was quite different: fascism tended to become a patronage system, a network of feudal barons and their retinue. Hitler and Mussolini undoubtedly possessed the charisma that the community demanded; the loyalty and enthusiasm they aroused cannot be explained solely by their political and economic success. To be sure, Hitler in an almost spectacular manner ended unemployment in Germany and seemed to overcome the economic depression, while Mussolini almost managed to keep Italy out of the depression altogether. Tangible success gained these leaders respect from even reluctant citizens. But the cult of the leader preceded such success.

The hunger for leadership in a leaderless world no doubt facilitated their endeavors, and they needed and got a dynamic mass movement with its liturgy and choreography. The democratic nature of this leadership meant shared myths, drawing the masses into a dialogue (as on Mussolini's famous balcony or through the rhythm of Hitler's speeches). Mussolini presented himself as the all-around man, running, harvesting, draining swamps, writing plays. Hitler, with his much more developed sense of liturgical form, sometimes became part of the mass himself, only to emerge for his speech and for dialogue with the people.

Yet the democratic leadership ideals of Hitler and Mussolini differed. The cult of the *Duce* existed almost independently of the Fascist party; those who regarded the party with suspicion still professed their loyalty and devotion to the *Duce*. As a result the fascist consensus in Italy was much more broadly based than in Germany. Mussolini rarely attempted to regulate cultural life; futurism, positivism, the exaltation of the Roman past, all existed side by side in Italy. Political conformity was enforced, but the rhetoric of confrontation and battle was much more violent than the prudent actions of the *Duce*. Both Hitler and Mussolini were objects of worship in word and picture, both identified themselves with the glorious national past, but the Nazi party was identical with Hitler. The political liturgy, however, was essential to both German national socialism and to Italian fascism. Typically enough, the first Nazi reaction to setbacks in World War II was the calling of mass meetings to perform rites of loyalty and hope. Mussolini also annexed the civic religion of nationalism to his own movement, introducing the cult of the "fasci," standing side by side with the traditional symbols of the nation, and creating his anthem which rivalled the national anthem. Both Italian fascism and national socialism with their own flags, anthems, rites, and ceremonies created a civic religion which co-opted nationalist traditions. Here the civic religion of nationalism found expression through the rites and ceremonies of the fascist movements.

Fascism as the inheritor of the community ideal of the radical right translated ideas of democratic leadership and camaraderie into practice. Nationalism had, at long last, provided that total community for which so many had longed since the age of the French Revolution. The abstract had been made concrete, the impersonal had been personalized; men had found shelter in a community of affinity. Politics and society were now, to use Adolf Hitler's phrase, based upon instinct and will.

Success brought failure. The weaknesses of this ideal were manifest: aggression was not content with the defeat of an internal enemy; it had sooner or later to redeem its territorial claims. The fascist consensus depended upon a permanent dynamic for continuing success, in spite of increasing use of terror and repression as the years went on. We must not forget that fascism was defeated by a lost war and not by internal upheaval or revolution. It is therefore impossible to say whether or not it was a foreordained failure. Yet its very success in war, its very aggressiveness, was bound to unite other nations against it. The defeat was complete as, after World War II, older political coalitions of liberals and conservatives reconstituted themselves and parliamentary government, long thought dead, proved very much alive.

All the factors that had furthered the radical right's ideal community still existed after World War II: the loneliness of man in an ever more depersonalized world was not arrested. Yet when the Bolshevik regimes of Europe practiced much of the political liturgy and even the ideals of that democratic leadership we have discussed, it was against the will of the vast majority of their population. What had been so successful as a means to mobilize the masses was not simply imposed from above, though neither Stalin nor the other Bolshevik leaders possessed the personal charisma of the fascist dictators. Moreover, political liturgy and the efforts at self-representation were stifled by regimes that lacked any dynamic and that, at their end, sinking under their own weight, could not even give the appearance of a viable movement. In the West, meanwhile, liberal ideas of freedom, the division between politics and life, triumphed once more. Even conservative parties like the Christian Democrats in Germany or Italy claimed the liberal heritage, while the Social Democrats actually occupied the liberal space in politics. The Jews who had survived the Holocaust were fully accepted back into these nations, though antisemitism as part of a more militant nationalism was by no means dead. Clearly, defeat in war had shown the tenuous nature of the rightist and nationalist ideal of community. The radical right did not, after all, answer the problems of modernity. In the end the nationalism of the radical right had compounded, not resolved, the dilemma of community in the modern age.

CHAPTER FOUR

Political Style and Political Theory: Totalitarian Democracy Revisited

> No shepherd and one herd! Everybody wants the same:
> whoever feels different goes voluntarily into a madhouse.
> —NIETZSCHE, *Thus Spoke Zarathustra*, Prologue

Over fifty years ago Jacob Talmon published a book of vast influence among historians, *The Rise of Totalitarian Democracy,* which introduced a new concept into our political vocabulary. It is time to reexamine this concept, taking the opportunity to look at the change from monarchical to modern politics—a change of special importance in the development of the new political style that went into the making of the civic religion of the nation. The Enlightenment and the French Revolution created totalitarian democracy, as Jacob Talmon saw it: their concepts of utopia, popular sovereignty, and the primacy of man in the natural order led to the abolition of those very liberties they had promised to protect. Tracing the "genealogy of ideas" of totalitarian democracy, Talmon tells us, provides an opportunity for stating some conclusions of a general nature. The most important lesson to be learnt from this inquiry is the incompatibility of an all-embracing and all-solving creed with liberty.[1] Though this statement comes at the end of his book, it points to its very beginning, where the collision between liberal-pragmatic democracy and totalitarian democracy is said to be at the root of the crisis of modern times.[2] He published his book in 1952, when fascism had been defeated only to give way to the menace of bolshevism, or so it seemed.

The Rise of Totalitarian Democracy was concerned with the continuity of political thought: tracing from the past those forces which led to the defeat of parliamentary government in the present. The emphasis upon the genealogy of ideas tended, however, to blur the profound change which came over European politics at the turn of the eighteenth to the nineteenth centuries. The French Revolution began a new age of mass politics, a visual age and one of the spoken word rather than one centered upon the printed page, the traditional vehicle of political thought. To be sure, the rise of the popular press provided an effective means of political propaganda, but such journalism was geared to produce an immediate effect and had few ties with traditional political thought. Political movements now had to project themselves upon the largely illiterate or semieducated masses, whose newly roused political consciousness had to be taken into account. They were moved by what they could see and touch, by politics as a drama which gave them a feeling of political participation. We witness a change, slow but sure, from written to iconographical language.[3] A new political liturgy was in the making, a new political style which articulated itself through festivals, rites, and symbols, adapting traditional religious liturgy to the needs of modern politics. More often than not, the new political style was accompanied by political journalism, which helped to project politics as a drama (and which both Winston Churchill and Benito Mussolini were to practice later).

The new politics emphasized style: politics was transformed into a civic religion. Here the age of the French Revolution did disrupt traditional politics, taking into account the rising political consciousness of the masses. Such was the foundation of antiparliamentarianism in the nineteenth and twentieth centuries, the result of changes in the historical situation—a new reality—rather than of a system of ideas like the Enlightenment, which was used to support liberalism and parliamentary government as well as the antiparliamentary tradition. Jacob Talmon came from a British tradition concerned with cohesion as against disruptive change. The so-called orderly unfolding of English liberties was his paradigm, as over against the trauma of revolution, perceived as the enemy of liberty.[4] This point of view was certainly arguable, and yet it tended to homogenize the antiparliamentary tradition of the nineteenth and twentieth centuries. The tradition varied, just as the history of constitutionalism was not cut from one cloth.

The term "totalitarian" obscured not only the different antiparliamentary traditions but also the nature and significance of the new political style.

Yet eventually, as we saw in the second chapter of this book, parliamentary governments themselves annexed the new politics for their own purposes, and totalitarian democracy as expressed through a liturgy of politics intruded upon the paradigm of representative government. The fear of mass politics has informed the use of the concept of totalitarianism ever since Hannah Arendt's *The Origins of Totalitarianism* (1951). Such a fear has blocked consideration of the new politics as more than just a means of manipulating the masses for the purposes of keeping the dictator in power. The contention of Montesquieu that tyranny depends upon the isolation of the tyrant from his subjects was accepted by Hannah Arendt and her successors.[5] The very opposite prevails in modern times. The dictator must reflect the wishes and hopes of his people and must share their attitude toward life. The dictator and the people do not confront each other. Instead, the new political style mediates between them, taking the place parliament occupies in the liberal state. Through rites and festivals, myths and symbols, the people are drawn into active participation. To millions this was the true democracy and the use of the pejorative term "totalitarianism" merely serves to obscure this fact.

The use of the new political style as an expression of democracy helped Italian fascism and national socialism to maintain a consensus, however tenuous, and to paper over for many years their social and economic failures. Moreover, mass terror, said to be an integral part of totalitarianism, was not at first used by fascist regimes. To be sure, there was much intimidation, some of it through well-directed acts of individual violence. But this was not mass terror, and, for the most part, the early years of fascism in power represented merely the climax of patterns of conformity basic to bourgeois society, a way of life fascism claimed to protect. The freedom advocated by bourgeois liberalism presupposed a consensus without which no society could function. But this consensus, while requiring a minimum of conformity in politics, relied upon a much more rigid conformity in manners and morals to maintain an ordered society. Nevertheless, the continuation and the heightening of established patterns of conformity were interpreted as produced by terror, to support the thesis that such regimes were imposed upon the innocent population, a contention that is nearer to the truth when looking at the Bolshevik regimes in post–World War II Europe. What Jacob Talmon called "totalitarian democracy," then, was a new political style, an alternative to parliamentary government, that met the exigencies of modern politics through its ability to integrate the masses and to provide the proper mediation between the government and the people.

The roots of totalitarian democracy lay in the French Revolution, inspired by certain *philosophes*. Yet the relationship of totalitarian democracy to the religious revival of the eighteenth century is crucial as well, because of what it can tell us about the kind of freedom historians who used that concept recognized and what freedoms they chose to ignore, and the insight this can give us into liberal attitudes to politics and society. For in pietism and evangelism we find the same unquestioning submission to authority as in Jacobinism, the identical effort to make the private public and to set standards of behavior that must be observed and about which there can be no argument. The religious revival, and not just the Jacobins, as Jacob Talmon had it, reduced everything to matters of morality and education.[6] Because the parallels between the Jacobins and the religious revival are ignored, it is possible to condemn the restrictions the Jacobins put upon individual freedom, and to accept the restrictions imposed by evangelism and pietism. Thus political freedom, which the Jacobins suppressed, was seen as individual freedom *tout court,* and the moral restraints imposed by evangelism and pietism were accepted as proper—or, better, as taken for granted, a part of the very fabric of society.

Thus political freedom was accompanied by authoritarian attitudes toward individual behavior advocated by pietism and evangelism. The concept of respectability was as great a restraint upon individuality as the commitment to virtue of the Jacobins. Perhaps even more so, for here there was no need of progress, no trust in the perfectibility of man, but rules of personal behavior laid down for all time and place. The very secularism which is condemned as leading to totalitarian democracy left more room for individuality than the morality decreed by John Wesley or the German pietists. Such respectability became an integral part of our society, and the line drawn between the normal and abnormal was and is taken for granted. Liberals tend to regard political freedom as identical with all other freedoms, thus legitimizing the restrictions upon the individual imposed by society, if not by parliaments.[7] From this point of view Jacob Talmon's English paradigm is closer to the Jacobin model than he would have cared to admit. Though we might agree that the liberal idea of political freedom did provide the best protection for liberty yet invented, the presupposition that favors this freedom above all others once again homogenizes the anti-liberal tradition. Liberals accepted the denial of liberty based upon evangelism and pietism and blamed the loss of freedom upon revolution.

Yet there was an important difference between evangelism and pietism, with their roots in the Reformation, and the newer doctrine of the Jacobins. Evangelism and pietism, like the Reformation itself, were indifferent to the form of political government, while Jacobinism attempted to control all aspects of life. The Jacobins reached out toward the totality of existence. The integration of the masses into the political system required encompassing political, aesthetic, and behavioral aspects of human life. Politics was supposed to provide a fully furnished house, where, to quote one popular German novel, "everything stands or lies in its accustomed place . . . one is immediately at home."[8] Especially in times of grave crisis, the liberal division between politics and other spheres of life proved ineffective: politics in such cases could no longer be defined through elections or political debate, but became an attitude toward life. Both nationalism and Marxism adopted such modern, as against traditional, politics.

Moreover, unlike pietism or evangelism, the new politics sought the devil on earth: it persecuted all those whom it thought to be different. To be sure, the religious revival also persecuted those who differed in manners and morals from the established norms, but at least it continued to believe in the possibility of conversion. Yet conformity was demanded by both these movements that served in large measure to define and legitimize modern politics and society.

The division between politics and life was basic to liberalism. It was founded upon the contract theory of government as against popular sovereignty. The fear that politics might become all-encompassing, a continuous Republic of Virtue of the Jacobins, underlies the concept of totalitarianism and totalitarian democracy.

The new political style attempted to integrate individualism and collectivity, personal and national renewal. These were contradictory aims that in the end meant submission to authority. Clearly, such a democracy did not provide that equilibrium between social and political forces which, as Jacob Talmon tells us, Robespierre had exchanged for commitment to a dictatorship of virtue.[9] Yet those who accepted the new democracy saw it as balancing liberty and authority through integration with a higher and immutable force, be it reason, the nation, or nature.

The religious revival of the eighteenth century and the new civic religion provided restfulness in the midst of change. Even the French Revolution did not necessarily seem as disruptive to contemporaries as it did to later historians. Take the Tree of Liberty as one example: its planting was the rite of a new beginning closely tied to the nation and nature. The tree, so Mona Ozouf writes, was a symbol not only of liberty but of continuity and stability as well, the "ancient tree of the nation."[10] Here the Tree of Liberty, as a much-vaunted symbol of revolution, was analogous to the tree as a national symbol. To be sure, the Tree of Liberty was also a symbol of change as it grew and spread its branches. Yet this was an organic growth, not a sudden disruption; in this sense it was similar to the tree as a symbol of the organic growth of the nation. Moreover, the tree was a revolutionary symbol opposed to violence; its planting was a sign that the use of force and reprisals had ended.[11]

The organic was always emphasized. Thus, during the revolution much was made of sunsets and the changing seasons, reminiscent of older folk festivals. The Jacobins knew instinctively what Gustav Le Bon, so much later, labeled the conservatism of crowds. Revolutionary festivals imitated the sacred, replacing the void left by the Church, sometimes quite literally. Thus it was decreed that a female Statue of Liberty should be set up in Notre Dame in place of the Virgin Mary.[12]

The price paid for this transference of Christian to civic religion was a homogenization of humanity. Rousseau had asserted that no citizen could stand apart from such rites: participation in festivals would purify men and prevent the corruption of government.[13] Solidarity purifies, not because it exalts man himself in the tradition of the Enlightenment, as some revolutionary theories might make us think, but, instead, because through the use of myth and symbol man becomes part of the nation and nature. Such a political style was ready-made for nationalism. The symbols of the Jacobins were universal: liberty, the republic, and reason, but it was the nation that gave aim and direction to the revolutionary rites.[14] Nationalism annexed the new political style and used it in order to mediate between the nation and its people.

Nationalism, rather than the Marxist left, was the inheritor of Jacobinism. Jacob Talmon himself was of two minds here: *The Rise of Totalitarian Democracy* stressed the similarity between Jacobinism and the thought of Karl Marx; both disrupted the existing order. However, in Talmon's *Political Messianism,* published eight years later, revolutionary nationalism entered into this broad heritage.[15] All nationalism was a revolutionary force at the beginning of the nineteenth century, yet, like the new politics, it did not present itself as a disruption of the existing order but rather as the revival of a usable past. All nationalism, quite unlike Marxism, appealed to a preindustrial past. The new political style itself was not given to modern symbols; even the Goddess of Reason was usually dressed in ancient garb. While Marianne was at first scantily dressed, a tomboy symbolizing the new order as against the old, another Marianne dressed in ancient armor or medieval dress made her appearance during the revolution and was destined to triumph as the symbol of the nation.[16] Nationalism was the first modern mass movement, yet it appealed to a tranquil past.

The radical nationalist right was not only aware of the political importance of the masses, but emphasized the integrative function of the "religion of patriotism." This is what P. Déroulède, the leader of La Lique des Patriotes, at the *fin de siècle* meant when he wrote that politics was the principal means of dissolving all distinctions among men.[17] Such ideas of equality attracted former Communards and Blanquists to the radical right. They had always opposed the elite politics of banquets and speeches, and had sought a populist political style. As heirs of the Jacobins they joined the radical right because its political style seemed to continue this democratic and revolutionary inheritance.[18] For them, as for the Jacobins, the nation concretized and expressed the general will. They continued that nationalization of the masses exemplified by the Jacobins. Their successors were the fascist movements. Hitler and Mussolini were influenced by Gustav Le Bon's classic analysis of the new politics, as they attempted a more thorough nationalization of the masses (this phrase itself was coined by Adolf Hitler).[19] The long speeches and the banquets, which had been retained by the far right, side by side with the new political style, were dropped and the new politics reigned supreme.

Fascism has been called the revolt of the senses against political philosophy.[20] By the use of the political style we have analyzed, it provided not only for stable government but also for personal fulfillment. Politics in a mass society assumed a therapeutic function which liberalism and socialism were unable to meet. Thus the young fascist Robert Brasillach, speaking in 1935 during the crisis of the postwar world, deplored that France was "without public rituals, religious sensuality, a Germanic unleashing of sexual frenzy . . . a passion for race and native soil, gigantic parades of a sombre . . . beauty."[21] He found all that France lacked at the Nuremberg

Nazi party rallies: a fully furnished house that provided an outlet for his sensual passions through the beauty of politics. His attachment to race and soil made sure that these passions did not escape into wide, empty, and frightening spaces but moved instead within a well-defined landscape in which he could find shelter and be at home. The unleashing of sexual frenzy was caught up and tamed: it did not threaten the fabric of bourgeois society, which the new politics, nationalism, and fascism were sworn to uphold and support.

The climax of the new politics came from the right and not from the left. Most important socialists liberalized their Jacobin heritage instead. When, for example, Jean Jaurés came to write his *History of French Socialism,* he praised Babeuf and Robespierre, not as forerunners of totalitarianism, but as confirming his own socialist humanism. Throughout the nineteenth century French socialists distinguished the French Revolution and Marxism from the Jacobin Terror.[22] Totalitarian democracy on the left was largely confined to Stalinism, itself a mixture of bolshevism and fascism, and it was the radical right with its nationalism that was the true heir of totalitarian democracy, as exemplified through the new political style. Indeed, Marxism failed to accept the new politics. The rationalism of Enlightenment proved too strong, and gave Marxism a lasting commitment to didacticism, which nationalism was able to avoid.[23]

To be sure, eventually the new political style informed most politics; in the age of mass politics even representative government could not do without it. French Republicans at the *fin de siècle* used festivals as a weapon against the authoritarian regime of Napoleon III, while the Third Republic found itself reviving a political liturgy because, as Gambetta put it (not unlike Rousseau himself), "a free nation needs national fêtes."[24] The spread of the new politics, once the expression of Jacobinism, demonstrates that the concept of totalitarian democracy was to a greater or lesser degree part of the imperative of mass politics. A preoccupation with formal political thought on the part of historians, to the neglect of the new political style, has led to an undue emphasis on liberalism as an unchanging reality supposedly exemplified by English institutions.

Because most modern political movements used the new political style as a way to integrate the masses, it is important to understand its function in largely replacing traditional political thought. Not only has the concept of totalitarianism stood in the way of such an understanding, but so has the myth of pragmatism in politics encouraged by historians who have contrasted the common sense of England and the United States with the intellectualism of the continent of Europe. "In our political life," Daniel Boorstin wrote in 1953 about the United States, "we have been like Molière's M. Jourdain, who was astonished to discover that all his life he had been speaking prose."[25] The American Revolution in contrast to the French, he goes on to tell us, was a revolution without dogma, reaffirming ancient British institutions.[26] Boorstin's laudatory view of American politics was similar to that which sees British history as a seamless web. Such analyses, for all that they reject both systematized political thought and the new political style as well, are themselves designed to support conservative and nationalist positions.

That America failed to produce important political thought, as Boorstin wrote,[27] is no proof of political pragmatism. Instead, it demonstrates once more how preoccupation with traditional political thought has prevented a proper analysis of mass politics. The United States eventually pioneered in the political uses of television and advertising, which, while attempting to capture the myths and symbols accepted by and acceptable to the masses, soon became of vital importance in the quest for political power by political parties and their candidates. Surely the United States made a vital contribution to the new political style. Far from rejecting the new politics, it extended the Jacobin heritage. The title of Murray Edelman's book about America, *The Symbolic Uses of Politics* (1967), is nearer to the truth than is Daniel Boorstin's conception of history.

For all that, individual nations differed in how much use they made of the new politics, depending upon their political landscape. Where liberalism was strong, the attempt was made to combine the new political style with the maintenance of political freedom or, indeed, to ignore the new politics altogether, surely one reason for the decline of liberalism. Conservatives, while at first declining the use of the new political style as revolutionary, made full use of it after World War I in their attempt to become a mass movement.[28] Those like the socialists who shared a rational heritage in the tradition of the Enlightenment opposed the human passions necessary to the very existence of the new politics. So-called national socialism as an antiparliamentary movement at the *fin de siècle* entered fully into the new politics and transmitted them to the twentieth century. The analysis of political style rather than systems of belief helps us to understand this genealogy and the historic significance of what Jacob Talmon called totalitarian democracy.

Such criticism does not detract from the basic importance of Jacob Talmon's discovery, even though one might not agree that the Enlightenment was solely to blame, and might disagree with the use of the term totalitarianism itself and the concentration on Marxism as its heir. Extending the analysis of totalitarian democracy beyond formal political theory gives it a new importance detached from liberal preconceptions. The new political style had come to stay, and so had the antiparliamentary tradition of the nineteenth century, so closely linked to modern nationalism. *The Rise of Totalitarian Democracy,* written so long ago, raised a central problem of modern politics. How, then, did the fascists themselves view the French Revolution, which stood at the beginning of their own political style?

CHAPTER FIVE

Fascism and the French Revolution

Reexamining the relationship between two cataclysmic events of modern history, fascism and the French Revolution, can, as we saw in the last chapter, throw new light upon the changing concept of the nation and its political style. The French Revolution as a historical event did not play a crucial role in fascist thought or imagination. It was not considered as an ancestor which had influenced the movement, and if fascists thought about the French Revolution at all, it was for the most part either to oppose it as a symbol of materialism and liberalism, or to contrast it to their own true revolution. The French fascists, to be sure, had greater difficulty in coming to terms with a revolution that was part of their own national history and that had provided France with some of her most important military victories. And yet, for all such denial and ambivalence, the French Revolution did provide an important background for the fascist conception of politics. The French Revolution, as we saw, put its stamp on a novel view of the sacred: it created a full-blown civic religion that modern nationalism made its own, and fascism, whatever its variety, was, above all, a nationalist movement. Moreover, some fascisms, almost in spite of themselves, did show some continuity of mind with the French Revolution.

At this point in research, it may well be impossible to prove any direct connection between the French Revolution and fascist political practice or ideology. Fascist leaders were conscious of the Revolution and its leadership within a polemical rather than historical context. The relationship between fascism and the Revolution involved a general reorientation of post-revolutionary European politics, rather than specific points of contact—a reorientation adopted at first by modern European nationalism, but subsequently by many other political movements as well. The basis of this reorientation was Rousseau's concept of the general will, that only when men act together as an assembled people can the individual be a citizen.[1] The general will became a secular religion under the Jacobin dictatorship—the people worshiping themselves—while the political leadership sought to guide and formalize this worship. Fascism saw the French Revolution as a whole through the eyes of the Jacobin dictatorship, and it was this aspect of the Revolution that exercised its influence upon it. The parliamentary phase of the French Revolution was nonexistent as far as the fascists were concerned, and it is of interest only for contrast in any comparison between the two movements, providing the opposite pole of the political spectrum. But one would learn little from such a comparison about either fascism or the French Revolution. During the Jacobin dictatorship, the unity of the people was cemented by common citizenship, by the worship of a supreme being, but also through appeals to an awakening national consciousness. The nation was no longer in the custody of a dynasty, but belonged to all of the people. The worship of the people thus became the worship of the nation, and the Jacobins sought to express this unity through the creation of a new political style based upon a civic religion.

This new politics attempted to draw the people into active participation in the new order and to discipline them at the same time through rites and festivals, myths and symbols, that gave concrete expression to the general will. The festivals of the Revolution, which reached their fullest expression under the Jacobins, had their own sacred space, such as the Champs-de-Mars or the Tuileries, and they contained processions, competitions, songs, dances, and speaking choruses. Symbolic gestures were also important, as at times people fell into each other's arms in order to document the over-riding theme of revolutionary and national unity. The mise-en-scène mattered as well: allegories of fraternity taken from the classics might surround the crowd, as well as temples and pyramids. There was joy in color and form while even nature was far from forgotten; the Revolution endowed the early rays of the sun with symbolic and political meaning.[2] The general will became a new religion expressed through an aesthetic of politics. Though revolutionary festivals took a variety of forms, they pointed to the new age of mass politics.

The chaotic crowd of the "people" became a disciplined mass movement during the Revolution, participating in the orchestrated drama of politics. But apart from political rites and festivals during the Jacobin dictatorship, an increasing conformity saw to it that the new order would not degenerate into chaos: dress, comportment, and even songs were enlisted to support that effort, and so were a multitude of organizations to which people were supposed to belong. Eventually, the revolutionary armies further strengthened the authority of the revolutionary state. Such conformity was placed in the service of the passion for liberty, closely associated with patriotism and the cult of reason.[3] This new politics attempted the politicization of the masses, which, for the first time in modern history, functioned as a pressure group and not just through episodic uprisings or short-lived riots. The age of modern mass politics had begun.

Stressing this aspect of the French Revolution should clarify its importance for fascism, especially as nationalism took up the new politics with its carefully organized festivals, rites, myths, and symbols. Modern nationalism from the very beginning presented itself as a democratic movement through which the general will of the nation would be put into practice. The drama of politics was meant to awaken the passion of the people for their nation. Just as some Frenchmen bewailed the decline of republican passion in the fourth year of the Revolution, so democratic nationalism thought itself dependent upon a continuing revolutionary spirit. This nationalism was largely tamed after the lost revolutions of 1848, coopted by established states and dynasties. Yet some of the revolutionary impetus of nationalism survived, in the form of a democratic nationalism based not on hierarchy and privilege but upon the general will of the people. This nationalism provides the link between the French Revolution and fascism: the nationalization of the masses was a common bond between the French and the fascist revolutions.

However much fascist movements and democratic nationalism differed from nation to nation, the instruments of self-representation and the need for popular participation were common to both. Moreover, all fascisms shared the utopianism which was said to have inspired the masses during the French Revolution: the longing to create a new man or a new nation.[4] Many other comparisons will be made in this essay, such as the fascination with death and the use of martyrs, or the preoccupation with youth, beauty, and war. But all such specifics are part of the general reorientation of European politics that we have mentioned already, and that began with the French Revolution. The Revolution, as it were, set the tone and the example for a new mass politics whose real triumph came only after the First World War. This was not a consciously adopted example, and many who took it up after the Revolution in order to organize the masses hated the Revolution, and saw the rites and ceremonies of the Jacobins only as a part of the Terror. This makes tracing any continuity difficult indeed, and yet, as a matter of fact, Jacobin politics were adapted to quite different ends. Early German nationalists, for example, who stressed the importance of festivals, of a political liturgy which centered upon the myths and symbols of the nation—using processions, folk dances, speaking choruses, and the singing of hymns—seemed to have few ideological contacts with the Jacobins, and yet the democratic impetus, and the means through which it expressed itself, constituted a bond between the two movements.

Nationalism was the inheritor of Jacobin politics, a modern, democratic, and, at first, revolutionary nationalism as opposed to the nationalism that supported the existing political and social order. This democratic nationalism which fought against the *ancien régime* for a more meaningful national unity was perhaps the most important single link between the French Revolution and fascism. Popular sovereignty was affirmed and controlled through giving the people a means of participation in the political process—not in reality, but through a feeling of participating, of belonging to a true and meaningful community. Whether in fascist mass meetings or the great festivals of the Revolution, men and women considered themselves active participants, and for many of them this was to prove a more important involvement than representative government could provide, removed as it was from any direct contact with the people. Revolutionary ardor or ideological commitment needed to express itself in a more direct manner. But such enthusiasm—an often messianic political faith—grips masses of men and women mostly in times of crisis, and this inheritance of the Revolution was operative mostly in turbulent times, as the Jacobin dictatorship and fascism itself demonstrate.

For all that, this inheritance is difficult to disentangle from others, not in its ideal of "the people" or the organization of festivals, but as a source for the aesthetic of politics. Italy was a Catholic country and Adolf Hitler grew up in Catholic Austria, and Catholic in this context meant the baroque with its theatricality, its love of symbols and gestures. Hitler was much influenced by the revival of the Viennese baroque at the end of the nineteenth century, with its grandiose buildings, its festivals, and the royal parades on the famous Ringstrasse.[5] Gabriele D'Annunzio's use of Christian themes in his festivals during his rule over the city of Fiume was obviously indebted to the Catholicism of the baroque, creating rites taken over by Italian fascism.

Some of the festivals of the French Revolution had themselves borrowed from Christian liturgy, and modern, democratic nationalism depended on it to an even greater extent. Thus the holy flame, so common in nationalist festivals, derived from the holy flame above the altar in Catholic churches, while declarations of faith were made, not to God, but to the nation. The dialogue between leader and crowd was in its stylized responses indebted to that between the priest and the congregation. Such borrowing from the Christian liturgy was especially important in Germany, where the new national consciousness was set upon pietistic foundations, and where practically all the early leaders of the nationalist movement came from a pietistic Lutheran background. For example, Ernst Moritz Arndt, the poet of German national unity, held in 1814 that prayers must accompany national festivals.[6]

German nationalism used Christian terminology to express itself, a trend which was to reach its climax in national socialism. There was the "resurrection of the Greater German Reich," "the blood of the martyrs," and constant appeals to providence. Hitler, at one point, called the martyrs of the movement his apostles.[7] The French Revolution had also created a new language for itself, but this had no effect in Germany. People were familiar with Christian terminology, and this was coopted by the Nazis. Furthermore, the Nazis imitated the interiors of churches as appropriate for their own kind of worship. The Jacobins had done the same, holding one of their important festivals in the Cathedral of Notre Dame.[8] No takeover of churches took place in Nazi Germany; instead, Christian forms were consciously used in order to construct a rival religion.

The so-called "sacred chambers" (*Weiheräume*) in factories and big businesses that were reserved for party festivities were arranged like a church; where the altar would be stood Hitler's bust and the banners of eagles decorated with swastikas as the symbol of unity between the nation and the Nazi movement. And yet, all this overt borrowing from Christianity must not obliterate the basic importance of the French Revolution even here: for the concept of the general will, of the people worshiping themselves, was the presupposition upon which all this borrowing rested. Popular sovereignty was not merely appealed to in Nazi speeches, but in one ceremony during the party day at Nuremberg, as we mentioned in an earlier chapter, Hitler advanced toward the holy flame as one of a crowd, emerging only at the last moment.[9] The creation of a political liturgy based upon the aesthetic of politics was a consequence of the belief in the artificial construct of "the people": they had to be mobilized, shaped, and disciplined, and the way in which this was done was influenced—if not directly determined—by the French Revolution. The Revolution signaled the break between the old politics of dynasty and privilege, and the new democratic politics supposedly based on the will of the people.

The overt attitude of national socialists toward the French Revolution was one of hatred: it symbolized all that had gone wrong with Germany. Historians used to explain what they regarded as the aggressive nature of German nationalism, and therefore of national socialism, through the fact that Germany had been untouched by the ideals of the French Revolution, and that subsequently it had missed the benign influence of the Enlightenment. Thus Germany came to differ from Western Europe. Such a view of German history can no longer be upheld. German nationalism, even as it fought against Napoleon, at first internalized ideas of freedom and humanity which the French Revolution projected. Love of fatherland and freedom were the slogans under which the German Wars of Liberation against France were fought, and freedom for many of those involved meant freedom both within the nation itself and for other nations wanting independence.[10] To be sure, as the struggle became more intense, opposition to the French Revolution and what it stood for increased, and proclamations of freedom rang increasingly hollow, or meant merely national independence; now only the fatherland counted. But just as the ideal of liberty exemplified by the French Revolution was repudiated, its influence reasserted itself through the idea of popular sovereignty and its consequences, which German nationalism, embattled against the reaction, accepted.

German nationalism, like all modern nationalism, involved the mobilizing and control of the masses. To achieve this, it constructed a world of illusion which in its content bore no resemblance to the French Revolution. This world, which the Nazis adopted as their own, was a rural, not an urban world (like that of the Revolution), one in which a mythical German past had remained alive, pointing to a better future. Most nations represented themselves through preindustrial symbols like the native landscape, projecting a feeling of continuity and harmony in contrast to the modern age. Hitler boasted that with the rise of national socialism "the nervous nineteenth century had come to an end."[11] The images and the rhetoric of nationalism were opposed to that which the Jacobins had projected. The storming of the Bastille was made into a metaphor symbolizing the perils of modernity.

All nationalism claimed to provide stability in a restless world, seeing itself as a civic religion with a claim to timelessness. National symbols looked backward rather than forward; these were no Goddesses of Reason who lacked a past.[12] While the Festivals of Revolution had a short memory, honoring the death of Marat or of the revolutionary martyrs, the martyrs of movements like national socialism were immediately assimilated to heroes who had fought for the fatherland in the medieval past or during the Wars of National Liberation. Nationalism had a different sense of history than the French Revolution; it looked to conventional, non-Enlightenment sources for its inspiration. And though the revolutionary festivals in the countryside also built upon ancient peasant traditions,[13] the thrust of these festivals was not directed toward recapturing the past in order to control the future.

The content of most nineteenth- and twentieth-century nationalism was different from that of the French Revolution, but its method of politics and self-representation was similar. For example, Robespierre might have felt at home in Nazi mass meetings, except for their huge dimensions and the kind of precedent and imagery used. He would have recognized the rhythms of such meetings, their songs and speaking choruses, as a political statement, and their play upon light and shadow would not have been strange, for the Revolution was fond of annexing to its own festivals sunrises, sunsets, and dawns.

The Nazis were particularly disturbed by the Revolution's break with the past, its repudiation of history, which seemed to them a logical consequence of the Enlightenment. Indeed, the triumphant Revolution had forgotten history; for example, the Pantheon, which was at first opened to great men of all nations and ages, was finally restricted only to those who had followed the turns and twists of the Revolution.[14] The Nazis and the fascists in general saw socialist and Bolshevik revolutions as the logical consequence of such a break with history: rootless and opportunistic, devoid of principles. All these revolutions were, so they claimed, controlled by the Jews, eternal strangers and antinationals. Hitler in *Mein Kampf* criticized just such a revolution. A revolution that is a true blessing, he wrote, will not be ashamed to make use of already existing truths. After all, human culture and man himself are merely the end-products of a long historical development for which each generation has furnished the building blocks. The purpose of a revolution is not to tear down the whole building, but to remove what is unsuitable and to build again upon the space thus vacated. Here was the model of a revolution that was pitted against that which France had provided. Such was Hitler's most consistent position toward the revolution, even if, at times, he admired its destructive power, which had served to put an end to the old order and had led to a new beginning.[15] This was, after all, what he himself wanted to achieve. But, in the last resort, the French Revolution, manipulated by the Jews, according to Hitler, had produced evil rather than good.

Nervousness was the disease most feared in the nineteenth century as leading to a general degeneration, not only of individuals, but of the state. The fascists were haunted by fear of degeneration, a word they applied liberally to their enemies. The answer to such fears, in their eyes, was the maintenance of respectability and racial purity. Keeping control over one's sexuality was vital to Adolf Hitler, who was obsessed with the spread of syphilis.[16] A clear division of functions between the sexes was basic to moral and physical health. The accusation that the Nazi ideologist Alfred Rosenberg in his *Der Mythos des 20. Jahrhunderts* (1930) leveled against the French Revolution was telling in this context. The collapse of the *ancien régime,* he wrote, had as its necessary and natural consequence the establishment of the overbearing influence of women, many of whom took on functions that had been the preserve of men. Had the ideals of that Revolution not included the liberation of women, whose forerunners, according to Rosenberg, were two demimondaines, Olympe de Gouges and Theroigne de Mericourt?[17] Rosenberg linked women's liberation to prostitution, and this within the framework of a confusion of sexes. The accusation of immorality leveled by the nationalist right against the French Revolution in most of Europe was more than just the reaction of prudes. It symbolized the destruction of the social and political order.

But here, once again, bitter opposition should not disguise certain similarities that point back to that general reorientation of European politics I have mentioned before. The Jacobins also insisted on clear and unambiguous distinctions between morality and immorality. Those who supported the Revolution and those who opposed it should be clearly distinguished. Robespierre loved to divide the enemies of the Revolution into various groups,[18] and to create order even among those destined for execution.

The uncompromising distinction between enemy and friend, supporters
and those who must be eliminated, was drawn in the name of the general
will of the people. Even as the guillotine was kept busy, it was claimed that
the people themselves wanted the Terror put on their daily agenda.[19] Hitler
made the same claim somewhat more theoretically: the people themselves
saw in a ruthless attack against the enemy proof of a just cause, and in the
refusal to exterminate him a sign of weakness.[20] He made these remarks
in the context of the nationalization of the masses, as he called it, crucial
to the reawakening of Germany. The emphasis upon unambiguous distinctions, in politics as well as social life, formed a common bond between
Jacobins and fascists. The either/or cast of mind, which put a premium
upon decisiveness, was a means to impose a new and untraditional leadership upon the nation. Such leadership was dependent upon the successful
nationalization of the masses, and this meant decisiveness, clarity, and conformity, projected in action as well as through the revolutionary or national
cult.

The general will of the people, if not mediated through representative
government, needed coherence, and as we have seen in reference to Jacob
Talmon's *Rise of Totalitarian Democracy*, political and personal conformity were essential to the existence of such a direct democracy. The myths
and symbols—the whole of the civic religion with its cult as the objecti-
fication of the general will—focused and directed the faith of the people.
Jean-Jacques Rousseau himself had recommended to the government of
Poland the institution of games, festivities, and ceremonies in order to
create republican habits of mind which would be impossible to uproot.[21]
But what about the leader himself as focusing and directing the faith of the
people? Here the legacy the French Revolution left to fascism was at best
ambivalent.

During the Jacobin dictatorship, the public leadership function was exercised through speeches and proclamations. Robespierre and other members of the Committee of Public Safety were compelling speakers, but they
were never the center of a cult or an integral part of the myths and symbols
of the civic religion. They were closer to Rousseau's original concept of the
general will, which foresaw a legislator but no charismatic leader as the
object of popular adoration and enthusiasm. The deeds of the Revolution
were carried out in the name of abstract principles, such as freedom or
reason, and not in the name of one man. To be sure, martyred leaders became part of the revolutionary pantheon. Jacques-Louis David cast his

painting of the assassinated Marat in the form of a timeless monument.[22] However, David never painted a living leader of the Revolution; for example, no such monument was erected to Robespierre. Jacobins were willing to celebrate collective deeds, but accepted individual heroes only when they were dead.[23] Leadership during the Revolution was, after all, collective leadership; the ideal of equality was maintained in theory and not yet objectified by one leader acting on behalf of the nation. Napoleon would change all that in a direction leading, not forward to future fascist leaders, but backward to monarchy and empire.

Fascist ideals of leadership could find no comfort here. The only connection between these ideas and the Revolution was, once again, the political liturgy, which could serve to support and to frame the leader, even if at times, as we have mentioned, it was used to demonstrate that the leader was one among equals. The theory of democratic leadership adopted by Hitler and Mussolini emerged as a consequence of the growth of urban and industrial society. Gustav Le Bon's *The Crowd* (1889) was a milestone on the road to modern dictatorship, a work, as I have mentioned before, known by and important to both Hitler and Mussolini.[24] That book was inspired by the crowds mobilized by General Boulanger between 1886 and 1889 in his bid for dictatorship, one of the first modern mass movements with a truly cross-class appeal. The Boulangist movement sparked a concern with the role of the masses in politics, illustrated by a spate of works dealing with collective psychology.[25] Le Bon stressed the effect of what he called "theatrical representations" upon the crowd, but also the necessity of providing a leader through whom the crowd attains its identity.[26] Such a leader must himself be hypnotized by the idea whose apostle he has become. Here Le Bon refers to the men of the French Revolution, together with Savonarola, Luther, and Peter the Hermit, as having exercised their fascination over the crowd only after having themselves been fascinated by a creed.[27] Le Bon had observed well. This was the kind of leadership needed in an age when the mobilized masses could sway politics in a manner which had not been possible earlier—with the exception of the French Revolution. Here again the Revolution prefigures a reorientation of European politics that, properly speaking, became effective only in industrialized Europe.

The use which the fascist leaders themselves made of a political liturgy, and the appeal of democratic leadership, varied from nation to nation. While Hitler made thorough use of this manner of self-representation, Mussolini seemed to have greater difficulty grasping its importance for the integration of the masses into the fascist movement. However, this was a matter of degree, for fascism also wanted to become a civic religion. Though much, as we shall see, was borrowed from D'Annunzio's rule over Fiume, Mussolini was also influenced by the political cult of the Revolution and the educational and integrative function it had served. Moreover, unlike Hitler, he borrowed from the Revolution the idea of a new calendar, in which the year One was the year of the final attainment of power.[28] What better signal could be devised to show that the old order was finished and a new age about to commence? The civic religion of nationalism, wherever it took roots, had little choice but to draw, however indirectly, on the only serviceable past within reach: the example of the Jacobins, with their attempt to unite, through mass rituals and easily understood symbols, the people, the state, and the nation. Mussolini would let the development of a speech depend upon the eyes and voices of the thousands who packed the piazza.[29] He posed for a photograph beside a statue of Augustus, and on another occasion was presented with a Roman sword; but such episodes are only part of a fully fledged political cult, with festivals like those celebrated by the Revolution, or like Nazi mass meetings.

While Italy was well on the road to a civic religion in the first ten years of fascism, later the cult of the Duce became more personal, as it came to be projected upon one man and the state, rather than upon the leader as a symbol of the ideology of his movement—an ideology now supposedly shared by all the people. Indeed, the cult of the Duce was kept almost separate from the Fascist party.[30] Hitler, on the other hand, in the long term, attempted to restrict the impact of a single individual upon the ritual. The ceremony itself should have an independent life, he believed, because this would ensure the continuity of the Third Reich even after his death; for his successor would not possess his own magic and the use of the liturgy would disguise this fact.[31] Mussolini never exalted a political liturgy in this manner,[32] nor did he have the illusion that it might function to keep the leader all-powerful through giving him the appearance of a priest at the altar of a baroque church.

Politics as a theater filled with passion had come into its own in Italy with Gabriele D'Annunzio's rule over the city of Fiume (1919–21). The succession of festivals in which D'Annunzio played a leading role was supposed to abolish the distance between leader and led, and the speeches from the balcony of the town hall to the crowd below (accompanied by trumpets) were to accomplish the same purpose.[33] D'Annunzio used secular and religious symbols side by side in order to create a civic religion. His was a fully worked-out political liturgy intended to keep Fiume in a state of continual excitement and euphoria, uniting the city against its enemies and projecting it as a symbol for a new Italy. The French Revolution was involved in such a political theater only in a most indirect way. D'Annunzio's rule over Fiume was the first time in the postrevolutionary age that the aesthetics of politics had been used once again as a principal means of governance. But the immediate inspiration for such politics was the poet's own fertile imagination, inspired by the artistic movements of his age.

Mussolini did take from Fiume some of his way of doing politics and many of the fascist rites and ceremonials through which the collectivity fused with the leader.[34] However, eventually the Duce was at the center of such politics, as we saw, becoming less the symbol of some transcendent principle—such as the Volk's soul or the race—than a political leader, the living creator of a new state. Nationalism in Italy had retained a liberal core and until the 1930s had avoided fusing with racism, or with that mysticism of the Volk which was to bedevil Germany. The state, not the Volk, played a dominant role in Italian nationalism, and here important groups such as the army saw the nation as symbolized by the king rather than by Mussolini. Moreover, unlike Hitler, Mussolini was not so much visually oriented, but focused upon the printed word and oral expression. The Mirabeaus, Andre Chéniers, and Davids, who helped to shape the festivals of revolutionary France, would have found no peers in fascist Italy, where the political liturgy did not excite such attention, and the names of those who organized fascist rites—men like Italo Balbo, Augusto Turati, or Achille Starace—were noted for other services rendered to the Fascist state. Germany, on the other hand, had its Albert Speer and Joseph Goebbels, who managed the aesthetic of politics.

We have found links and differences between the French and the fascist revolutions, not by examining specific attitudes, but through more general principles. The political liturgy, the aesthetic of politics, forms the core of continuity between the two revolutions, together with the quest for totality and the either/or mentality as the spur to decisiveness in politics. Basic to all of these links was the democratization of politics, the rule of the general will, that informed the nationalism upon which fascism was built. Fascism and the French Revolution, each in its own way, saw themselves as democratic movements directed against the establishment. Fascism as a movement had a revolutionary thrust, and even in power—having itself become the establishment—made full use of an antiestablishment rhetoric directed against the bourgeoisie.

There are two further connections between the French Revolution and fascism that bear mention: the preoccupations with death and youth. Funeral symbolism played a large role in revolutionary festivals, often acted out around an empty tomb.[35] These were the tombs of the martyrs of the Revolution, whose actual funerals were grandiose mise-en-scènes, at whose end stood the Pantheon. The Revolution attempted to redesign cemeteries as places of eternal sleep rather than Christian resurrection. Architects experimented with tombs containing the ashes of great men to be placed at the center of such cemeteries.[36] The cult of the martyred dead, or of those who had played an important role in the Revolution, was celebrated during Jacobin rule and the Directory. Fascism celebrated a similar cult of the dead. Italo Balbo first organized fascist funerals in Italy as mass events combining religious with patriotic ceremony.[37] Such funerals were part of many fascist rites organized by Balbo, providing perhaps another inspiration for the fascist ceremonial so splendidly displayed by D'Annunzio.

The fascist cult of the dead was not confined to the martyrs of the movement, but included the fallen of the First World War. Both Italian fascism and national socialism regarded themselves as the true inheritors of the war experience, guardians of the cult of the fallen soldier. Fascist Italy built some of the most spectacular war cemeteries—such as that at Redipuglia in the Alps—using Christian symbolism, as, for example, the three crosses of Calvary, to proclaim the resurrection of those who gave their life for the fatherland. All nations who had been at war gave singular honor to their war dead, but in fascism such remembrance was close to the center of its political ritual, never to be lost from sight. The martyrs of the movement were assimilated to the fallen soldier of the First World War; both had sacrificed their lives for the nation. Italian fascism's cult of the dead, in contrast to that of Nazi Germany, has only now received attention, and therefore statements about it must be tentative. But in a movement which saw itself in the light of the First World War, and which was pledged to continue the fight for Italy's victory, sacrificial death was bound to occupy an important place in the rhetoric and ceremonial of the party.

There can be no doubt about the pride of place held by the memory of the war dead and martyrs in national socialism. Some of the most spectacular ceremonies at the Nuremberg rallies were devoted to this cult, including perhaps the central ceremony where Hitler stood alone in front of the eternal flame against the background of massed party formations. Christian symbolism was once again part of this cult: for example, the bullet which killed Albert Leo Schlageter, considered a Nazi martyr, was kept in a silver reliquary.[38] State funerals were carefully programmed ceremonies of great splendor. Thus, when the body of the assassinated Nazi leader of Switzerland, Wilhelm Gustloff, was transferred to his home in northern Germany in 1936, the journey took fifteen hours. There was a ceremony at every station on the way, and the partially open coach with the coffin and guard of honor was flanked by two coaches reserved for wreaths.[39] State funerals, though infrequent, were an integral part of the cult of the dead which the Nazis practiced.

State funerals were celebrated with great pomp throughout the nineteenth century, but these were funerals of rulers, generals, and members of the government. The French Revolution and fascism democratized state funerals: not birth or privilege, but service to the cause, warranted such display, regardless of the person's social origin or standing. France took up this revolutionary tradition with the founding of the Third Republic; for example, the funeral of Victor Hugo in 1885 has been called one of the first fruits of the mass age, with its procession past the catafalque standing under the Arch of Triumph and ending at the Pantheon, which was opened for the first time in thirty-five years.[40] The precedents for such a funeral were those of Marat or Mirabeau, and, although Napoleon III had refined and elaborated the practice of state funerals, these did not have the same overall national and educational purpose. Yet here, once more, there was no straight line connecting the two movements, but a gray zone, which complicates the tracing of influence. For example, the actual pomp and circumstance of state funerals began, not with the French Revolution, but with the baroque. The theatricality of the baroque, and its fascination with death, led to a surfeit of funeral pomp, with interminable processions and elaborate decorations: the catafalque came into its own as a kind of stage for the corpse. Though fascism, like the French Revolution, preferred a simpler, classical style for its decorations, baroque funeral pomp remained a fixture in the Catholic regions of Europe. The tradition of the baroque, familiar to fascist leaders, obscures the influence of the French Revolution. Nevertheless, while baroque funerals were religious rites without any political purpose, both the French Revolution and the fascists integrated such funerals and the cult of the dead into their political style, as part of their own self-representation.

Why this preoccupation with death by revolutions seeking to usher in a new and dynamic age, be it the Republic of Virtue, the Thousand-Year Reich, or the drive to create a new fascist man who would put everything right? The fascist call to sacrifice made use of the Christian dialectic of death and resurrection. The transcendence of death was closely linked in fascism to the fallen of the First World War, as documented by the design of military cemeteries with their crosses and frequent representations of soldiers touched by Christ.[41] The Nazis, for example, took the cult of the fallen soldier and applied it to their own martyrs. Death and life were not contraries, but linked to one another. For some Italian fascists, like the futurists discussed in the next chapter, death had to be accepted; it was sober and devoid of sentiment, a test of individual discipline. But, for the most part, fascists held to the traditional idea that sacrifice for the nation transcended death. Thus fascism sought to abolish death, just as it attempted to make time stand still. Such an emphasis in its ideology is hardly astounding in a movement dedicated to perpetual war.

The French Revolution could not make use of the Christian theme of death and resurrection. Instead, as we have mentioned, death was defined as perpetual sleep. Indeed, the redesign of cemeteries was part of the attempted de-Christianization of France. The cult of the martyrs helped to legitimize the Revolution, and the funerals of so-called "great men" in the Pantheon were seen as a means to educate the public in virtue.[42] These were men of the past like Rousseau, Voltaire, or Descartes (whom the Revolution could claim as its ancestors), the martyrs of the Revolution, and a few of its leaders. This cult of death was obviously different from that of fascism: it lacked the dialectic of death and resurrection. Only through the preservation of his memory in the minds of his countrymen could the martyr of the Revolution or the "great man" be assured of eternal life. With fascism, on the other hand, the dead return to inspire the living.[43] As soldiers fell in the wars of the French Revolution and Napoleon, there was a slow return to the idea of the sacredness of their last resting-place, as Christianity reasserted itself as a doctrine of consolation.[44] Though the nature of death was different, both the French Revolution and fascism practiced a cult of death in order to legitimize their revolution through its martyrs, to justify the call for sacrifice now or in the future, and perhaps also because they were under the spell of the apocalyptic vision that the scourges of God had to be overcome before time could be abolished. What Ernst

Bloch called the "hidden revolution" was never far below the surface even of those revolutions which rejected it.[45]

The cult of youth is easier to analyze: both revolutions sought to present themselves as youth movements filled with energy, resolve, and beauty. Yet, here also, there were important differences in practice and theory. Fascist movements were youth movements in fact and in theory, but the militants of the French Revolution were often family men, settled in life.[46] To be sure, young men went off to war, giving rise to songs and poems which extolled their youthful qualities as soldiers of the Revolution. Though the Marseillaise called all citizens to arms, according to the third verse it was "our young heroes" who fell in battle, while the earth stamped out new heroes to take their place. Fascist worship of youth hardly needs underlining. It is documented by the statues surrounding the Forum Mussolini in Rome, or the figures crowning the Führer's rostrum at the Nuremberg party rallies, showing a Goddess of Victory flanked by three figures of naked youths. But here, again, the connection is indirect, indeed even less certain than in the case of the cult of death. The cult of youth was a product of war, not of the French Revolution, while its revival at the *fin de siècle* directly influenced fascism.

It is easier to find general rather than specific links between fascism and the French Revolution and I have tried to sketch some of them here. If they are to be summarized, it might be simplest to state that the French Revolution marked the beginning of a democratization of politics that climaxed in twentieth-century fascism. I have attempted to analyze the legacy of the French Revolution as it applied to both national socialism and Italian fascism. But this legacy differed, just as the two fascisms were different in many respects. National socialism was the true inheritor of the aesthetics of politics. Though Mussolini also made use of the new mass politics, his dictatorship was more personal than that of Hitler, who tended to cast his power in symbolic form. But Italian fascism forged its own link to the Revolution, absent in Germany. The French Revolution had regarded itself as a new departure, creating a nation of brothers, while some of its radicals had talked about creating a new man. That was precisely what Mussolini had in mind: that fascism should create a new type of man, no longer a product of the present order.[47] He never told us exactly what this new man should look like or how he should behave, though this can be inferred from the new fascist style. The new man proclaimed that fascism must pass beyond the present into a yet uncharted future.

This seems one reason why some Italian fascists did not stop at the usual condemnation of the French Revolution, but called upon fascism to surpass it with a new kind of democracy to be run by producers. The fascist ideal of the new man inherits from the hated Enlightenment the concept that a new man can be created through education and experience.[48] The Nazis, and especially the SS, also envisaged a new man, but he was to exemplify ancient Germanic virtues, a man from the past unspoilt by the present. The primacy of historical myth in national socialism could not tolerate a revolutionary concept of man. Their different concepts of a new man was the nearest both Italian fascism and national socialism came to providing an official guide to utopia. But here, once more, differences between the two fascisms affected their view of the French Revolution. Mussolini, at least nominally, was opposed to utopias, to concepts standing outside history, and in his article on fascism in the *Encyclopedia Italiana* he linked the idea of utopia to Jacobin innovations based upon evil and abstract principles. Fascism was supposed to be a realistic doctrine which wanted to solve problems arising from historical development. For all that, the new man could not be allowed to exist outside the fascist state, but was an integral part of this state on the road to utopia. In spite of the repeated attacks upon utopianism, the fascist state itself tended to become a Republic of Virtue.[49]

The French Revolution was condemned, not only for its utopianism and materialism, but also for its passion for absolutes, as Jacobin thought was characterized by another article in the *Encyclopedia*[50]—surely an odd condemnation from a movement which believed in absolutes, from the myths and symbols of the nation to the infallibility of the Duce. The Jacobins were also attacked by Italian fascists for being too rigid and formalistic, but even this attack focused upon their love for absolutes. This meant, for one historian writing in the *Encyclopedia*, the attempt to purify France through the shedding of blood on behalf of abstract principles, such as the Supreme Being or the Republic of Virtue.[51] Once more, fascism itself was mirrored in this condemnation—it, too, wanted to enforce public virtue and was not averse to the shedding of blood, if not on behalf of the Republic of Virtue, then on behalf of a virtuous Nation.

Were such accusations due to the fact that fascism could not see the mote in its own eye, or do we see one revolution attacking a rival? While the first hypothesis was certainly true, the latter was of greater consequence. Hitler, as we have seen, constructed his own model of revolution, quite different from that of France; Mussolini, too, claimed originality for his revolution, which wanted to create a new man and a new nation through its own momentum, based upon its peculiar mixture of left- and right-wing doctrine. Perhaps because of the liberal tradition of the Risorgimento, and the syndicalists and futurists who joined with fascism, Mussolini's revolution was closer to the French model than that proclaimed by Nazi Germany. The Nazi condemnation of the French Revolution was on the whole straightforward: it was liberal and materialist, the work of Jews and Masons.

But what did French fascists themselves make of their own national revolution? Many of them had passed through the Action Française, with its exaltation of the *ancien régime* and hatred for the Revolution that had so wantonly destroyed it. We cannot describe here the attitudes of each French fascist movement to the Revolution; in any case, this would mean telling a repetitive tale accusing the Revolution of having begun a process which culminated in the corrupt Third Republic. Nevertheless, we can find ambivalent attitudes toward the Revolution on the part of some French fascists, different from those in Italy or Germany. George Valois, one of the founders of French fascism, saw the French Revolution as the beginning of a movement, both socialist and nationalist, which the fascists would complete.[52] Unlike George Valois, who never ceased to flirt with the left, the young fascist intellectuals who edited the journal *Je Suis Partout* in the 1930s and 1940s did not find their roots in the French Revolution, but were ambivalent about its heritage. This *équipe* reveled in their youth, worshiped energy, and cultivated an outrageous polemical style directed against republican France. *Je Suis Partout* published a special issue on the French Revolution in 1939, dedicated to those who had fought against the Revolution, especially the peasants of the Vendée, who were said to have sacrificed their lives for the truth, and to Charlotte Corday, who had assassinated Marat.[53] There was nothing ambivalent here, nor about the headline claiming war and inflation to be the driving forces behind the Revolution. The Revolution, so we hear, had opened the door to speculators long before present deputies had demonstrated once more the link between corruption and republican parliaments. And yet there was a certain admiration for Robespierre, "genie inhumain et abstrait," himself unique in his incorruptibility.[54]

However, once more Robespierre, the Jacobin, is condemned for his passion for absolutes, his "religious passions"—and this from Robert

Brasillach, the leader of this *équipe,* who could be said to exemplify just such a passion.[55] Brasillach, as one of his contemporaries put it, was himself a sentimental romantic, who was attracted to the aesthetic of politics, greatly admiring the Nuremberg party rallies as already mentioned.[56] This did not prevent him during World War II from accusing the Gaullists of possessing the religious spirit of a militant Robespierrism, which left no room for open-eyed realism.[57] These strictures were echoes of Mussolini's criticism of the Revolution, and in this case what we have called the mirror effect was present as well: the Revolution was accused of attitudes, many of which were, in fact, shared by fascists. Brasillach and his friends had broken with the Action Française precisely because it was too sober and stodgy, not passionate enough, and because it looked to the *ancien régime* rather than to a future revolution. Their revolution meant hatred for capitalism, Jews, and parliamentary democracy, a love of youth, and a fascination with violence.

Speaking about the French Revolution, Brasillach exclaimed that it had set the world on fire and that it had been a beautiful conflagration.[58] Revolution itself was praised, even if its content was denied. Similarly, Drieu la Rochelle praised the truly virile republicanism manifested by Jacobin authoritarians during the French Revolution.[59] For these young fascists the French Revolution served as an example of how to bring down the old order, manifesting the beauty of violence and of manliness. But even here they were not consistent. Thus, in the special number of *Je Suis Partout* on the Revolution, Brasillach condemned the Jacobin Terror and called for a general reconciliation—with the Vichy government in mind.[60] There was always the pull of conservative attitudes toward the Revolution, and it was the historian Pierre Gaxotte of the Action Française who wrote the leading article, claiming war and inflation to be the motors of the Revolution, in the special issue of *Je Suis Partout*. There, he roundly condemned all revolution: a revolution without the guillotine, without looting and denunciation, without dictatorship and prisons, was said to be an impossibility.[61] And this was written in a journal of which Robert Brasillach was the driving force.

The Jacobin lurked close to the surface among these French fascists and, as in the case of Mussolini, mirrored some of their own commitments and practices. The "abstract" was rejected in favor of a greater realism, but what was more abstract than a national mystique which demanded unquestioning loyalty, or a view of men and women through their stereotypes? For was not the so-called new man, after all, an ideal type?

The Jacobin Terror was at least momentarily rehabilitated by Marcel Déat's Rassemblement National Populaire (RNP) when, as the Germans occupied all of France, the collaborationists wanted to show themselves worthy of being trusted by the Nazis. Now a leader of the RNP wrote that, as in Robespierre's time, terror must be the order of the day. The sworn enemies of the national revolution should pay with their lives for treason or resistance.[62] But such praise for the Terror merely grasped a convenient precedent and hardly touched upon the influence the French Revolution itself may have had upon Marcel Déat and his political party.

The rejection of the French Revolution as a model for change was general among fascists, although, as we have seen, this was graduated in the Latin nations rather than one-dimensional as in Germany. But, when all is said and done, the most important influence exercised by the Revolution upon fascism was its inauguration of a new kind of politics designed to mobilize the masses and to integrate them into a political system—through rites and ceremonies in which they could participate, and through an aesthetic of politics which appealed to the longing for community and comradeship in an industrial age. As Adolf Hitler put it, when a man leaves his small workshop, or the big factory where he feels small, and enters a mass meeting where he is surrounded by thousands of people who share his convictions, he becomes convinced of the righteousness of the cause, gaining personal strength through fighting within an all-encompassing confraternity.[63] This was a language the members of the Committee of Public Safety might have understood.

Tracing the connection between the French Revolution and fascism means emphasizing degrees of difference, nuances, and inferences. No body of research exists that might encourage more authoritative statements about the link between the two movements, starting with the influence of the Revolution upon important fascist leaders. We would also have to know what, if anything, those who organized fascist rites and ceremonials actually borrowed from the Jacobins: only in the case of Nazi Germany can it be said with some certainty that the earlier movement provided little or no detailed inspiration. For all that, important connections existed, and even the manner in which fascist movements rejected the French Revolution can cast some light upon fascism itself. In the last resort, the political culture of fascism was indebted to the French Revolution in general, as the first modern movement to make use of a new kind of politics in order to mobilize the masses and to end the alienation of man from his society and his nation.

Every fascism had its own character, and Italian fascism received much of its dynamic and sometimes revolutionary fervor not from the distant past, but more directly from the futurist movement that was at one and the same time artistic, revolutionary, and political.

CHAPTER SIX

The Political Culture of Italian Futurism

Futurism has long been recognized as an important and influential artistic movement, part of the avant-garde which had its beginning in the early years of this century. The contribution of futurism to the political culture of the twentieth century has often been characterized as bizarre or amusing—of little consequence after the interventionist struggle during the First World War, or once the fascist movement had become established.[1] This judgment is certainly correct as far as any direct futurist influence upon the political events of its time was concerned, and yet it rests upon a very narrow definition of politics: instrumental and institutional as against the thrust of political culture. Political culture as I use it here means politics as the expression of a lifestyle, an attitude toward the totality of human experience. Viewed this way, futurism made its own important contribution to the civic religion of nationalism.

When the artistic importance of futurism is acknowledged but its political relevance denied, the aesthetic is torn from its political frame of reference. Yet culture and politics cannot be so readily separated. It was precisely because of its cultural orientation that futurism was able to make a distinct contribution to modern politics, giving nationalism a different kind of base than that which has filled this book.

While our political culture has been determined to a great extent by social struggles and political necessity, both modern culture and politics have been haunted by a specter that has been referred to repeatedly as crucial to the civic religion of nationalism: how to integrate the masses of the population into society and politics. The French and Industrial Revolutions raised this problem as more men and women than ever before lived in concentrated urban spaces, where they could be easily roused by political appeals and mobilized into the new citizen armies that came into being during the wars of the French Revolution and Napoleon.

Nationalism was the first modern movement that attempted to integrate all citizens into society and politics, and the way it went about its task was to determine much of the future. From the very beginning most national movements allowed no separation between politics and culture. They wanted to possess the entire man and brooked no rival allegiances. The very metaphors used by volunteers during the revolutionary and Napoleonic wars to describe their relationship to the fatherland illustrated this totality: they were its children, it was the mother and bride; nowhere do we find the nation confined, exiled as it were, to the political sphere.[2] The national anthems as part of the self-representation of the nation, discussed in the first chapter of this book, can furnish additional evidence. While national anthems focusing upon a king or emperor had stressed his fame and glory, the new national anthems emphasized brotherhood and the preeminent claims of the nation over the individual.

To be sure, liberalism attempted to build its politics upon the autonomy of the individual without denying the needs of the nation, and its balancing act between politics and the maintenance of individuality was by no means unsuccessful. Yet during serious economic, political, and social crises the demand for a totality of life was heard loud and clear until it managed to restrict effectively the space in which individuals could determine their own fate. Just as in earlier and present crises people flocked to the Church, so they were apt to look for security and shelter in the civic religion of nationalism—and as in their churches they saw the meaning of their own life represented by the symbols which surrounded them, hell as well as paradise, so, as we have seen in previous chapters, they reached a new level of perception through national symbols and ceremonial.

Futurism cannot be torn from this context, and its so-called political statements must be evaluated as an integral part of the futurist's literary and artistic purpose. To be sure, the futurist political program of 1918 sought to make a distinction between political and artistic futurism. But it did so because the futurist avant-garde was thought to have outstripped the artistic sensibility of the people. This sensibility, so the futurists thought, was essential for the political regeneration of Italy. Only the artist, through the fire of his intuitive genius, F. T. Marinetti tells us, can regenerate the nation and prepare it for the coming futurist age.[3]

This program reflects the changes of human perception which determined many of the attitudes and fears of the age when futurism was born, for not only the specter of integration haunted modern culture and politics, but also the new speed of time, the rapid change in the pace of life which the futurist manifestoes capture so well.[4] The futurist's joy in the simultaneity of experience summarized the change which, as the twentieth century opened, was pressing in upon all sides, symbolized by the revolution of communications—by railways, the automobile, and even the bicycle—as the culture of space and time was being transformed.[5] It was not only the futurists who saw in this revolution a challenge to the present order of things. For example, the constitution of the first French bicyclist association of 1870 called for a struggle against routine as the enemy of all progress.[6] The earliest reaction to the telephone was that one could now be two places at one and the same time, while the English Prime Minister Lord Salisbury marveled, in 1889, that the telegraph—an Italian invention that aroused the special enthusiasm of futurists—". . . combined almost in one moment . . . the opinions of the whole intelligent world."[7] Futurism took up and heightened already present perceptions of a world in rapid motion, a new dynamic that must be taken into account when assessing its influence upon political culture.

This revolution in time was accompanied by a revolution in visual communication: not only through the work of avant-garde artists, but also by the widespread use of photography and the beginnings of the cinema. They, too, seemed to involve a simultaneity of experience: being several places at the same time, unsettling for most people who before the turn of the century had lived in a more one-dimensional world.

The new speed of time related closely to the need for integration within a community able to provide some immutability, while at the same time giving new meaning, to life. But did this mean that such a community had to be rooted and static, communicating a feeling of belonging through organic growth analogous to nature and history? Traditionally nationalism had presented itself this way, condemning all that was rootless and that refused to pay its respect to ancient or medieval traditions. To be sure, at one point nationalism itself had been a movement directed against the establishment, but by the end of the nineteenth century it had become firmly established. Nationalism had its own dynamic, but this was increasingly directed toward outward expansion and against internal enemies. The new speed of time, the dynamic that threatened to escape all control, was caught up and tamed by its eternal verities. Nationalism seemed to have become the cement and not the yeast of society.

Such nationalism was a reactionary ideology that apparently slowed down change and restrained the onslaught of modernity. Surely this static quality enhanced the success of this dominant nationalism as an integrative force of diverse groups of the population. Yet it was the renewed dynamic, the appropriation of the new speed of time by another kind of nationalism exemplified by the futurists in their acceptance of modernity, that must make us revise our approach to the means through which this integration was accomplished. While most twentieth-century nationalism retained its role as an immutable and unchanging force, the repository of eternal and unchanging truth, a different nationalism, as we shall see—just as enthusiastic and single-minded—integrated men and masses through noninte-gration.[8] Modern technology was incorporated into such a nationalist system as a vital national symbol, and the individual rather than the masses supposedly stood at its center.

The individual was not tied to the weight of past history or the product of organic growth. He could take off into uncharted spaces, proclaiming, for example, Italy's glory through his personal drive and energy. Yet he must also be disciplined, integrated with like-minded men, not through a set world view, but through a personal and political style: a way of perceiving the world, of acting, and behaving based upon the sober and un-sentimental acceptance of the new speed of time, as well as upon a love of combat and confrontation. The end product was not the resurrection of past ideals, but a so-called new man—symbolic both of modernity and of the power and strength of the nation. This new man of futurism, then, was not, properly speaking, an autonomous individual—though he was given freedom of choice—but part of an elite of supermen voluntarily sharing an identical attitude toward life, discipline, and claims to national leadership. Individualism meant possessing the strength of will to rise above the mass of men in order to accept futurism and its consequences. Such an ideal catered successfully to youthful desires to be part of a community, and yet to retain their individual identity.

When in the spring of 1934 Filippo Marinetti visited the Germany of Adolf Hitler, he was greeted in the name of the National Socialist Writers

Union by Gottfried Benn, then Germany's greatest poet. After the obligatory reference to the Führer, Benn praised the futurist's love of danger, rebellious spirit, his joy in speed and lack of fear. He went on to declare that the fundamental contribution of futurism to fascism were the black shirt—"the color of terror and death"—(whose real origins had no connection with futurism), the battle cry "a noi," and the fascist anthem, the "Giovinezza." Benn concluded by exclaiming that Marinetti had demonstrated the immortality of the artist through his contribution to the political ideals of the nation.[9] Here fascism was defined through its style and discipline, "the toughness of creative life,"[10] to quote Benn once again—that resolute sobriety which was said to constitute the essence of both artistic and political form. Political style was substituted for ideology in the name of a new nation that looked to the future without the burdens of the past. This substitution was crucial to the fascist style, though futurism in alliance with fascism pursued its own cause and created its particular propaganda, which was not always identical with that of fascism. For all that, the artist was given a heightened importance in futurist and fascist political culture—a new immortality as Benn put it, though he himself was excluded from making a contribution to Nazi ideals. National socialism was based upon traditional nationalism and used its political style to a different effect than that of the futurists: not as a substitute for historical memories, but in order to make the past come alive as a model for the present and future.

Yet Italian fascism, once in power, was not able to share Benn's futurist model of politics; a more solid integrating force was needed than the wearing of a black shirt, a battle cry, an anthem, and the example of an elite of so-called new men. Nevertheless, the Italian fascist political style attempted to concretize the glorious past even while calling for the new man of the future. Partly because of this ambiguity, some of the most creative artistic minds in Europe were attracted to Italian fascism: men like W. B. Yeats, Ezra Pound, or T. S. Eliot—to cite merely some English examples—while national socialism was devoid of all real literary and artistic talent once Benn had left the party.[11] These men looked for the discipline of classical form and found it in the kind of fascism Benn had praised. Young French intellectuals like Robert Brasillach misinterpreted the Nazi ceremonial they admired, in a way that fit their own undisciplined and youthful drives, their love of style rather than ideological imperatives. This emphasis upon style rather than ideology was captured by Léon Degrelle, the youthful Rexist leader, when he called the fascist dictators the "poets of revolution."[12]

To be sure, these intellectuals were deluded about the course fascist regimes were to follow. No nation could rein in the new speed of time and provide an integrating force merely through discipline and political style. Yet the futurists were highly successful as propagandists for their own cause, using all means of publicity in order to attract attention. Their *serata* perhaps served this purpose best: grand happenings in a rented theater involving the audience as participants; being insulted and repaying in kind. Such evenings included political statements—for example, in 1914 eight Austrian flags were burned on the stage—as well as lectures and demonstrations of futurist art. The audience at these evenings was truly cross-class: bourgeois, students, workers, and intellectuals.[13] These *serata* were one of the chief means through which futurism became one of the first popular avant-garde movements. Most important from our point of view, Marinetti's statement of 1920 that while we do not live in a terrestrial paradise, economic hell can be overcome through the staging of innumerable artistic festivals,[14] anticipates the success and function of much of the political liturgy of European fascism.

Nevertheless, to popularize art and to aid people to escape for a brief time the routine of their lives was different from the attempt to mobilize the masses in order to take over power, and from the use made of such a liturgy once power had been attained. The futurists themselves realized this fact in their attempt to create a political movement after the First World War; more concrete and continuous signposts were needed. But for the futurists these did not include the past as an example for the present; instead they sought to institutionalize the avant-garde of a youthful elite. With the example of Marinetti and D'Annunzio before them, young writers like Robert Brasillach in France could be excused for believing that the avant-garde artist had a role to play within the political culture of Italian fascism, that the gulf between art and politics might finally be bridged.

This nationalism, then, was not weighted down by volkish ideals. It accepted technology and with it a new speed of time, using the forces unleashed by modernity in order to integrate men and nations. The political culture of futurism was expressed through a political style that sought to propel nationalism into modernity, to give it clarity and form without restraining its dynamic drive. Once this nationalism has been disentangled from völkish nationalism, the futurists become part of a more general movement seeking to gain dominance for the new as over the old nationalism. The First World War was a crucial phase in the development of both nationalisms: though the traditional was apt to emphasize the defensive nature of war together with its glory and challenge, the other saw the war as the beginning of a permanent revolution, as a good in itself. These attitudes were not exclusive. The radical right in much of Europe after the war harbored both nationalisms in an uneasy alliance.

When Marinetti called the war a *guerra festa*,[15] he was articulating the sentiments of volunteers all over Europe who had rushed to the colors as war was declared, seeking to transcend the boredom and responsibilities of their daily lives. These volunteers, as I have mentioned earlier in the book, created a myth of their war experience which, with its ideals of camaraderie and sacrifice, influenced the politics of postwar Europe. Everywhere the radical right broke out of its ghetto after the war, organizing veterans and attempting to become a mass movement.

Political liturgy, centered upon myth and symbol, became firmly rooted as an integral part of the postwar right-wing political culture, with its mass meetings, its choreographing of crowds, and its creation of the proper solemn and monumental environment. All this had been in the making for a century as part and parcel of modern nationalism. However, the futurist ideal of the political avant-garde had stripped it of most of its ideological weight. The war gave futurism an added momentum even as it encouraged the use of political liturgy by the radical right: where the mainstream of the right had sought to convey a sense of security and order as well as a certain dynamic, the nationalist right, which the futurists represented, rejected the appeal to normalcy and focused upon the insecurity of perpetual war. It took concepts like manliness, energy, violence, and death, and sought to tear them loose from the moorings of history and immutability in which more traditionalist nationalist movements had anchored them. Here modernity was again in conflict with tradition, nostalgia with the avant-garde.

Death constantly preoccupied the futurists—especially after the First World War, the test of their attitude toward life. During and after the war, as mentioned earlier, the unprecedented experience of mass death was made generally acceptable for the nation, tamed, as it were, through the cult of the fallen soldier with its constant analogy to Christ's death and resurrection. Death and resurrection were central to the iconography of military cemeteries as national shrines of worship, just as the ordered rows of graves in their natural setting also helped to transcend death in war.[16] Futurists demanded confrontation with the reality of death, instead: death was to be a test of self-discipline devoid of any transcendence. Sacrificing one's life for the fatherland was not beautiful or mystical, but must be taken for granted. During the war, in 1915, Marinetti wrote that "we commemorate our dead in shorthand; in this way we can avoid smelling their stench for too long."[17] For the advocates of heroism in life and war, there was nothing heroic about the war dead. Futurism, Marinetti had written earlier, exalts life and ignores death.[18] Here futurism demonstrated a bloody-mindedness, a calculated brutality, that through their rhetoric was transformed into a demand for battle without quarter, a fight to the finish—an extremism which at times outdid the vocabulary which fascists or Nazis applied to their own enemies.

The young French fascist, Robert Brasillach, saw the attitude toward death advocated by the futurists as central to the fascist myth, and pointed to the example set in the Spanish Civil War by the eighteen-year-old son of the commander of the Alcazar of Toledo—held hostage by republican troops—who faced death rather than urge his father to surrender the fortress in order that he might gain his freedom. The son was allowed to telephone his father in order to press him to surrender. "What is it little one," the commander asked; "nothing at all," the son replied, "they say they will shoot me if you don't surrender." "You know how I feel," the father replied, "if it is certain that they will shoot you commend your soul to God, give a thought to Spain and another to Christ." Shortly thereafter the son was shot. (To this day the telephone on which this conversation took place is displayed like a shrine in the fortress.)[19] It was the matter-of-fact and unsentimental attitude toward his own death, and the father's equally matter-of-fact assumption that the son's sacrifice was necessary, that impressed futurists and Italian fascists alike.[20]

Such an ideal of death for the fatherland can also be found among certain youthful members of the fascist and national socialist movements after the seizure of power. Here it was the often proclaimed principle of hardness toward one's self and others, facing death as part of one's regular duty, not to be sentimentalized but taken for granted, that led to attitudes parallel to those the futurists had advocated. Yet these attitudes were confined to a small and distinct minority—youths who thought of themselves as leaders of the future—such as, for example, those adolescents who attended the Nazi party boarding schools. After they graduated from these schools, such young men were likely to join the German army or the Waffen-SS before and during the Second World War.[21] Thus, death for the fatherland was accepted by these youths soberly and without sentiment, a test of the individual discipline which was supposed to unite the fascist elite. Fascism in power, however, identified with the traditional ideal of sacrificial death. The hall devoted to the memory of war heroes at the war cemetery of Redipuglia, which in 1938 was decorated with a frieze showing a fallen soldier lying in the arms of Christ, was typical of this attitude.[22] Here, at the very center of worship of the civic religion, tradition triumphed over a new futurist and fascist political style.

The ideal of manliness, always a part of the nationalist mystique, was an important metaphor through which futurists perceived their dynamic, the active and energetic élan of their movement. Marinetti endowed the beauty of speed with a militant masculinity.[23] I have shown elsewhere the close connection between nationalism and manliness in the nineteenth and twentieth centuries.[24] The masculine ideal as the principle of creativity put forward by Otto Weininger in his influential and racist *Sex and Character* (1903) had an immediate following among the radical Italian right, including important futurists. They took from this really quite unfuturist book whatever they needed. Weininger's exaltation of virility, as opposed to the feminine, struck a chord in the nationalist journals *Lacerba* and *La Voce,* where it was interpreted as contempt for the average human being by a youthful manly elite.[25] Moreover, the clear and unambiguous distinction Weininger drew between the sexes, encompassing moral and ethical judgment, drew those tight, clear lines which were the essence of the political style of futurist nationalism. Here there was no room for an "indefinite wobble," as Ezra Pound described liberalism and parliamentary democracy,[26] but clarity of form and decisiveness prevailed. Masculinity meant combat, and in Germany as well as Italy or France, one version of the ideal male after the First World War was a warrior represented by classical figures of youths on war memorials.[27]

We have drawn our examples not only from the Italian futurists but from men of other nations as well, in order to illustrate the general appeal of this kind of politics. However, if the Italian and French fascist concepts of manliness were similar, they differed from that current among the Nazis. The futurists loved brutal sincerity, combat, and what they saw as rough masculine energy, but this did not lead them to abandon, in theory at least, individualism in favor of the tightly knit male camaraderie characteristic of the Nazi SA or SS. Their emphasis was upon integration through disintegration, each man practicing in an autonomous manner what he regarded as the fascist style and discipline. This new man, as Marinetti defined him, was a disciple of the engine, the enemy of books, a believer in personal experience.[28] Moreover, he was the product, not of an inherited culture, but of his own activity—disciplined and lucid, sober, and contemptuous of death. This new man was no worshiper of ancient beauty, like Nietzsche's Superman, but for all his individuality he practiced his discipline and style in the service of the nation. The acceptance of modernity was shaped through faith in the power and glory of Italy. But at what price?

The search for a new man was a part of postwar political culture—not only a concern of the futurists, but also of Oswald Spengler's barbarians or Ernst Jünger's worker. Once again they share certain traits with the Italian futurists: the love of war and danger, the repudiation of the past and of books, and the self-discipline they imposed upon themselves. All these new men are the result of the war experience: the front-line soldier— a new race of men, as Ernst Jünger called them—energy come alive.[29] And yet it is precisely at this point that such new men met in an unholy alliance. The new man of the futurists, and that of Italian fascism, inspired by their vision, was confined to a certain style and discipline, which we have mentioned so often, while his actions had a definite goal and prescribed conduct. He may have been imagined as energy come alive, but it was well-controlled and disciplined energy. This avant-garde could not, after all, escape into orbits of their own choosing. They were tied to a certain definition of courage and manliness, fulfilling the destiny of the nation. Their integration through disintegration resulted in an ideal type rather than in ideal individuals.

The evolution of Ernst Jünger's thought in Germany from an emphasis upon the individual to the construction of just such a type is relevant in this context, symptomatic of the potential for depersonalization that existed even in that nationalism which accepted modernity and sought to transcend the weight of history. Jünger's writings during the war seemed to concentrate upon individual experience, the role of self-discipline, of energy, and the exaltation of battle. In his famous war diary, *The Storm of Steel* (1920), Jünger denied that infantry battles had degenerated into an impersonal butchery. "On the contrary, today more than ever, it is the individual that counts."[30] The challenge of battle has created foolhardy fighters. This sounds not so different from Marinetti's exaltation of war as both an individual and a national experience. Yet, as the book was being revised after the war, Jünger began to strike a different note: the condition of battle depersonalized man; stripped to his primeval instincts by the domination of machinery, man's personal feeling had to yield.[31] Now death in battle was for Jünger symbolic of an individualism destined for extinction. A new man will arise out of this war experience, one whose heroism consists in treating his body as a mere instrument beyond all instincts of self-preservation.[32] Such a man, when seen in group photographs, we are told, has lost all individuality. His penetrating look is steady and focused, practiced upon objects that have to be grasped while in rapid motion.[33] This "worker" has experienced a process of integration, and represents the transformation of the undisciplined masses into a disciplined army.[34]

Here the speed of time has lost its challenge, and modernity has created a human type which has successfully absorbed it. Ernst Jünger, like Marinetti, had no use for the guidance of history or volkish ideals (his opposition to national socialism on this count is well enough known), but in his case style and discipline have themselves led to a conformity no less stifling than that advocated by volkish nationalism.

Marinetti and the futurists did not mean to travel down Jünger's road. They opposed all that could end the speed of time, the march forward into uncharted spaces: artistic movements like *Strapaese* that idealized a rural and provincial past, and political devices like racism. Germany was attacked for staging an Exhibition of Degenerate Art, for believing in a photographic static.[35] Perhaps Wyndham Lewis, the futurists' sometime English disciple, expressed best the difference between the German tradition and their own taut political style, as they saw it, and this during the First World War before the rise of national socialism: "Germany stands for romance and should not win the war."[36] Futurists resisted Mussolini's imitation of German racial laws; anyone—presumably even a Jew—could become "a new man": it was his will and discipline which counted. Yet no modern mass movement could do without sentimentality and the appeal to tradition. No yardstick of an avant-garde elite could be used to reassure all citizens. Fascist movements were populist, and Marinetti was closer to Ernst Jünger or the young French fascists, who made no pretense at leading a popular movement.

Even so, futurism was eventually slowed down by the need for the representational, even the commemorative, in its fascist political art. The futurist contributions to the exhibition which celebrated the first ten years of the Fascist Revolution (The Mostra della rivoluzione fascista, 1932) are instructive in this regard. Enrico Prampolini dedicated a panel to the futurists and the Arditi which reflected something of their supposedly fiery and iron will,[37] but there were other paintings and statues attributed by the catalogue to the futurists that are monumental and static. Above all, the Hall of Martyrs with its giant cross and multitude of names, though apparently of futurist design, contradicted their own view of matter-of-fact death though, apparently, Mussolini himself had a hand in the planning of this sanctuary and ordered the construction of the cross as the centerpiece. The symbols of the Hall of Martyrs speak of transcendence, not of sober acceptance.[38]

Any consideration of futurism and political culture must address the questions of whether a nationalism based solely upon the challenge of modernity can be successful, and whether style can take the place of traditional content in nationalist politics. The love of technology, the fascination with speed, with machinery, was common to fascisms all over Europe, shared by many conservatives as well. For example, the engineers who flocked in such numbers to the Nazi cause were not simply technocrats—whatever that may mean—but saw only two alternatives before them: effeminate and cowardly escape into a pastoral past, or masculine and courageous flight into the German future.[39] Yet technology became a part of their self-identity with its roots thrust into the Germanic past; the "liberation" of technology that the Nazi regime was to bring about was said to be synonymous with the recovery of the German soul.[40] Here, despite these alternatives, the new technology was absorbed by traditional nationalism.

Such "reactionary modernism" was an attempt to reconcile modernist nationalism with tradition—the dominance of a romantic and historically oriented system of thought—most often the victor. Modernity created its own necessities as well: the longing for immutability in a changing world, and the need for order. Adolf Hitler expressed it well when he wrote, as mentioned in the last chapter, that with the seizure of power by national socialism the nervous nineteenth century had come to an end.[41] Nervousness was, after all, that disease thought basic to most other bodily and mental illnesses, projected upon all those who refused to conform to accepted norms. The political culture of futurism could not address nationalism as a new civic religion. Nevertheless, futurism did make a vital contribution to this nationalism, though the futurists themselves would have thought it wasted.

Nationalism as a civic religion now contained a dynamic, a drive, which must carry with it ever new generations. This involved not only the praise of war, the urge to take action, but also that style and discipline which the futurists championed. Here Gottfried Benn was correct: the shirt, the battle cry, the Giovinezza—symbols of action—projected a dynamic which was always present and at times difficult for European fascist parties to control.[42] This difficulty proved much greater in Italy than in Germany, for the "reactionary modernism" of the north was anchored securely in nationalism as a historical and civic religion. Here, in Italy, where the system upon which traditional nationalism was based was much thinner, porous, and liberal, the futurist élan could have a larger scope. The ideal of a "new man" of a yet undefined future was built into Italian fascism—even if he was a type rather than an individual—while in Germany such a "new man" exemplified a past resurrected: from the fallen in the war or Germanic heroes of ancient times.

However, futurist contributions to political culture, to politics as a way of life, had a still broader scope. They reflected the manner in which after 1918 many people built war into their lives, accepted and even glorified violent struggle as a purpose in and of itself. Discipline and style were put in the service of permanent war as a way of life. This outlook appealed to the same kind of youth who had volunteered for war in 1914. Marinetti's emphasis upon war as a festival, upon life as a constant happening, paralleled the wish for the extraordinary which was so strong in the minds of European youth satiated with bourgeois life. The *vita festa* with its heroism of the spirit, manliness, and will of iron—to stand the test of battle—addressed the hopes of prewar and postwar youth, to be institutionalized and tamed by the political liturgy of the nationalist right. Futurism heightened this longing without institutionalizing it, pushing what is known as the "spirit of 1914" to its extreme. As such it can be found in various movements of the radical right between the two world wars.[43]

The so-called German Free Corps in the years immediately after the war can provide one of the best examples of the implications of the futurist political style. Here this style came alive, and quite unconsciously expressed a felt need of postwar youth which was not confined to Italy. The German Free Corps was made up of former soldiers who chose to fight on once the First World War had ended in order to protect Germany's eastern frontier and to put down revolution at home. They thought themselves, not without reason, deserted by their own government, and for some of them the very concept of a German nation was no longer a political reality.[44] After the Corps had been disbanded, a myth grew up around these "soldiers without banners," *condotierri* fighting battles for their own sake, exemplifying self-discipline and creating their own political style. As one Free Corps leader wrote, ". . . we are an army of those men who must act."[45] The identical myth can be found more recently in works that have sought to glorify the courage, tenacity, and discipline of those volunteers who joined Hitler's foreign armies under the auspices of the SS. Here were men, to cite a French memoir, who ". . . had arrived at the outermost edge of Nietzsche's world view."[46]

This love of struggle, the assertion of manliness in a degenerate world, runs like a red thread throughout the first half of our own century, attracting much the same European youth to which futurism appealed; here, however, it was without the necessity of a modernist aesthetic. Futurism was stripped of the bizarre and the artistic in these movements; there remained only a stark and dynamic nationalism that had discarded all traditional and historical restraints. However, many of these later volunteers also believed in the new man of the future—thought of themselves as such new men—and asserted that the Free Corps or the SS had given firm contours to an otherwise vague ideal.[47] Clearly, the future was no longer open-ended for such men. Like Jünger's race of supermen or Spengler's barbarians, the future had arrived and the new man was a finished product.

In spite of all their differences from the futurists, such new men show us how the political culture of futurism might have looked when pushed to its extreme. They brought out something of the implications within the political culture of futurism. There was no direct connection between the futurists and these troops of volunteers, but the parallels help us to understand a political culture of which the futurists were a part, a political culture which sought to integrate men and masses, even as it attempted to accept the chaos of modernity. Yet in this process it ran the danger of depersonalizing and brutalizing politics.

The new man, symbol of a new age, who was to form an elite that would lead the nation into the uncharted future, proved in the end to be but another stereotype: a symbol not of an open-ended modernity but of the fact that twentieth-century nationalism in the last resort was tragically bound to be true to itself.

The futurists had rejected nationalism as a civic religion, but even here the general trend toward conformity inherent in all nationalism was evident as well. Where nationalism became a civic religion it was apt to foreclose all room for individuality. Futurists had rejected racism and accepted Jews as fellow fascists, but at the climax of the civic religion of nationalism Jews were discriminated against or expelled. There is no more poignant example of this thrust of modern nationalism than the transformation of intellectuals who had considered themselves guardians of individuality into obedient servants of the nation.

CHAPTER SEVEN

Bookburning and Betrayal by the German Intellectuals

In 1983, West German intellectuals commemorated the 1933 Nazi consolidation of power by holding talks, discussions, and conferences throughout the country. Every significant episode was recalled, and none is more relevant to academics and educators than the bookburning that was staged in all university towns on May 10, 1933. Since the Nazi party, professors, and students had collaborated closely in the preparation of this event, the betrayal by the intellectuals in their roles as humanists was fully revealed in this act. Coming at the start of the Nazi regime, it foreshadowed the exclusion of the Jews and dissidents from the nation which was to follow, for it was their books that were being burned.

The bookburnings were a spectacular act on the public stage, performed by a regime that relied on myths, symbols, representative art, and human stereotypes. It is well to recall the events that took place on this stage: over twenty thousand books blazed in Berlin, and over two thousand in other large cities of the Reich.[1] Professors of German and professors of law gave speeches, and students, almost all of them "Burschenschaftler" (fraternity boys), supplied the signal fire and the applause. But we must also look behind the curtain. The so-called "cultured circles," predominantly academics, were the ones who ignited the fire—not the Volk or the people without a book, but precisely that part of the nation that lived by the book. How did it come to that? Why did the middle-class intellectuals or the "Bildungsbürger" burn their own books? We must understand the background of this betrayal by the intellectuals—not only the immediate background, but how the flames of May can be placed within the development of German culture and society. With the help of the speech "Struggle against the Un-German Spirit," made by the then prominent professor of German literature Hans Naumann, and the jurist Eugen Lüthgens, at the bookburning in Bonn, we will attempt to trace the historical influences that led to such a narrowing of their field of vision. After that, we will focus on the classical concept of *Bildung,* which had played a crucial role in Jewish emancipation (as we shall see in a later chapter), and which departed from German history as abruptly as it had entered it.

Hans Naumann set the tone: this bookburning is a symbolic action, he exclaimed, a spring's awakening of youth, similar to that of the so-called rush to the colors of 1914.[2] Yet the heroic, the stormy impulse of youth, is mentioned only tangentially in the speeches; in the center stands the urge to renew the traditional bonds of family and homeland, Volk and blood.[3] The flames are meant to send a signal for the awakening of youth, for the heroic, for spring's awakening, but tamed by bourgeois virtues. We hear much about the fulfillment of duty and respectability, of enemies such as disintegration and dissolution, materialism and class struggle. It is not the individual heroism in war that is conjured up, but the myth of the war experience as the comradeship of the Volk, as service and sacrifice. What is necessary is an inwardness that provides support in the midst of the decadent world that surrounds us, as Eugen Lüthgens formulates it, rooted in Volk and race.[4]

Activism is embedded in a sense of rootedness and settledness, typical for the German political right. The nation as a civic religion supports the respectability of bourgeois society. It is symptomatic of this alliance that a bronze bust of Magnus Hirschfeld, who pioneered a new understanding of sexuality, was burnt in Berlin together with his books and the files of the Institute for Sexual Research, which he had founded in 1909: not only Jewish and dissident elements were involved here, but also an offense against bourgeois morals, the collapse of respectability. The tossing of the bust of Hirschfeld into the flames is the sole instance where an image was burned along with the books. Certainly Hirschfeld's so-called "typically Jewish" appearance also played a role that one ought not to underestimate.

Thus, an image of youth, similar to the "generation of 1914," was conjured up, not to abolish the existing order, but to cleanse it: like Walter Flex's protagonist Ernst Wurche in the *Wanderer between Two Worlds*

(1917), the young wished to "remain pure and become mature" and wanted to sense the whiff of "a religious spring."[5] They agreed here with England's Rupert Brooke, who, in one of his most famous poems of 1914, had compared the outbreak of World War I with a leap into clear water.[6] The students of 1933, like the volunteers of 1914, wanted to purify themselves and the nation by means of an inner rebirth. Even a brief overview demonstrates that the ideals of Führer and Reich had in 1933 already become the focus for images of regeneration dating from 1914.[7] But this was nothing new since in the nineteenth century the search for eternal values and inner rebirth was already characteristic of bourgeois youth. Yet, at the Wartburg Festival of the German fraternities in 1817, dedicated to the search for German unity, the students had not merely burnt so-called antinational books, but had also thrown a powdered pigtail into the flames as a protest against the ruling classes.

Such turning inward was not only a German phenomenon. During the rapid social and economic changes of the nineteenth century the European middle class in distress sought to call to its aid immutable powers that seemed impervious to change: the nation, nature, or revealed religion. In this way, bourgeois norms took on the appearance of immutability. World War I strengthened the yearning to believe in eternal values; nature, religion, and the nation stood for a safe and sound world, surrounded by death and destruction.[8]

In Germany, however, this craving for inwardness was especially strong and made it more difficult than in other Western states to save the tradition of the Enlightenment and reason, and with it the classical ideas of *Bildung*. Here there were not enough antibodies against the decline of the Enlightenment available; these were, for example, easier to obtain in England and France, where no war had been lost. While tendencies to burn books existed in all of Europe, it was in Germany that the flames were lit in May 1933. In addition to the defeat and collapse experienced by Germans, the opposition to rationalism was deeply rooted in a tradition that should not be overlooked, one that even coined a new terminology.

The German craving for inwardness was strengthened not only by the romantic era and the influence of Pietism but by a certain revolutionary tradition. We find this tradition in other countries as well, but in Germany it was stronger and longer lasting. Ernst Bloch called it the "secret revolution"; Jacob Böhme and Paracelsus were two of its prophets. It built upon the apocalyptic tradition with its special emphasis on suspending time and overcoming death. This was a revolution of inwardness which early on mobilized the disenfranchised against the rulers, but which then was coopted relatively easily by the existing society. It was not a big step from the "dawn of the apocalypse" to the flight into myth. The paradise of an eternal Germanic past was to be recaptured. The world, which, according to Ernst Bloch's dictum of 1921, was rushing toward the revolutionary apocalypse, in reality feverishly approached a reactionary utopia.[9] The heralds were prophets of a new religion; however, the great "conquerors" were those who waited until the time was ripe. Böhme and Paracelsus had their successors: Wagner, the impeded savior,[10] and Stefan George, whom Hans Naumann so boundlessly admired.[11] Not only do the speeches at the bookburnings allude to the "secret Germany,"[12] but Naumann saw the Führer hand in hand with George—like Zarathustra descending to earth. Already, much earlier, Naumann had quoted George's aphorism of flame: "He who loses the flame from view is driven, vanishing, into the universe."[13] ("Wer die Flamme aus dem Blick verliert, den treibt es zerstiebend ins All.")

The German "predisposition for a life of the spirit," as a schoolbook of the nineteenth century formulated it, was also encouraged by Lutheranism, by the fact, which Robert Minder has analyzed so well, that so many of the most influential German thinkers and poets came from Lutheran parsonages.[14] Germany produced no anticlerical Protestant poet of note, perhaps owing to the general craving to embody all possible eternal values. The overwhelming majority of the bourgeoisie did not question authority; the nation and the existing order were the driving forces through which eternal values were brought down into their personal lives. They made life holy and gave daily life new meaning. The inner life pressed for an outer confirmation; here, Lutheran inwardness had long ago proved insufficient. Thus, the young volunteer, who in 1914 was blessed in church before departing with his regiment, said, "Now we are made holy."[15]

The students at the Wartburg had come forth against the will of the authorities; however, the students of 1933, like the volunteers of 1914, were called up by the powers that be. No Bastille was stormed, no human rights were proclaimed. On the contrary, an inner purification was the goal, a purification that would then automatically bring about a better, healthier world. Yet, upon closer inspection, this great spring cleaning proves to be a dusting off of old furniture and a sweeping out of the parlor.

The "Burschenschaftler" of 1933, like the volunteer of 1914, saw himself as the true representative of the nation. Such a fiction was still preserved in 1933, although the student in modern society—in contrast to under-developed nations—no longer exercised this function: most social groups were now capable of articulating their own concerns. The students of 1933, indeed even those of 1914, could not perform the function of the students at the Wartburg Festival where, in a certain sense, they did speak for the nation. The yearning remained, however, and it was not only left-wing bourgeois youth who wanted to move down among the Volk; the right had exactly the same wish. The bookburnings were symbolic of the path that would lead the educated out of their isolation from the Volk. Thus, the leader of the students at the bookburning in Würzburg stated: "The work of Bismarck is now being crowned." And he meant the national socialist takeover. "This work," he continued, "was done by a simple man of the Volk without any academic education, . . . it is not the academic education that is decisive, but rather the living will."[16] The path to the Volk was complete; Adolf Hitler was the model, and the concept of *Bildung* had to conform to Hitler's "ideals." The academic was now enabled to take part in a living community, an exalting and refreshing experience, particularly since he was to become a leader of the Volk and pioneer of the Reich. Thus, the claim of the educated to leadership could be democratized through ar-ticulating and formulating the will of the entire nation. Such fictions are part of the history of intellectuals in an era of masses, whether of the right or the left.

But it was the right that made it easier for artists, writers, poets, and students to maintain this fiction by assigning them a political function which the workers' movement or a parliamentary republic could not offer. They helped build the bridge between the "secret Germany" and the mod-ern mass movement by giving shape to a political liturgy. Politics as a drama expressed itself through rites and symbols. Here the educated had a po-sition that gave them the appearance of a *praeceptor Germaniae,* of which Naumann, for example, then unctuously made the most. Architects, artists, and poets of the Third Reich found here a path to a community with the Volk,[17] which seemed to validate their claim as leaders. The artistic and the political had united in the nationalization of the masses, in which the one complemented the other in order to disguise reality and make it palatable.

Gabriele D'Annunzio, as we saw in previous chapters, exemplified the way in which a poet could shape political reality, and he found imitators even where leaders like Mussolini and Hitler pulled the strings. Here the poet as prophet became reality. D'Annunzio himself continually dealt with the symbol of the flame in much the same way in which it appeared so much later at the bookburnings.[18] The flame was not a predominantly negative symbol, although it was that, too: the burnings of heretics and witches had long preceded the bookburnings. But with the modern nation the flame became one of the most important symbols of resurrection, return, and purification—it united the Christian motif of resurrection (i.e., the Easter fire) with the pagan motif of spring. The bookburnings must be understood as a fire of purification, of awakening, as analogies to the generation of 1914 made clear again and again. Successful mass movements cannot be inspired by negative symbols. The bookburnings were to represent a positive symbolic action within the bounds of the Third Reich.

Already in the course of the nineteenth century a bourgeois society searching for stability and eternal values had sharply isolated the outsider, and Naumann's description of members of a foreign race as shameless, dissolute, and decadent reflects here, too, a historical development upon which the Third Reich could build.[19] The outsider was understood as that person who deviated from the norms of bourgeois society and thus placed them in question. Not only in Germany was the outsider increasingly locked into place; outsiders in most countries were measured by the same yardstick, brought into line (*gleichgeschaltet*), long before such a process became identified with the policies of national socialism. The concept of race chiefly affected Jews, but the medicalization of the outsider, as Sander Gilman has called it—the stylization of the outsider into a medical case—placed all of them firmly beyond society's norms. The mentally ill, habitual criminals, homosexuals, and Jews were ever more firmly fixed within their so-called abnormality by means of the concept of illness. They were sick, as one can read in the medical reference works of the time, nervous and fidgety in a time when calmness was demanded; the outsiders were exhausted when energy was the call of the day.[20] How similar the antisemitic iconography was to that of the mentally ill in the nineteenth century: ungainly, always in motion, disproportioned. In every outsider the much praised manly virtues were missing, especially self-control and a love for the finer things in life.[21]

Jews and homosexuals were often accused of acting like women: they sowed confusion where order was imperative; they menaced the division of labor on the basis of sex and did so within a society that was largely based on such a division of labor. Here we have arrived again at that respectability which guarantees a sex-specific division of labor, in addition to control over sexual drives—all of that which the outsiders lack and which made the work of Magnus Hirschfeld so particularly symbolic.

The sick were contagious, and the entire medical vocabulary of infection, used so much by the Nazis, was based upon the medicalization of the outsider. But the sick could be healed, and the Nazis initially attempted this—naturally, only with Aryans, not with Jews. Yet here a fundamental theme reappears: the alliance of national socialism and bourgeois respectability. To cure, therefore, meant to spur the outsider on to strenuous labor, to obey a rigid moral code, to take on a normal appearance, as far as that was possible. Such was the treatment in many cases for homosexuals in the concentration camps. And such were the instructions for the asylums in reference to euthanasia: whoever could not be cured from "outsiderdom" had to die. For the outsider existed against the natural order of things, an order that had been monopolized by society, the nation, the current norms, as we have seen.[22] To appropriate a piece of eternity for oneself was pointless if it did not serve to restore cleanliness, harmony, and beauty to the world.

The bookburnings were a further step in this direction, for not only books written by Jews were burned, but also those that were branded as shameless and decadent. The Zionist *Jüdische Rundschau* of Berlin wrote on May 10 with great insight: "The big spotlights at the *Opernplatz* (in Berlin) shone also into our tangled existence and our fate. Not only Jews, but men of pure German blood, too, were accused. They will be judged individually according to their actions. But for the Jews no individual reasons are needed; there the old proverb applies: 'The Jew will be burned.'"[23]

These, then, seem to me to be the most important factors leading to the betrayal of the intellectuals. All of these factors: the turning inward, the ideal of rebirth, of purification, the craving for eternal values, for being at one with the people, the primary importance of respectability, the exclusion and isolation of the outsider as well as his homogenization left their traces in the brief speeches at the bookburnings. Speakers like Naumann, and the fraternities listening to him, saw themselves as acting for the nation—but in reality it was *Bildungsbürger* speaking to *Bildungsbürger*.

What had the educator betrayed? A concept of *Bildung*, which represented exactly the opposite of the myth of eternal values and everlasting order, one that focused upon the individual and upon the power of his own reason. The content of this "neohumanist" concept of *Bildung* at the turn of the eighteenth to the nineteenth century was "the development of the intellectual, moral, and aesthetic capabilities of the individual in order to further his independence and self-determination," as Rudolf Vierhaus formulated it. The educated person, he continues, is not a *Bürger* because he belongs to some class or profession, but because of his love for humanity.[24] Goethe's Wilhelm Meister expressed in one sentence the wish that accompanied him throughout his life: "to educate (*ausbilden*) myself, just the way I am."[25] This self-cultivation, according to Wilhelm von Humboldt, was to take place at the university through the study of classical and aesthetic subjects. The state was to have no say here. "Academic freedom" was supposed to reign, and the university was to be more an institution of independent research than of teaching. The new university of Berlin, founded in 1810, was intended to exemplify these principles.

Individuality, freedom, and reason stood at the center of the concept of *Bildung*, modeled on ancient Greece, where, so Humboldt tells us, individuality and citizenship were identical. Both were accompanied by classical beauty, which Humboldt defined as "clarity of mind."[26] It cannot be overlooked that the concept of *Bildung* was optimistic and somewhat vague, too individualistic—and Humboldt himself had great difficulty in defining a concept of community. His highest ideal of community consisted in the coexistence of human beings in which each strives to develop himself from his essential nature and for his own sake.[27] Such an ideal could not easily be reconciled with demands of life or politics.

Yet, in the age of the Wars of Liberation against Napoleon, German national consciousness was not yet estranged from this ideal of *Bildung*. Personal freedom was often perceived as an intrinsic component of patriotism, and tolerance as well as cosmopolitanism were part of what it meant to be German. Certainly Ernst Moritz Arndt must be read in this way: not only did he want to protect ordinary people from exploitation by tyrants, but for him the ideal of the fatherland was inconceivable without the freedom of all mankind. And yet, here, too, as with Fichte, who was discussed at the beginning of our study, portents of the future are present as, for example, when German warriors were said to exemplify "freedom, valor, masculinity, chastity, order, and propriety."[28] The vision of Germany became restricted in the struggle with "immoral France"; nevertheless, liberalism remained alive, not in opposition to but as a prerequisite for the existence of the nation. Over one hundred years later, however, Professor Lüthgens castigated what he called the "fiction of individual freedom," which had led men to ignore the wider goals of society and the nation.[29]

Precisely because the concept of *Bildung* was so open—theoretically, everyone could acquire *Bildung*—it came into conflict with the formation of an elite in bourgeois society. This was a necessity that every rising middle class felt; in England, a bourgeois elite took form at the same time, the product of the reformed "public school" as well as of Oxford and Cambridge. In Germany, the educated became the elite, as Humboldt had desired, but in the process they transformed themselves into a closed, self-renewing caste: the academics with their own hierarchy as the guardians of *Bildung* and therefore of national consciousness.

Many of these academics were liberal, even reformers. The evolution from the old to the new ideal of *Bildung* did not proceed in a straightforward manner. For example, professors along with artists, writers, and liberal politicians, prevented the introduction of strict censorship in Wilhelminian Germany.[30] Nevertheless, a further constriction of their field of vision resulted from the concept of *Bildung* itself, because, now that *Bildung* had been professionalized, neohumanism was downgraded to a pedagogy. *Bildung* was no longer perceived as a continuing development of the personality; only the end product counted. At this point during the nineteenth century, *Bildung* as a profession and the ever narrowing vision of society met, and perhaps one can view the alliance of professors and Prussian bureaucrats in the "Kaiserreich" as the decisive stage of this development.[31] Therefore it was almost logical that the word *Bildung* was trivialized and came to describe the yearning for something more elevated—it did not really matter what that something was, it only had to provide an uplifting experience. Fontane strikingly portrayed this trivialization of *Bildung* when he wrote that Jenny Treibel, despite poetry and exalted feelings, was still the Jenny Bürstenbinder of old, exclusively concerned with externals.[32] Whether in fraternities, at the podium, or in Jenny Treibel's drawing room, the concept of *Bildung* had largely lost its openness, its liberality, and its reason. The fraternities accepted the narrowed concept of *Bildung* and the academic caste system as they attempted to regenerate themselves by means of a symbolic leap into the Volk.

The concept of *Bildung* led to yet another unforeseen consequence: the primacy of culture. Already for Humboldt, *Bildung* was oriented toward aesthetic values and the classics—it stood above the mundane. Academics, whether liberal or conservative, saw themselves, therefore, as standing above politics and political parties.[33] The Volk articulated itself through culture, a culture which easily became myth. The old ideal of *Bildung* had passed into the hands of the learned, and they felt themselves to be the furthest advanced in the process of *Bildung*, obliged to be teachers and educators of mankind.[34] The old ideal of *Bildung* was still alive among many intellectuals who were self-employed, among the liberals of the old school, and especially among the so-called left-wing intellectuals of the Weimar Republic. But such intellectuals were being pushed more and more to the edges of society, particularly since they were often Jews. Finally, many of their books were then burned.

Humboldt's old concept of *Bildung* had weaknesses; certainly the greatest among them was its distance from reality on the basis of the primacy of culture. It was because of this distance that the noble concept helped liquidate itself. What was latent in all of Europe became reality in Germany. The concept of national socialism itself, as discussed earlier, is of French origin, and France, not Germany, experienced the first modern mass movement, as well as the Dreyfus Trial. But concrete historical developments brought the right to power in Germany, facilitated by those intellectual currents I have analyzed here, which so largely shaped the consciousness of the ruling classes—articulated by the educated as the *praeceptores Germaniae*. Reality exists as humans perceive it, as their consciousness determines its nature. Everyone lives his own myth. Too few Germans met the crisis in their lives and in society during and after the war in a reasoned way. Too few made use of the old concept of *Bildung*, which did offer an alternative, however archaic it may have been.

The old concept of *Bildung* was not tailored to the era of mass politics. The Nazi nationalization of the masses, on the other hand—politics as the drama of lofty values—was. Yet even in the midst of all the intoxication and enthusiasm the craving for self-cultivation lived on in free spaces not occupied by the state, the Volk, or official culture. When, in February 1936, a magazine of the "Strength Through Joy" movement, *Woman at Work*, took a poll of working women, 81 percent of those who answered said that they wanted to use their leisure time in their own ways. Of these, 32 percent felt a hunger for good books, and it was not the official Nazi literature they had in mind.[35] Thus, below the surface continuities believed long dead were present. Even if total control can transform historical reality, it apparently does not change all of human nature.

And yet, one part of the German bourgeoisie continued to see itself as guardians of neohumanist *Bildung*, in spite of the new currents of the time, in the face of national socialism, and even in the face of death. The German-Jewish *Bildungsbürgertum* had been assimilated into the German bourgeoisie during the relatively brief epoch of classical *Bildung*, and it viewed as its own this tradition which had helped make Jewish assimilation possible. Two examples must suffice to illustrate their continued adherence to the old concept of *Bildung*: no other group so consistently cultivated the Goethe myth in its positivist Enlightenment interpretation; most of the Goethe biographies were written by German Jews, while an answer of the leaders of German Jewry to the antisemitic wave of the 1890s was to call for subscriptions to a Lessing monument. If one analyzes the cultural aspects of the German-Jewish emigration and the Jüdischer Kulturbund (the officially permitted Jewish cultural organization) under the Nazis, one soon notices that here the neohumanist ideal of *Bildung* was, in a certain sense, rescued and transmitted to our times.[36]

And still the ashes glow. What in 1933 illuminated the "Opernplätze" of Berlin and Bonn, among others, is still latently present. We still do not know how the true ideal of *Bildung* can be brought into harmony with the modern mass society. Bourgeois respectability is still too often maintained at the outsider's expense. The estrangement from reality of many young people is frightening—irrational currents often possess political significance. The list of latent dangers is long and not to be overlooked if we remind ourselves of the consensus upon which national socialism rested so long—it ultimately fell, not from within, but only as the result of a lost war. That must sober us, since we know, as has been stressed throughout this book, that the dangers and temptations exist in all countries as an integral part of all nationalism. But bourgeois society, which determines our entire attitude and our lifestyle, even in large part for those who view themselves as antibourgeois, also needs reexamination. At one time its ideals were based on true *Bildung*, on tolerance and freedom. Can these values also survive times of crisis? Can we learn the lessons from the ever narrowing vision of the bourgeois world?

Here it is not a matter of exorcising a past, which, like all history, was tied to its specific time. Those who so gladly shout "fascism" today trivialize the past. To see the fascism or national socialism of the period between the world wars as existing today only diverts from the real dangers and turns fascism itself into an eternal value. Instead, it is a matter of scattered piecework: components of fascist or Nazi prejudices and myths still lie about—after all, like racism, they were only a heightened nationalism— still tempting, and because of that it has been useful to examine one of the pieces and to confront it with Humboldt's concept of *Bildung*. Each nation is a mix of many, often contradictory traditions, and Germany was no exception.

Such traditions transcend the left and right, although the right has been especially susceptible to the search for eternal values, to the fear of chaos— yet, bourgeois respectability and many of its attitudes toward life have been held in common by all classes along with all of the attendant dangers. In just the same way the old concept of *Bildung* somehow lived on in Germany in different classes: among the left intellectuals, some liberals, and especially the German-Jewish bourgeoisie, and, as we saw, also among those women who had answered the poll of the "Strength Through Joy" movement, most of whom were not formally educated. One did not have to burn books to be part of the betrayal by the intellectuals. National socialism could build its consciousness upon a perversion of the idea of *Bildung*. Still, we know who burned the books—the educated themselves. The Jews saw themselves excluded from the *Bildungsbürgertum* which had once welcomed them; the bookburning was evidence that their status as outsiders was being consolidated, that there was now no room for them in the civic religion of nationalism.

PART TWO

The Jews and the Modern Nation

CHAPTER EIGHT

The Jews and the Civic Religion
of Nationalism

The nation by its very nature demanded a thorough assimilation by Jews long before the civic religion of nationalism threatened their membership in the community. Nevertheless, nationalism was not simply good or evil but contained many layers of meaning. This statement was especially relevant for Jews in Western and Central Europe after emancipation. For while it was the state, then in formation, which emancipated them, it was the nation they faced once they were emancipated. Jews up to that time had been treated as an altogether separate nation, referred to as the "Jewish Nation" in distinction to the nation in which they lived; now they had to leave their own nation and integrate themselves into the host nation. The adjustments and the problems of such integration have been analyzed many times in religious, social, and economic terms, and indeed these factors were crucial to Jewish assimilation. But on another level as well Jews had to come to terms with the modern nation as a unifying force which tried to assimilate not only the Jewish nation but many other diverse groups of the population.

The myths and symbols of nationalism, with their liturgical rites and ceremonies, seemed one important avenue through which the people united with the nation. During most of the nineteenth century they had served to document the loyalty of Jews to the nation as well. Jews took part in national festivals, sang national anthems, and admired national monuments. Here the Nation tended to become a civic religion, as defined throughout this book; even if at times it showed itself flexible and even tolerant, in the end its claims became ever more absolute. The nation was defined primarily in cultural terms, as for example in Germany, and many of its national heroes like Goethe and Schiller came from the Enlightenment with its promise of toleration in return for good citizenship.[1] Nationalism itself, then, was not simply one-dimensional: it could make alliances with liberalism and even socialism; it was not yet mainly conservative or chauvinistic in spite of the way in which it displayed itself. A liberal and rather tolerant nationalism characterized the period of Jewish emancipation, and the Jews themselves supported this nationalism which continued to make their assimilation possible. Nevertheless, even apart from its hymns and its liturgy, certain foundations of national identity were taken for granted regardless of the variety of politics nationalism could accommodate.

The belief in the existence of a "national character" was present from the beginning of modern nationhood.[2] Romanticism, with its emphasis on organic development, on the totality of life, was at the root of this search. It meant that regardless of the unity in diversity advocated by some nationalisms, cohesion and uniformity were always potentially present. The foundation upon which national character was built did not differ greatly from nation to nation: a certain morality, comportment, and appearance were crucial, usually linking the nation with the moral attitudes of the newly triumphant middle classes.[3] The Napoleonic Wars, in which so many nations found their national identity at the beginning of the nineteenth century, added ideals of manly strength, heroism, and camaraderie. At the same time, the preoccupation with ideals of beauty in an ever more materialistic and urban civilization gave shape to such ideals through the elaboration of a national stereotype. The important role played by the admiration of art among the nineteenth-century bourgeoisie is well known: art as a projection of beauty stood for the true, the good, and the holy, and so did the national stereotype, which reflected and personalized the character of the nation.

Here the nation set additional conditions on Jewish assimilation, and, though the now dominant manners and morals were no real obstacle, as we shall see in the next chapter, the national stereotype was potentially dangerous. For in all constructions of a national character the distinction between insider and outsider was sharply drawn. The antisemitic literature opposed to Jewish emancipation cast the Jew as the very opposite of national ideals as reflected in the stereotype of national character, lacking in respectability, truthfulness, and manly beauty. The Jews, and indeed all of those who stood outside of respectable society and therefore of the national ideal, were always characterized for what they were not rather than for what they were, measured against the ideals represented by the nation.

Within the evolution of nationalism the relationship between insider and outsider needs closer examination. How important was the counter-image, the stereotype of the Jew, to the image of nationalism; how important, that is, was the outsider to the very existence of society itself? Nationalism had its origins in the needs of the times, but its evolution toward a full-blown civic religion was sharpened and further defined as it faced real and putative enemies. And all these enemies, some of whom have been mentioned already in the preceding chapter, whether so-called unassimilable Jews or, for example, those who in Germany were called the scoundrels without a fatherland—namely the socialists—were seen as possessing identical morals, manners, and looks, directly opposed to the national stereotype. Here we may have touched upon a hidden need of all of modern society, through which insider and outsider are indissolubly linked.

Most Jews before the 1930s entered fully into the civic religion of nationalism—within the ever narrower nationalism of Germany or, much more easily, into what remained of the liberal nationalism of Italy or France. Jews accepted the demands of modern nationalism and kept their identity through their faith or family tradition. The barriers to their assimilation, just mentioned, were potential rather than actual warning signs. Where national ideals expressed themselves largely through comportment and looks, conditions were created which eventually encouraged antisemitism and even racism, but only in the end did this mean total integration or total exclusion.

The civic religion of nationalism was a secularization of revealed religion, and yet Christianity remained an active element, another indication that Jews might easily become outsiders. The connection between nationalism and Christianity was most obvious, so it seems, at the start of modern nationalism and then again during the First World War. During the first part of the nineteenth century, national monuments were proposed in which crosses played a part. Churches themselves were designed as national monuments, such as the Cathedral of Cologne in Germany, or the Madeleine in Paris, and churches could provide the settings for national festivals. But the influence of Christianity was mostly felt in less obvious ways, as, for example, in the production and choreography of national festivals. After all, the civic religion was a secularization of revealed religion and always kept something of its origins. This problem has not yet been properly investigated, except for Germany,[4] and until the period of the First World War all statements must be tentative. But in that war, as hundreds of thousands sacrificed themselves for the nation, the link between nationalism and Christianity became obvious. Christian symbols, indeed the very figure of Christ, were present in the cult of the fallen soldier—and, in Germany, Italy, and France, familiar Christian symbols represented national sacrifice.[5] The First World War was a climax in the evolution of modern nationalism, and in its quest for totality the nation sought to coopt Christianity. We are concerned with modern nations which practiced their own civic religion, and not with nations like Rumania where nationalism and Christianity were virtually identical in a predominantly peasant society, and where, during the Second World War, the Legion of the Archangel Michael, better known through its shock troupe, the Iron Guard, staged bloody pogroms against the usurious and infidel Jews who had killed Christ.

For many Jews the First World War seemed to present a new opportunity for a more perfect integration into the nation at the precise time that the civic religion of nationalism became ever more menacing through its cultural imperatives, which tended to homogenize its members. This civic religion, especially after the First World War, was supported by much of the center and most of the political right. Now its effect in many nations with an antisemitic tradition was a de-emancipation of the Jews rather than the integration of outsiders into the nation. Most European Jews were patriots and remained liberals. This meant a certain reluctance to participate in a nationalism which had shed its earlier tolerance and was becoming increasingly militant—an integral nationalism which sought control over all aspects of life and thought. The more developed the religion of nationalism, the greater the need for external and internal enemies against which it could define itself and strengthen its resolve, and here the Jews were a ready-made target.

But what about the civic religion of nationalism among the Jews themselves, as some attempted and then succeeded in founding a Jewish nation? The Zionist movement, similar to other European nationalisms, contained many social and political attitudes: it could absorb socialists, liberals, and conservatives. And yet, at first, liberalism predominated, reflecting the self-interest of Jews in their period of assimilation. But this liberal impetus did not entail a neglect of the civic religion of nationalism. Theodor Herzl himself is a good illustration of how both liberal attitudes and the civic religion were joined. Herzl, in 1902, published his Zionist utopia, *Altneuland*. The Palestine of the novel is a land where "supreme tolerance" reigns, where Arabs and Jews live harmoniously side by side, and where religion is largely removed from public life. To be sure, a chauvinist faction, led, typically enough, by an Orthodox rabbi, struggles for power in *Altneuland*. But the hero of the book strongly affirms that there can be no distinction between one man and another, that one should not inquire after a man's religion or race. And indeed, the hero's best friend is an Arab of an old Palestinian family.[6] Herzl's departure from liberal dogma comes only in his praise of an economy based on the model of the English cooperative movement.

National symbols and national rites were an integral part of the Palestine of Herzl's imagination. The care with which Herzl personally designed the symbols of Zionism and the staging of his Zionist congresses is now well known; as he put it in his *Judenstaat* (1896): ". . . if anyone wants to lead many men he must raise symbols over their heads."[7] He paid close attention to the creation of a flag for the movement, and devoted his energies to the design for a new parliament building. Many more examples of the conscious creation of national symbols could be given, from creating songs for the movement to the often elaborate ceremonials at Zionist congresses. The invention of national festivals also engaged Herzl's attention, and Martin Buber's call in 1899 for a national rite which would link the victory of the Maccabees to the new Jewish national movement reflected his own intentions. But in this particular case the Maccabees did not stand for an aggressive spirit; indeed, the nationalism which accompanied the creation of this civic religion was centered largely upon the inner renewal of the Jew, a renewal which would make the Jew one with the land and his people. Hans Kohn, an important early theoretician of the Zionist movement, called this the "nationalism of inwardness." An inner spiritual reality would be created through membership in a real community based upon shared experience. Martin Buber and his Zionist friends considered this the true "Hebrew Humanism."[8] This was not the revolution of inwardness of the "secret Germany" mentioned in the last chapter, which all too often resulted in a cry for battle. For Herzl, as for Buber, the civic religion of nationalism was not a call to battle but an educational process for the individual Jew who must recapture his dignity as a human being.

Martin Buber and many other Zionists saw national unity as a prerequisite for a greater unity among peoples, between humanity and all living creatures, between God and the world. Their creation of a civic religion was accompanied by a certain cosmopolitanism more resonant with the old, more tolerant nationalism than with the all-encompassing and chauvinistic nationalism which was reaching for victory after the turn of the century.

The First World War strengthened such so-called integral nationalism all over Europe, and it penetrated Zionism as well. Vladimir Jabotinsky founded his Revisionist movement in 1925, and this movement subordinated considerations of justice and morality to the central goal of founding a sovereign and exclusively Jewish state in all of Palestine. For Jabotinsky, old-fashioned liberalism was irrelevant, as good as dead in a world which knew no mercy. The result was a Zionism which called itself a movement rather than a party, and which attempted to rely upon a mass base. Jabotinsky in his novel *Samson the Nazarite* (1930) said of his hero that in the spectacle of thousands obeying a single will, "... he had caught a glimpse of the great secret of the builders of nations."[9] Jabotinsky paradoxically never rid himself completely of the liberalism of his Russian youth. He himself remained a liberal in his social and economic outlook, and regarded his more militant nationalism as a pragmatic response to a given situation, the only way in which Jews could obtain a state. He saw no value in the state as such other than as a framework for the nation in the making, and he rejected a leadership cult.[10] However, his movement did put forward claims to dominance in the name of the civic religion of nationalism, and its youth set store by a paramilitary spirit and discipline. Revisionism as a whole projected a modern nationalism as over against the kind of liberal nationalism the majority of Zionists at that time advocated. Here Zionism caught up with the normative nationalism of the postwar age. Jabotinsky also believed in political ritual and ceremonies, centered in this case upon Trumpeldor and other heroes of a Jewish militant and heroic past. Tel Hai, the Jewish settlement Trumpeldor had defended against Arab forces, where he had been killed in 1920, became the center of a Revisionist cult, a place of Jewish heroism and bloody sacrifice; while for socialist Zionists Trumpeldor remained above all a committed socialist, a symbol of work and toil on the land.[11]

However, a modern, more thorough nationalism was inherent even in those liberal attitudes cherished by the Zionist movement over so long a time. Here, once more, the civic religion of nationalism played its part, especially in the search for a national character, which, as we have seen, entailed the belief in an ideal type—in the stereotype of rooted men and women. It is not astonishing that Zionism was concerned with creating a "new Jew," for other national movements toward the turn of the century also wanted to create their own "new man": a national stereotype, strong, filled with energy, well-proportioned according to Greek models.

Max Nordau's famous speech at the Second Zionist Congress of 1898 set the tone for Zionism with its distinction between "muscle" and "coffeehouse Jews," the latter pale and stunted, the former deep-chested, sturdy, and sharp-eyed. We shall discuss Nordau's "new Jew" as part of his wider thought in a later chapter, but this was an effort as a Zionist to shake off the stereotype of the ghetto Jew and to normalize Jewish men, to construct them in contrast to those rootless intellectuals who fill Nordau's famous book *Degeneration* (1892).

All national movements had stressed bodily rejuvenation and founded gymnastic clubs as a means of forming a "new man." The Zionists, however, felt a special urgency to create a "new Jew" who would signal a break with the so-called physical weakness and nervous condition of Jews in the diaspora. Jews must reconnect with their ancient and heroic past, symbolized, for example, by Bar Kochba's uprising against Rome. The bodily degeneration among Jews caused by shattered nerves became a popular topic in Zionist publications—indeed, physicians at the time considered nervousness the chief sign of degeneracy. Zionists added overintellectualizing as another cause typical of city life, where men sat up all night in coffeehouses.[12]

Zionism, like all modern national liberation movements, was hostile to the modern city, the "whore of Babylon," which encouraged rootlessness. Here, once more, Zionism felt a special urgency, as most Jews were indeed city dwellers and therefore exposed to temptations which would lead to shattered nerves and the destruction of strength and beauty. The coffeehouse served as symbol for the rootlessness of the city, for German as well as for Jewish nationalism, however different their evolution proved to be in the end. Coffeehouse Jews were said to lack willpower and courage, exactly the two characteristics thought indispensable for those who wanted to build a nation. Nervousness marked all those who stood outside or were marginalized by European society and the nation—Jews, the insane, habitual criminals, sexual deviants, and gypsies by and large shared the same stereotype, the counter-type to the normal, healthy, vigorous, and self-controlled male. Zionism was no exception in the way it marginalized those who did not conform to national ideals, in this case the ghetto and the coffeehouse Jew. Here also it was the belief in a Jewish "national character" which mattered, symbolized by outward appearance. The ideal of manly strength and beauty, represented through a well-proportioned, steeled, and muscular body, was celebrated in much of Zionist literature and art, just as it was propagated, for example, in England and Germany as their national stereotype at the same time. As a recent historian of Zionism has written, "The physical ideal was entailed by the national ideal to the point where it was impossible to separate the two . . ."[13]

Despite the influence of a more cosmopolitan and liberal nationalism, the iconography of Zionist nationalism was similar to that of other nations, not only in the importance assigned to the "new man," but also in its flag, national anthem, and sacred flames, and in the use of nature, its sunsets and dawns, to arouse a national spirit. After all, Theodor Herzl saw no contradiction between the tolerance and openness of *Altneuland* and the necessity of creating a civic religion—the nation displaying itself—in order to integrate a disparate people into one nation.

However, in the history of the Zionist movement the uniformity latent in the civic religion of nationalism never quite won a victory over that individualism which Herzl had praised. It is true that between the two world wars nationalism easily became racism, and some few Zionists at times came close to approving such a nationalism.[14] And yet, the individualism of a liberal nationalism retained its hold for a long time, first upon Zionism and then in the State of Israel, even as it fought wars which might have foreclosed this option. Certainly, one crucial aspect of the civic religion of the State of Israel largely reflects this tradition, and not the militancy or integral nationalism which might have been expected. War monuments and the commemoration of its fallen soldiers are close to the core of the civic religion of all nations. In Europe the commemoration of fallen soldiers, as we saw in earlier chapters, was usually combined with praise for their heroism and the glorification of the nation. Across Israel there are about a thousand war memorials and memorial sites, and from the vast majority of them any kind of aggressiveness, glorification of the nation, or hero-worship is absent.[15] The astonishing density of memorials and memorial sites (about one for every sixteen fallen soldiers) does not mean, as it would have in Europe, an effort to make war acceptable through masking or disguising its terror.

Indeed, heroic abstraction or patriotic inscriptions are avoided by most

Israeli war monuments, though some came into existence after the victory in the Six-Day War of 1967. Nevertheless, the individualism present even in the most nationalistic approaches shines through in most of them. Thus there are some memorials of naked youths, but they are not presented as ancient Greeks or as symbols of heroism, as, for example, in Germany, but as individuals instead. Just so, the nicknames of soldiers are inscribed together with their proper names on even the few aggressive monuments, depriving them, according to European tradition, of an aura of sanctity. Here also the individual latitude allowed in the decoration of graves in the national military cemetery in Jerusalem is startling. The graves in European military cemeteries, from the First World War onward, are uniform, subordinated to the symbolism of the nation and of Christianity, which promises the resurrection of the fallen. The decoration and, for the most part, the inscriptions on the gravestones are laid down by the War Graves Commissions of the respective nations. But, while the form of the Israeli war graves in the national military cemetery in Jerusalem is uniform, their decoration is entirely left to the families of the soldiers themselves. They choose the flowers and even the artifacts to be placed upon the grave—this in contrast to the British Military Cemetery on the other side of Jerusalem, on Mount Scopus, where uniform gravestones are imbedded in a well-manicured, impersonal lawn.

The memorial (*yizkor*) books that families or comrades assemble for fallen soldiers do not exist in Europe; thus, for example, every one of the 1,200 soldiers of the famed Golani Brigade who were killed in Israel's wars is commemorated in such an album. The format of these booklets is uniform but their contents are highly personal: pictures, diplomas, reminiscences by friends, essays and poems written by the fallen soldier himself. The culture of commemoration in Israel projects a feeling of personal mourning rather than national triumph.

The fact that Zionist nationalism had managed to retain some of the liberal nationalism of its birth is one factor which made it possible to combine individualism and the cult of the fallen soldiers—a centerpiece of the civic religion of nationalism—in this unique manner. Yet other specific factors also went into the retention of individualism in the face of a nationalist imperative. The tradition of Judaism encouraged such personal mourning; here there is no Christian linkage between death and resurrection so crucial for the mythology of the fallen in European nations. Moreover, the country itself is small and intimate; practically everyone knew some fallen soldier or his family. The memorial books of East European *landsmanshaftn* (communities) may have provided a certain background for the *yizkor* books.[16] Still, the broader considerations related to the history of nationalism must not be lost from sight. Even when it came to building their own Zionist nation, the nationalism involved for a long time tended to remain archaic in contrast to that modern nationalism which dominated Europe after the First World War.

Yet, through the Revisionist movement, modern nationalism made inroads into Zionism as well, even while Zionism through its attempt to develop a stereotype symbolizing national character, and to adopt other elements of the civic religion of nationalism, began to contradict within itself the openness and relative tolerance it had taken from the older liberal nationalism. Clearly, a people's history and present situation decided what kind of nationalism was going to triumph, and a newly built mid-twentieth-century nation living in a state of permanent war—with a cohesive civic religion already in place—might well feel the pull toward modern integral nationalism. That in Israel the battle between the old and the new nationalism was joined for such a long time, that the urge toward uniformity always inherent in a civic religion of nationalism has not yet won out in the midst of a pitched struggle for national survival, points to the strong heritage of an open and tolerant nationalism, which in the Diaspora had given the Jews their chance at citizenship. Here the tradition of the age of Jewish emancipation, of the Enlightenment, however beleaguered and challenged by modern nationalism, continued and continues to have its effect.[17]

CHAPTER NINE

Jewish Emancipation: Between Bildung *and Respectability*

The nation presented a greater challenge to Jewish emancipation than society itself. Here Jews, while they had to adjust to new circumstances, found it relatively easier to integrate. How they adjusted on their entry into Gentile society was, in turn, relevant to their place in the national community. The attainment of social respectability was a prerequisite for nationhood. The process of German-Jewish emancipation has often been explored by historians, and yet several decisive aspects relevant to the attainment of social respectability remain to be discussed. The categories of legal, economic, and political history have been used to analyze the integration of Jews into German life, while the history of ideas has served to clarify the place Jews held in German thought. Factors not so readily assumed within traditional historical categories, however, also played an important part in the process of Jewish emancipation. I will be concerned here with the ideal of self-education or character formation, and with those manners and morals that constitute the idea of respectability. The course of Jewish emancipation took in all aspects of living: Jews wanted to join a way of life that Germans claimed as their own. Emancipated Jews did not merely shed their old clothes in order to put on new, but attempted to become radically changed men and women. Every aspect of this change was part of the totality of the German-Jewish relationship.

The age into which a minority is emancipated will, to a large extent, determine the priorities of its self-identification, not only at the time of emancipation itself but into the future as well. Jewish emancipation in Germany took place in the first decades of the nineteenth century, which, for a relatively short period of time, saw many members of the middle class and even some members of the aristocracy ready and willing to transcend differences in background or religion. Jews were emancipated into the autumn of the Enlightenment, when the ideals of rationalism, pragmatism, and tolerance still retained their appeal. Jewish emancipation in Prussia—which will be our principal concern—was a result of defeat at the hands of Napoleon and the brief era of reform that followed, during which it seemed as if the middle classes might break the monopoly of power held by the Junker caste. The annulment of bondage (serfdom in Prussia was abolished in 1807, four years before the emancipation of the Jews) and the upsurge of individualism promised well for the future. As part of this spirit of reform and liberality, the concept of *Bildung* was meant to open careers to talent and better citizenship through a process of self-cultivation based upon classical learning and the development of aesthetic sensibilities.[1] I have addressed the concept of *Bildung* in chapter 7 of this book, concentrating on its contradiction. This, in turn, was part of the development of German nationalism into a civic religion whose effect on Jewish citizenship was addressed in the chapter on "The Jews and the Civic Religion of Nationalism." Here I am primarily concerned with its beginning, before it disappointed the hopes which the Jews had placed in it. Yet, at the very same time that the concept of *Bildung* helped open the gates to Jewish citizenship, society was engaged in a search for stability and cohesion in the midst of social and political upheaval. Nationalism provided some of this cohesion and stability, but basic to the quest for social consolidation was the belief in a certain moral order expressed through the concept of respectability.

Both *Bildung* and respectability served to define the middle as over against the lower classes and the aristocracy. Jews were emancipated into *Bildung* and respectability, or, as it was expressed at the time, *Bildung* and *Sittlichkeit*—words much used by the German-Jewish press, in the sermons of rabbis, and in German-Jewish literature as well, exhorting Jews to acquire these entrance tickets to German society. To be sure, baptism was still the final certificate of acceptance; nevertheless, *Bildung* and *Sittlichkeit* played a less visible but almost equally important part in the acceptance of Jews by an ever more secular Gentile society and as members of the nation as well. Jews, then, were emancipated into a society where *Bildung* prom-

ised equality and citizenship, while respectability demanded a greater conformity in manners and morals than had existed earlier.

The importance of the ideal of *Bildung* as a key to German-Jewish emancipation has only recently received attention, and yet *Bildung* was considered the "knighthood of modernity," the possession of which signified
membership in the bourgeoisie. *Bildung* meant considerably more than the
difference between those who were educated and others who had little formal education; the concept combined the meaning carried by the word
"education" with character formation. Man must grow like a plant, as
Johann Gottfried von Herder put it, striving to unfold his personality until
he becomes a harmonious, autonomous individual engaged in a continuous
quest for knowledge.[2] Johann Wolfgang von Goethe's Wilhelm Meister
(1795–96), already cited in a previous chapter, always kept in mind "the
cultivation of my individual self just as I am."[3] The tools used in furthering
the process of self-education were the study of the Greek and Roman classics and the cultivation of aesthetic sensibilities, once more exemplified by
classical ideals of beauty. During his brief year as Prussian minister of education (1809–10), Wilhelm von Humboldt institutionalized the ideal of
Bildung in the Gymnasium as well as in the university. Citizenship and
Bildung were considered identical; after all it was one of the goals of Humboldt's education reform to provide the Prussian state with better civil
servants.

Bildung was readily embraced by Jews as helping to complete the process
of emancipation. Berthold Auerbach, for example, wrote in 1846 that while
"formerly the religious spirit proceeded from revelation, the present starts
with *Bildung*."[4] Though most Jews sent their children to the more prag-
matically oriented Realgymnasium rather than to Humboldt's humanistic
Gymnasium, this was rationalized by *Sulamith,* a journal devoted to the
cause of Jewish emancipation, which wrote in 1818 that Jews could not
very well attend a "school for scholars" because they had to earn their
living by trade. Nevertheless the Realschule taught "bourgeois vocations"
while at the same time inculcating virtue and self-cultivation. Right thinking, so we are told, was taught through the study of mathematics, natural
science, and history, a continuation of the Enlightenment approach to education that must have struck a responsive chord in German Jewry.[5]

Bildung was paired with *Sittlichkeit*; the open-endedness and individualism thought necessary for character formation were anchored in a restrictive moral order. The famous German dictionary by the brothers

Grimm (begun in 1845 and not finished until 1931) defined *Sittlichkeit* as the proper moral comportment. Human actions based upon a moral imperative must express themselves through "decent" behavior and the "correct" attitudes toward the human body and its sexuality.[6] When, for example, *Sulamith* in 1807 examined the state of *Sittlichkeit* among Frankfurt Jews, it focused upon their cleanliness, sexual attitudes, and personal behavior. Decent and correct behavior was considered the outward sign of respectability.[7]

The concept of respectability was rather new in the age of Jewish emancipation, the result of the eighteenth-century pietistic and evangelical revivals, encouraged by the wars against "immoral France."[8] Respectability was not confined to the refinement of manners as part of the civilizing process that had begun with the change from feudal to court society, but set norms for all aspects of human life. These proved congenial to the upward mobility of the middle classes with their emphasis upon self-control, moderation, and quiet strength. Human passions and fantasies that might escape control were regarded as enemies of respectability, endangering social norms. Respectability provided social cohesion and set signposts that determined proper and improper behavior, the correct or incorrect attitudes toward the human body. Historians have barely begun to examine the concept of respectability, for it has been taken for granted, and yet it was a result of specific historical forces that met the needs of European society on the threshold of modernity.

Historians analyzing Jewish emancipation are beginning to refer to the concept of *Bildung* as aiding in the transformation of Jews into German Jews, but *Sittlichkeit* has been ignored, even though Jews had to adjust their traditional ways to a new moral order of mostly Protestant inspiration. While some of the armor in the antisemitic arsenal consisted of the accusation that Jews were incapable of *Bildung*, a still more telling and long-lasting slander was that they undermined society through their uncontrolled sexual passions, their supposed slovenly looks and behavior—accusations that made *Sulamith* not only examine the comportment of Frankfurt Jews from the point of view of social respectability, as we mentioned, but also claim in its very first number that every people, including the Jews, is capable not only of *Bildung* but also of improving its "personal morality."[9]

To be sure, the quest for *Bildung* was in the forefront of those aiming at emancipation—"*Bildung* must be our principal business," asserted

Sulamith[10]—but the need to teach respectable behavior and attitudes was recognized as well. The embourgeoisement of the Jews was crucial for their entry into German society at a time when middle-class social attitudes were making their mark, even though the Junker class retained political power. The embourgeoisement of the Jews must be seen as part of a more general trend—after all, the many lithographs that popularized Queen Luise of Prussia as a heroine of resistance against Napoleon showed her no longer in the midst of the royal court but surrounded by her husband and children, a middle-class family in royal dress.[11] Jews were judged by the standards of what was now considered decent, not only by Gentiles but by their own rabbis and press. The Frankfurt Jews, according to *Sulamith* in 1807, were passing through the childhood of culture; they lacked politesse, although their cleanliness was praiseworthy in spite of their crowded living conditions, and flirting and indecent sexual actions (*Unzucht*) had declined. They still did not know how to act with *Anstand*—according to decent and correct manners.[12] Many rabbinical sermons during the first decades of the nineteenth century repeat these concerns. Gotthold Salomon, for example, one of the most celebrated preachers of the time, called upon parents to teach children to enjoy pleasure only in moderation and to shun ill-concealed sensuousness encouraged by mixed dancing. "To be moderate in one's public amusements is part of . . . the refinement of manners."[13]

The "refinement of the Israelites" ("die veredelung der Israeliten") was forever on the lips of famous rabbis and filled the pages of *Sulamith*. Jews were called to enter the process of *Bildung* and to show their devotion to social norms through their comportment. They were, in short, to adjust to the way of life of the middle classes. They must reactivate, we hear again and again, the urge to be virtuous, present in all men but lost to Jews during centuries of oppression. Men must get rid of their instinctual drives; to quote *Sulamith* once more, mere sensual pleasures must be rejected, "For what else is the meaning of virtue than the ruling of our passion through reason."[14] Jews were trying to escape their stereotype, in part encouraged by Gentiles and in part accompanied by taunts that Jews could never enter into respectability and join the national community.

The ghetto Jew was seen by the Gentile world as unproductive, earning his living through usury and by his wits, a *Schnorrer* incapable of "honest work." The gospel of work was an article of faith in the age of the industrial revolution, but for Jews it had a special significance if they were to enter the German middle class. Working for a living, Jews were repeatedly told, was the principal part of one's earthly vocation: "serving the Divinity entails work as a sacred duty." This service demanded restraint and the rejection of pleasure. Self-control led to contentment, and "no one who is idle attains happiness."[15] Just as the stereotype of the unproductive ghetto Jew was accepted in order to be exorcised, so the fear of Jews, who were perceived as unsteady and without roots, pervades the sermons and writings of men committed to Jewish emancipation. During the 1830s Gotthold Salomon inveighed against the danger presented by vacillating men who were described as effeminate and debauched. Like his Protestant colleagues, he blamed such unsteadiness upon the fulfillment of desire, just as gratification of sensuality must needs produce criminals.[16] But there is a tone of urgency here, an effort to stress the image of masculinity so central to the concept of respectability, as over against the prevailing stereotype of the Jew.

Indeed, Jewish religious service itself had become a metaphor for chaos and disorder in the Gentile world; the "Jew-school" seemed to exemplify irreverence and undignified behavior.[17] Leopold Zunz demanded in the 1830s that "wailing must be banished from the temple."[18] Jewish religious service had already been changed in order to conform to the ideal of orderly and reverential behavior accepted by Christians as fitting the occasion. While Jews proceeded to reform their own services, some of the rulers of the German states decreed Jewish religious reform in order to force the Jews to behave in a respectable manner, using Jewish worship itself to teach proper manners and morals. In 1823, for example, the Grand Duke of Sachsen-Weimar-Eisenach promulgated rules for Jewish religious service without, apparently, consulting rabbinical authority. Not only were prayers to be said in the German language but all moving around during services was strictly forbidden—as were all the noise and merriment that might take place inside the synagogue on Purim. Decent dress must be worn at all times, and the wearing of burial shrouds on Yom Kippur (customary among German Jews) was forbidden forthwith.[19]

The chief rabbi of the small duchy protested this decree, arguing that the state must not interfere with the life of individuals or individual organizations provided the moral fabric of society is upheld. Here the duke and the rabbi agreed, for the protest was directed only against having to say Hebrew prayers in German, while the chief rabbi himself saw the need for services to proceed in "true reverence, quiet and order"; for the rabbi as for the duke such reverential behavior symbolized the moral order. Small wonder that the rabbi's protest was ignored, though the new rules were enforced only in 1837 and choral singing introduced at the same time.[20]

Not only this chief rabbi, but most of the German-Jewish leadership understood only too well the importance of respectability for the cause of Jewish emancipation, and they were ready and eager to accept its dictates of conformity, the more so as respectability provided tangible signs as to how life should be lived in Gentile society. *Sulamith,* during the first decades of the nineteenth century, was filled with descriptions of Jewish schools dedicated to the teaching of virtue, emphasizing the duty of work as over against the temptations of idleness. Ludwig Philippson, rabbi and founder of the *Allgemeine Zeitung des Judentums,* writing on the Prussian king's birthday in 1837, stated with approval the basic presuppositions of respectability. "I am a Prussian," he began his tribute to the king, and he continued by asserting that the equality which the king grants to his subjects excludes sectarianism and divisiveness; instead, government must encourage order and quiet. When the majority wants to retain all that is decent and proper, Philippson concluded, one or two persons cannot be allowed to create a disturbance or to frustrate its will.[21]

Philippson linked civic equality to a respectable conformity. He assumed that this moral order corresponded to the wishes of the majority; patterns of thought and behavior that had not been generally accepted in the last century were now taken for granted. Philippson foreshadows a time toward the end of the nineteenth century when laws punishing so-called abnormal behavior—the sodomy laws, in England and Germany, for example—no longer appealed to religious truth for their justification but to the people's sense of justice instead. The norms of society must prevail; they were a goal to be attained in the process of assimilation.

Jews brought into their process of emancipation attitudes crucial to respectability, and the usual stereotype of the rootless ghetto Jew did not correspond to realities, though both Gentiles and a large number of Jews accepted it as obvious truth. Above all, the traditional quality of Jewish family life could not be overlooked. Jews seemed to lead an exemplary family life even before the nuclear family was regarded as basic to the health of society and the state. After emancipation, family bonds tended to take the place of rapidly loosening religious ties. "How much lack of order and confusion would rule in the world if God had not created this beneficent institution (the family) and elevated it into a sacred law." The well-being of all human society depends upon it, in the words of this rabbinical ser mon, and the state has a stake in seeing to it that order and decency are preserved.[22] Once again, Jews offer their loyalty and collaboration to the state viewed as moral authority. For Jews themselves, those who possessed *Bildung* and the proper comportment exemplified both "Germanness" and "Jewishness," and for many of them this provided the meaning that religion and tradition once had.[23]

Jewish identity was linked to family pride, which was often the reason why German Jews refused baptism. When Moritz Oppenheim, one of the first German-Jewish painters, wanted to document Jewish patriotism in 1833–34, he painted a Jewish volunteer freshly returned from the German Wars of Liberation, sitting in the midst of his admiring family. Oppenheim painted many scenes from Jewish family life, projecting German middle-class values into his pictures of ghetto life as well. Here Jewish tradition was not merely compatible with the demands of citizenship but was, both before and after, exemplary of the middle-class way of life.[24]

Thus Jews found it easy to enter into this aspect of respectability, for they had exemplified the bourgeois family before it was born, and perhaps because of this long tradition they were able to modernize their family structure more easily than the Gentiles. As Shulamit Volkov has shown, by the end of the nineteenth century German Jews not only had fewer children than other Germans but took better medical care of their infants.[25] The Jewish family was a constant irritant to antisemites, as we hope to have shown elsewhere;[26] they were forced to argue that, though Jews themselves lived the ideal bourgeois family life, this did not keep them from seducing Christian women and trafficking in white slavery. Indeed, the very success of Jewish embourgeoisement was turned by antisemites against the Jews, especially by racists like Richard Wagner, for whom the Jews not only exemplified the power of gold and a sterile legal order but also the undue restraint put upon human passions.[27]

Sittlichkeit narrowed the perspective of *Bildung* and tended to focus upon the finished product rather than upon the never-ending process of self-cultivation. Manners and morals were considered not subject to change but laid down for all time and place. The resulting way of life was described in Georg Hermann's novel *Jettchen Gebert* (1906), required reading for most German Jews. Jewishness in the novel is expressed through family pride, the "good name" of the Geberts, who are respected for their probity by Jews and Gentiles alike. The family business symbolized family worth and was the visible proof that the Jew had become an honest bourgeois and respected citizen—a theme that is carried in German-Jewish literature from the Geberts to Lion Feuchtwanger's *Geschwister Oppenheim* (The Oppermanns, 1933), written as the Nazis came to power, where the sale of the family business signaled the end of German Jewry. The older Geberts still lived in the world of the Enlightenment, but all of them wanted "a steady pace of life in the most perfect harmony." This pace of life is disrupted in the novel when Jettchen attempts to marry a penniless Christian writer. Jettchen's worldly, tolerant, and cultivated uncle gives two reasons why, despite the couple's love for each other, Jettchen cannot be allowed to marry, and both of them sum up widespread attitudes among German Jews. First of all, the writer does not belong to the bourgeoisie, while Jettchen cannot be torn from the middle classes; all her roots are there. Second, the writer is a Christian, and such a marriage would betray family pride, the Geberts having refused to trade their religion for advantage of position or title.[28] Opposition to intermarriage did constitute the bottom line of Jewish assimilation, while being regarded as a solid bourgeois was its reward. When in 1933 Jews were expelled from active participation in German life and had to establish their own cultural organization, Georg Hermann's novel was still praised as recalling the finest tradition of the German-Jewish past.[29]

The contradiction between the openness and tolerance of *Bildung* and the restrictive vision of respectability was not obvious to those living in the age of Jewish emancipation, though *Bildung* itself soon became a monopoly of a caste rather than accessible to anyone willing and able to participate in the process of self-cultivation. The alliance between academics and bureaucrats took control, guarding the concept from those without the proper humanistic education. *Bildung* was nationalized as well—becoming an attribute of those who could boast Germanic roots and who alone could appreciate the good, the true, and the beautiful.[30] Not only *Bildung,* but respectability itself, contracted, refining the distinctions between those inside and those outside society. These narrowing visions were perhaps a greater menace to the continuing process of Jewish assimilation than the often crude and violent accusations of antisemites against the Jews. Here means of integration were cut off or made more difficult to use, not primarily because of unreasoning hatred against the Jews but because of the fear of social change, the attempt to find the solid ground in the midst of the chaos.

Those who were thought to lack respectability were branded as abnormal, hostile to the norms that society had established. Medicine came to the aid of respectability, defining normal or abnormal behavior as matters of sickness and health. The physician played a crucial part in elaborating the stereotype of the outsider, so different from that of the respectable citizen: unable to control his passions, his nerves shattered, weak of body and mind. Thus the stereotype of the insane, and the antisemitic stereotype of the Jew shared the same "movable physiognomy."[31]

The medicalization of the outsider—those who did not fit society's image of itself, such as the insane, homosexuals, or habitual criminals—was accompanied by the medicalization of the Jew. Famous physicians at the turn of the nineteenth century, like Richard von Krafft-Ebing or J. M. Charcot, thought that Jews were inclined to nervousness because of weak nerves, the result of inbreeding.[32] Nervousness undermined that calm resolve respectability demanded. To be sure, these physicians believed that Jewish nervousness was a tendency that could be cured, while for the enemies of the Jews it became a racial characteristic that doomed them for all time. The alliance between medicine and respectability meant that health and sickness were to a large extent dependent upon the acceptance of the moral order. Those who stood outside the limits of respectability must be easily recognized through their looks and bodily posture as a warning to all normal persons. Superior health implies superior beauty, so the wisdom of both doctors and laymen ran; health and beauty always went together according to the Greek example.[33]

Strength and vigor were rewards for moral rectitude and proper comportment, the ideal of manliness that accompanied the rise of respectability. *Sulamith* cited Proverbs 31 as the justification for woman's passive role, in which learning to dance took the place that gymnastics and the toughening of the body held in male education. The toughening of the male body became an obsession at the end of the nineteenth century, though gymnastics had been practiced throughout the century in order to form a manly body as well as to strengthen the Volk. Jews had been members of gymnastic associations, though many local groups excluded them from membership. Toward the turn of the century Jews founded their own gymnastic associations. The cultivation of the body through sport was supposed to produce "muscle Jews," as Max Nordau told the Second Zionist Congress.[34] The *Jüdische Turnerzeitung* wrote in 1910 that sitting in cafes led to neurasthenia: Jews should feel ashamed for failing to steel their bodies.[35] Such Zionists believed, as we shall see in the chapter devoted to Max Nordau, that in the Diaspora some type of degenerative process had indeed taken place among Jews, mirrored in the appearance of neurasthenia. Not only Zionists but those, like Cesare Lombroso, committed to assimilation, shared these preoccupations.[36] They were based upon the need to repudiate the stereotype of the ghetto Jew of the past who through his appearance and behavior seemed to deny that ideal of manliness basic to respectability and, therefore, to the process of Jewish assimilation. The same fear of rootless outsiderdom that had haunted Gotthold Salomon at the actual time of emancipation remained to haunt German-Jewish history.

Jews who practiced sport, rode, or climbed mountains are rare in nineteenth- and even twentieth-century literature. Until the mid-nineteenth century, for example, Jews portrayed on the German stage were usually old men, lonely and without a family that would document their bourgeois status.[37] This image of old age was symbolic for lack of manly vigor, and even when young Jews appeared in plays, they were usually pictured as weak and puny. Small wonder, then, that some members of the German Youth Movement stated that because of their weak bodies Jews could never become Germans.[38] Adolf Hitler himself summed up the thrust behind this accusation: the Jew drains from all races their energy and power, trying to deprive them of all that might serve to steel the muscles. The Jew turns healthy morals upside down, lacks hygiene, and transforms night into day[39] (the latter an example, by the way, that Hitler himself seems to have followed). The outsider was the focus of all that presented a danger to the norms of society, a menace to respectability. Through his supposed bodily weakness the Jew menaced the ideal of masculinity; as an unmanly man he threatened the clear and distinct division of roles between the sexes. We have shown elsewhere how racists accused the Jews of being feminine, an accusation based upon the stereotype of women as the antitype of manliness: passive, in need of protection, not in control of their passions.[40] The sexual division of labor was at the root of respectability, as important for social cohesion as the economic division of labor that G. W. F. Hegel and Karl Marx saw as essential for the existence of capitalism.

Jews attempted to pass the test of their manhood and citizenship by volunteering in the German Wars of Liberation, and, in two versions of the painting of the returned soldier, Moritz Oppenheim depicted him either showing the Iron Cross, the highest decoration for valor, to his family, or as bearing a wound home from battle. Thus Jews were emancipated not only into the age of *Bildung* and *Sittlichkeit* but also into the Wars of Liberation against Napoleon. However well they performed in battle, the imputation of outsiderdom still lingered, and Jews passing the test of their manhood in war, side by side with their Christian comrades, were often accused of cowardice when it came to the point of danger. The antisemitic campaign against supposed Jewish shirkers in the First World War induced the high command to gather statistics on how many Jewish soldiers served in the front lines. Jews had to embrace the ideal of manliness and bodily strength as part of their embourgeoisement, but this imperative did not silence the suspicion of cowardice and bodily weakness that followed the emancipated Jew as a potential outsider.

Respectability itself was part of the narrowing vision of German society. Liberalism could remain alive even while respectability attempted to tighten the reigns, for political and economic freedoms were not supposed to entail freedom of manners and morals; rather the cohesion respectability provided was thought necessary to supply liberal freedoms with a stable base. The menace of potential outsiderdom threatened by respectability was not perceived by Jews at the time. Liberalism seemed to provide a secure anchor for Jewish assimilation, despite the remaining obstacles to full citizenship. The harmonious life of the Geberts, with hardly a cloud on the horizon, was typical of many German-Jewish families before the First World War. The narrowing social vision seemed latent rather than operative, lying in wait until after the war when it found a mass base in its onslaught against Jewish emancipation. More research is needed on how *Sittlichkeit* both made Jewish emancipation easier and ultimately facilitated the image of the Jew as the outsider.

The concept of *Bildung,* once so promising for the process of assimilation, was detached from the idea of citizenship and increasingly devoted to a search for the good, the true, and the beautiful that stand above the concerns of daily life. Moreover, this search ended in the arms of the nation. I have already mentioned in an earlier chapter how *Bildung* substituted pedagogy for self-cultivation; now the product rather than the process counted. Jews resisted the ever-narrowing concept of *Bildung* and sought to cling to its earlier humanistic ideal. For example, it has been calculated, as I explained earlier, that most Goethe biographies were written by Jews in order to recall that Germany's cultural hero was committed to the humanistic ideals of *Bildung* and the Enlightenment.[41] Eventually even a writer like Berthold Litzmann, who in 1914 still pleaded for reconciliation with the French, took it for granted that "today, in contrast to the nineteenth century, intellectual independence and individuality can only flourish if they are rooted in the nation."[42]

Jewish commitment to the humanistic ideal of *Bildung* was based on the correct perception that only through transcending a German past, which the Jews did not share, could Jew meet German on equal terms. Historical roots had played no part in Humboldt's concept of *Bildung,* and the classics upon whose knowledge the concept so largely depended were considered a universal heritage. Similarly, the concept of respectability was based upon a moral order and did not necessarily depend upon shared historical roots.

Emancipation meant not only a flight from the ghetto past but also from German history regarded as an obstacle to integration, for even if the national past was myth rather than reality, the Jews were, through no fault of their own, excluded from participating in the roots of the nation. The search for common ground transcending history was one reason why Jews as a group tended to support cultural and artistic innovation to a greater extent than did Gentiles. Jews provided a disproportionate share of support for the avant-garde and for educational experiments as well. This avant-garde in arts and letters broke with past traditions but did not really menace respectability. Thus one could remain *sittlich* and support expressionist or impressionist painters, or the avant-garde theater—even if it presented nudity upon the stage and experimented with all forms of sexual expression. Supporting cultural innovation not only helped overcome the handicap of a separate past but also continued the impetus of *Bildung* as a process of self-cultivation. But then, *Bildung* had always concentrated upon culture and all but ignored politics and society.

Bildung furthered a cultural vision of the world. This facilitated the division between culture and other aspects of life that led many Germans to equate *Bildung* with a vague quest for "higher things," as we have seen, but it also made it easier to support cultural innovation while remaining traditionalist in politics and social life. Moreover, it blinded to political realities those who were committed to the primacy of humanistic culture. Jews tried to make contact with the masses of Germans, largely through literature,[43] but many were also suspicious of these masses, whom they viewed as easily aroused and carried away by passion. Jews shared fully what James Sheehan has called the lingering doubt of liberals about the relationship between what they regarded as the real Volk of enlightened and liberal men and the masses of the German nation. They feared what Jacob Auerbach castigated at midcentury as the fanaticized and misled masses—once again, not without reason.[44] The pressure of mass politics, the desire of the German masses for their political emancipation, introduced an emotional and irrational factor into politics rather easily captured by the antisemitic German right.

The necessity to transcend the past and the effort to continue the emancipatory ideal were common to most German Jews, whatever their political faith. Young Jewish socialists tried to concretize the ideal of a common humanity through the manner in which this transcendence could be accomplished. The final victory of socialism over present property relationships would issue in the triumph of humanity, the true unfolding of *Bildung* and the Enlightenment. Many early Zionists, in turn, attempted to humanize their nationalism, regarding the nation as a stepping stone to a shared humanity as we saw in the last chapter. However, all these young Jewish socialists or nationalists, despite their desire to transcend political liberalism, never really sought to attack *Sittlichkeit*. Indeed, the goal of the revolution or of the new Jewish nation was to strengthen *Bildung* and *Sittlichkeit,* not to abolish them. For assimilated German Jews, they provided the common ground upon which all Germans could meet, ignoring differences of religion or historical experience, and where, in the last resort, Germans could meet on terms of equality with the other members of the human race.

Bildung and *Sittlichkeit,* which had stood at the beginning of Jewish emancipation in Germany, accompanied German Jews to the end, blinding them, as many other Germans, to the menace of national socialism. Though the Centralverein deutscher Staatsbürger jüdischen Glaubens (the largest association of German Jews), waged a courageous fight against volkish nationalism, it seemed inconceivable that someone like Hitler, apparently without *Bildung* or the proper comportment, could occupy Otto von Bismarck's chair in the Reich's chancellery.

The embourgeoisement of the German Jews, in all its hopes and frustration, must be seen against the background of the embourgeoisement of German society as a whole. *Bildung* and respectability were two important aspects of the triumph of the middle classes, exemplified by the spread of decent and correct manners and morals—of a certain way of life—long before it was completed by the sharing of political power. The ideals of *Bildung* and respectability, once so promising, eventually proved dangerous to that process of Jewish emancipation which they had once encouraged. *Bildung* turned away from Humboldt's concept, falling into the hands of narrow-minded academics and bureaucrats. *Sittlichkeit* as respectability played a more complex role through stigmatizing and identifying those supposedly outside social norms, presenting a potential danger to Jews as new arrivals. Emancipation made all aspects of German life relevant to the Jewish situation in Germany, especially those social and cultural factors apt to be taken for granted as an integral part of a way of life that dated from the past and would never change.

The historical myths of nationalism both narrowed the base of this way of life and gave it a new dimension of immutability. Jews had to transcend this historical base even while attempting to maintain *Bildung* and respectability—ideas that in reality were not immutable but changing with the passage of time, just as they had triumphed only in the age of Jewish emancipation. Thus the process of emancipation reflected some basic demands of modern society that, for better or worse, both Jews and Germans were forced to fulfill. German Jews became *Bildungsbürger*, exemplifying the ideals current at the time of their emancipation, trying to preserve their liberal heritage all the way to the end.

CHAPTER TEN

German Jews and Liberalism in Retrospect

To analyze the relationship between German Jews and liberalism from hindsight runs the danger of foreshortening history, of ignoring the restraints of time. Nevertheless, it is worthwhile to undertake this task in order to draw some conclusions from this long-standing identification which might enable us better to understand problems inherent in liberalism itself, and those which haunted German Jews in their period of assimilation. Though I intend to approach this analysis from the point of view of German Jews, it is impossible to separate the problems of liberalism from those faced by the Jews in modern times; their identification was too close for that. I want to take stock of a relationship that went beyond the usual alliance between a political or ideological movement and a group of the population, determining, instead, the self-identification of many, and perhaps even most, German Jews.[1]

The overwhelming majority of Jews in Germany felt that they had no alternative but to accept the process of emancipation, however incomplete, and to enter into the process of assimilation—no Jew wanted to return to the ghetto, to a time of unfreedom, and every Jew wanted to become a citizen. Jews wanted to become Germans, but what sort of German?—for there were many different definitions of what it meant to be a part of the German nation. The liberal *Bildungsbürger* as defined by Wilhelm von Humboldt provided the model for German citizenship for newly emancipated Jews, as mentioned in the last chapter. Through fostering the growth of reason and aesthetic taste, each man would cultivate his own personality until he became an autonomous, harmonious individual. This was a process of education and character-building in which everyone could join regardless of religion or background; only the individual mattered. Liberalism during the age of Jewish emancipation was founded on an attitude of mind which, it was hoped, could be translated into liberal politics.

Yet this emancipation was not the result of political necessities, though considerations of usefulness to the state played an important part. Rather, it was due in large measure to the acceptance of Enlightenment thought with its belief in the potential of human reason, in the kind of self-education and *Bildung* that Wilhelm von Humboldt tried to make into an integral part of the Prussian educational system. The emancipation of the Jews in Germany was a cultural emancipation and its political consequences were only apparent much later. This historical development explains to a large extent the depth to which the concept of *Bildung* based upon the Enlightenment penetrated Jewish secular and religious thought: by acquiring the proper culture Jews would enter German citizenship. Liberal thought, destined to remain valid for German Jews because it had legitimized their emancipation, was conceived as a continuation of the Enlightenment. German citizenship meant developing one's own intellectual potential, a continuous process that depended upon self-cultivation. German liberalism in its origins was not, as in England, primarily a philosophy of prosperity,[2] though as it became attuned to the Railway Age it came to concentrate upon political and economic reality as well, but at the expense of its original impetus. That system of liberal thought which, as in England, found its roots above all in the Industrial Revolution, rather than in a philosophical system, was shared by Germany only toward the end of the nineteenth century. This difference is important for the distinction between liberal thought and liberal politics which, as we shall see, was to haunt the relationship between Jews and liberalism.

The hopes for a more complete Jewish emancipation were symbolized by the conviction of nineteenth-century liberals that intellectual development and national progress were identical.[3] Jews could freely enter into the process of *Bildung* through school and university, through the cultivation of their own personalities. The belief that those who entered into this process of *Bildung* would also make the best citizens seemed full of promise for Jews who desired to obtain equal rights with their Christian neighbors.

The difference between liberal thought and liberal politics provides one of the principal themes for any analysis of the symbiosis between Jews and liberalism. Many Jews, during the first half of the nineteenth century, inclined toward political conservatism, or thought that unquestioning obedience toward the state was part of their newly acquired citizenship; while others—perhaps the majority—were politically passive.[4] However, despite such diverse political attitudes, most German Jews accepted liberal thought as given, an article of faith upon which their hope for full emancipation depended.

Thus the expectation that the hopes placed in emancipation would be fulfilled was closely identified with belief in liberal ideals, and these, in turn, were an integral part of the German-Jewish identity. Lessing's *Nathan der Weise* became a *Magna Charta* of German Judaism, but the liberal heritage was also absorbed by a major trend of German-Jewish religious thought, to become an integral part of the essence of Judaism. This was a trend in Jewish theology that can be discerned from the very beginning of the process of emancipation,[5] and that was crowned by a work which many German Jews regarded as their second *Magna Charta*: Leo Baeck's *The Essence of Judaism (Das Wesen des Judentums,* 1906, a book that was presented by the Jewish community of Berlin during the Weimar Republic to every Jewish high school student who had passed his *Abitur). The Essence of Judaism* emphasized the autonomy of each individual; respect for his freedom as over against the state is designated as a religious duty. For Baeck the state was based upon bourgeois property rights, and, though it is part of the blessings such property confers to help the poor and the helpless, the principal task must be to prevent the existence of a propertyless class. Finally, as in Humboldt's definition of *Bildung,* neither the state nor the human personality is a fully formed product of history or circumstance, but in constant development. This development reaches out for the universal, to humanity, through the unremitting self-cultivation of the individual personality.[6] The much invoked "Mission of Judaism" was based upon such an ideal long before Leo Baeck wrote his famous book.

Even those Jews who fought against liberalism with all their might were influenced by liberal thought. Many of the most important Jewish socialists attempted to soften Marxist orthodoxy, using liberal thought in order to move the individual increasingly into the center of socialist theory. As I have shown elsewhere,[7] for such men the final victory of the working class and the abolition of existing property relationships would issue in the triumph of humanity, but this victory would be meaningless unless it was based upon *Bildung* and the Enlightenment. Such a revision of Marxism can be found to a greater or lesser extent in the thoughts of men like Kurt Eisner, the young George Lukacs, or the Frankfurt School, as well as amongst the so-called left-wing intellectuals during the Weimar Republic. These were men who used liberal ideals in order to transcend their outsiderdom in society and in the labor movement, even as they rejected liberalism as being the ideology of capitalism. Ernst Bloch stated, typically enough, that the humanism of the Enlightenment had been absorbed by Marxism, but it was the Italian Jewish socialist Carlo Roselli who formulated the connection between liberalism and socialism, dear to such men, with greatest clarity: the spiritual substance of liberalism can only be preserved in a socialist society.[8]

Even German Zionism, publicly the sworn enemy of liberalism, in reality absorbed much of its thought. Leaders such as Martin Buber, Robert Weltsch, or Georg Landauer saw in Jewish nationalism a necessary ingredient of the never-ending cultivation of their own personalities: such nationalism was not a purpose in and of itself, but instead a necessary step toward the union with all mankind.[9] The liberal ideals that derived from the period of emancipation were given equal weight with nationalism, a unique phenomenon in our own century and the only attempt I know of not to abolish but to humanize nationalism in an ever more nationalistic age. The disproportionate part Jews played in this enterprise cannot be ignored, though non-Jews were, of course, also involved. Beyond the evidence this phenomenon provides as to the penetration of liberal thought even among those Jews who would reject it, such use of liberalism raises two questions, the answers to which are of importance for the relationship of Jews and liberalism in retrospect: firstly, how intertwined were liberal theory and practice, and, secondly, to what extent did theory dominate or even displace practice in the alliance of liberalism and the Jews?

For most Jewish citizens the difference between liberal theory and practice must have been irrelevant, at least until the last years of the Weimar Republic. They supported liberal parties and organizations, and sought to transform liberal thought into practice through their support of political liberalism. Strong liberal parties during most of the empire encouraged such unity (it has been estimated that two-thirds of the Jews in the empire voted for the Progressive party).[10] This unity of theory and practice varied with the strength or weakness of liberal political parties. Thus, liberal thought existed without much of a political base in the age of Jewish emancipation, with a rapidly diminishing political infrastructure during the Weimar Republic and with none at all during the Third Reich. Such a changing relationship between liberal thought and its political structure must necessarily influence any analysis of the relationship of Jews to liberalism, and it raises the question of how one might evaluate the liberalism of German Jews, which during most of its history had little chance of realization: did the belief of most emancipated Jews that such a chance existed blind them to political realities, giving an almost fatal unreality to their political aspirations? This, of course, is seen merely in retrospect.

That so many Jews clung to liberal parties in Wilhelminian and Weimar Germany, even when these supported antisemitic candidates, shows to what extent the urge to establish a unity between theory and practice blocked the consideration of political alternatives. When the Social Democrats defended Jewish rights at the turn of the century, the leaders of the major Jewish organizations saw in such action a danger to their own respectability.[11] Theodor Barth, the leader of the Progressive Liberals, discovered by the turn of the century a liberal potential among the right wing of the Social Democrats and suggested an electoral alliance with that party. When such an alliance came about in 1912, it became easier for many Jews of the establishment to sympathize with the Social Democratic Party.[12] But the "red danger" was not exorcised so easily, and until 1930, at least, the vast majority of German Jews remained loyal to the liberal parties that were becoming an ever more insignificant political force. As historians we can see in retrospect that during the Weimar Republic the Social Democrats increasingly coopted the liberal space in German politics, but we cannot expect that the leaders of German Jewry and most of their followers, who had grown up before the First World War, would be aware of this fact. This was the more so as their allegiance to liberalism, despite the search for ideological and political unity, was based in the final resort upon their faith in liberal ideals, and not upon the primacy of political liberalism.

It was easier in the end phase of the Weimar Republic for Thomas Mann to confess his allegiance to social democracy than for the German Jews, who knew full well how much they owed to liberal thought, and who wanted to attain full membership in the bourgeoisie. This though Thomas Mann, himself a convinced bourgeois, used the same argument that Carlo Roselli and many Jewish socialists had voiced as well, namely that his new political engagement would preserve liberalism within Germany.[13] If after 1930 many Jews drew close to or even joined the Social Democratic party, now almost their only defender, many nevertheless remained with the Staatspartei, the insignificant remnant of political liberalism in Germany.[14]

Analyzing the alliance between German Jews and liberalism in retrospect means comprehending the problems inherent in this close relationship: above all, the depth of allegiance to that theory which had legitimized the process of Jewish emancipation, and the tenuous chance of its political realization determined by the fate of liberal political parties. The Third Reich put the relationship between Jews and liberalism to its crucial test, just as all German-Jewish problems were now up for reconsideration, seen, so to speak, through a magnifying glass. The relationship of liberal theory to liberal practice became part of the internal Jewish debate, not as an urge to modernize liberalism—which one can find among the socialists we have mentioned—but as a life belt instead.

Because the Third Reich forced Jews to reconsider a liberalism they had taken for granted, it tested both the depth of that allegiance and the extent to which ideals that had stood Jews in good stead during the process of emancipation and assimilation could be maintained or had to be discarded. Though liberal allegiance was tested throughout the German-Jewish community, I want to single out as an example a group that formed the most committed citadel of liberalism. Here one can follow the testing of a Jewish liberal identity at its most extreme, characterized through its unbending allegiance to the tenets of Enlightenment liberal thought. It does not matter for our purposes that the membership of the Jüdische Reformgemeinde (Jewish Reform Congregation) was as small as it was distinguished and influential; concentrating upon the reaction of the congregation to the new situation of Jews in Nazi Germany brings into sharper focus liberal dilemmas that were faced by more moderate liberal congregations as well.

The Jüdische Reformgemeinde was the most radical wing of liberal Judaism. It was founded in 1845 in order to eliminate from Jewish religious practice customs that seemed to conflict with German citizenship. All signs of particularism, like the Hebrew language and reference to Jerusalem, were thought to be out of place for Jews as German citizens. Between 1845 and 1932 no less than eleven revisions of the Prayer Book were undertaken, adjusting it to the changing times, until a book of only sixty-four small pages remained.[15] The goal of these reforms was to strengthen German identity, but the Germany with which this congregation identified was a liberal Germany.

To be sure, especially after the First World War, not all members of this congregation were committed liberals. Then the leaders of the Verband nationaldeutscher Juden (Association of National-German Jews) and some of their followers were members of the Reformgemeinde. They were, no doubt, attracted by the emphasis upon German citizenship, the rejection of any religious practices that might set Jews apart from Germans. The fact that this congregation attracted virtually no East European Jewish immigrants—regarded with open enmity by the Verband—must have given them satisfaction as well. But their conservative nationalist definition of what constituted a German differed from that of most of the congregation. The leaders of this Jewish Reform rejected what they saw as the radicalism of the Verband nationaldeutscher Juden,[16] even though a member of that Verband was for a time the president of the congregation. Moreover, many members were also part of the Reichsbund jüdischer Frontsoldaten (the National Association of Jewish War Veterans), whose leader sat on the board of the Jüdische Reformgemeinde. Such membership might have pushed the congregation to abandon its liberal stance, to recognize the realities of the new Germany which both the Nationaldeutsche Juden and the leadership of the Jewish veterans organization saw as the triumph of the ideal of a volkish community, the latter perhaps more for tactical than patriotic reasons.[17] But, as we shall see, the congregation itself refused to follow here: the contrast between the unanimous stand taken, for example, by the rabbis of the congregation under the tyranny of national socialism and the members of these organizations could not have been greater.

The fact that the Reformgemeinde even under the Nazis took their German identity for granted has obscured the discussion that took place at the time about the kind of German tradition they regarded as their own. Theirs was not the Germany of a conservative nationalism, for in the sermons of the rabbis and the pages of the congregation's journal, the *Mitteilungen der Jüdischen Reformgemeinde,* the basic principles of liberalism remained intact before and after the Nazi seizure of power. For example, the bar mitzvah candidates of 1931 were told that the triumph of the critical spirit over blind faith constituted the essence of Judaism.[18] Individualism was always in the forefront: thus we hear from the pulpit, in 1932, that individuals created religions and political parties, and this sermon on the theme of "Religion and Politics" ended with the exclamation "the human being first and foremost, and the human within all things" ("der Mensch über alles und der Mensch in allem").[19] The identical thoughts were repeated from the pulpit in 1935—that is, two years after the seizure of power: only out of the individual himself can a community be regenerated, and, though the concept of the community must be given its due, Jews must remain nonconformists who confront the present with the eternal worth of the individual in mind.[20] Surely for these men German *Patriotismus* could not be exclusive in the way of those Jews who professed to know only the German people and care only about the future of Germany, as the leader of the Verband nationaldeutscher Juden put it.[21] Their commitment to Germany pointed back to a time when patriotism had been paired with a concern for all humanity and where nationalism was seen as a step in the free development of the individual. Here liberal thought attempted to humanize nationalism, a function it also filled for the Zionists mentioned above. Certainly, a comparison of both such nationalisms, the Jewish-German and the German Zionist, might lead to interesting results. If, for example, men like the Zionist leader Robert Weltsch saw in nationalism a phase of personal development that would, in the end, benefit all mankind, so the chief rabbi of the Jewish Reform Congregation preached at a patriotic ceremony before the First World War that he who serves the fatherland serves all mankind, because this service will help develop his individual personality and thus enable him to benefit all communities.[22]

This liberal patriotism was bound to be tested in the radically changed environment after 1933; what seemed at risk, above all, was the individualism upon which their outlook on the world was based. It was the youth group of the Reformgemeinde that now called for more coherence among Jews, for the creation of a true community. This challenge to liberalism was not inspired by a wish to imitate the *Volksgemeinschaft* the Nazis proclaimed, but by the new situation of Jews thrown back upon their own resources, the creation of a ghetto even if its walls were completed only over a period of time. Surely the Jewish Reform Congregation had always regarded itself as a community, but as a religious community only, one dedicated to study and learning free from myths and symbols—an intellectual community lacking that appeal to the emotions that the German right, but also the German Youth Movement, had made their own. Because of the resistance by the leadership of the congregation to the acceptance of an emotion-laden concept of community, the debate initiated by the congregation's youth became a test of liberalism. The congregation's intellectualized concept of community was based once again upon individualism: nonconformity was a quality that would protect Jews against assimilation.[23] But after 1933 such a definition could no longer satisfy youth—

particularly those hard hit by Nazi discrimination—and it is possible to follow in the *Mitteilungsblätter der Jüdischen Reformgemeinde* how the youth group tried to infuse the liberalism of the congregation with the ideal of a true community based upon shared emotions. For example, they suggested ridding the *Heim-Abende* (congenial get-togethers) of more or less abstruse intellectual discussions in order to concentrate upon individual encounters instead.[24] But a retreat into the apparent comfort of close personal relationships was not a tactic designed to strengthen communal bonds. Thus, in 1934, the youth group of the congregation obtained a uniform, as well as a flag, and a special dress uniform to be worn on festive occasions. The first flag was consecrated on the 23rd of August 1934, and at the same time, roving through the countryside, became an important activity of the group.[25] The symbols and the spirit of the German Youth Movement were copied by the youth group at this late date in order to create the feeling of community.

However, in spite of this apparent acceptance of the German ideal of *Gemeinschaft,* traditional liberal values were not abandoned by the congregation, but reaffirmed instead. The Reformgemeinde saw itself even now as a liberal community asserting the need for pluralism in all walks of life. Not "Jewish-volkish" personalities were needed, Karl Rosenthal, one of the congregation's youthful and vigorous rabbis, tells us in a sermon entitled "Within the New *Reich*" (September 1933), but individual personalities; and yet, he continues, the religious community, through performing its spiritual tasks, must become a truer community.[26] The conflict between liberalism and the search for a true spiritual community had been fought out in Germany itself long ago, and the community had been the victor. But the symbiosis between Judaism and liberalism was too deep-seated and could not be destroyed at the first onslaught.

The liberal Jewish paper, *Der Morgen,* closer to the mainstream of German Jewry than the publications of the Reformgemeinde, published in June 1932 an article by the non-Jewish writer Wilhelm Michel in which he analyzed what he called the end of liberalism. It was time, he wrote, to join in the hopes and feelings that moved all Germans, to fight against the exaggerated concept of freedom that liberalism had advocated.[27] Liberal Jews themselves wrote frequently after 1933 about a "converted liberalism," one that did not ignore the need of order in its concern with freedom. Already during the crisis of 1920–21 with its upsurge of nationalism and anti-semitism, the *Mitteilungen der Jüdischen Reformgemeinde* had called for

putting some restraint upon the worship of reason in order to give enthusiasm and the emotions of the heart their rightful place.[28] At the same time
Leo Baeck, who in the original edition of his *The Essence of Judaism* had
condemned all mysticism, now in a revised edition of his work defined
mysticism as something within us which encourages men to unfold their
personality freely, joining men to God.[29] Such ideas reflected the hunger
for myth during the Weimar Republic, but they never got the upper hand
over the tradition of the Enlightenment; they were constantly negated
through an emphasis upon reason and the individual personality. But now,
under national socialism, among Jews of all liberal persuasions there was
a strenuous effort to "convert" their liberalism to a greater emphasis upon
the principle of order.

Nevertheless, the ". . . Jewish love for Humanity and the age of Humanism"[30]—to quote a 1936 article in the *Mitteilungen*—lived on. It did
so as part of a retreat from an unpalatable reality into that preoccupation
with culture as humanistic *Bildung* which had been prepared by the primacy of liberal thought over liberal practice, a theme that has accompanied
us throughout this analysis. The primacy of *Bildung* provided refuge during
the Third Reich for Jews and many Gentiles alike, but for the Jews the
attainment of *Bildung* as an extension of the Enlightenment had been one
of the chief signs of their emancipation. Within the increasingly narrow
bounds of their German ghetto, culture, severed from political, social, or
economic reality, became a refuge and at the same time the guarantee of
their German-Jewish identity. Thus in 1934 it was proudly stated that the
Kulturbund deutscher Juden (the newly created Jewish organization that,
under Nazi auspices, sponsored all cultural activity) considered culture as
a good in itself, not related to any extraneous goals or activities. And in
1937 the Jüdische Reformgemeinde mourned the decline, caused by economic pressures, of *Bildung* among its hard-pressed youth. *Bildung* as art,
philosophy, and history would never become unfashionable and there could
be no excuse for abandoning one's self-cultivation.[31]

The conflict between liberalism and ideas of community was not abolished but disguised through emphasis upon the cultural inheritance that,
as these German Jews viewed it, was a liberal bequest. There were many
established leaders of the Jewish community who explicitly demanded the
separation of liberalism from its political infrastructure—a demand that,
as we saw, young Jewish Socialists like Carlo Roselli had made much earlier.
Manfred Swarsensky, a young rabbi at an important Berlin liberal syn-

agogue, wrote in 1933, speaking for many others, that Jewish liberalism was a child of European liberalism and could not be traced to specifically Jewish roots like the Talmud and Torah. Thus the crisis of general liberalism had affected Jewish liberalism as well. Nevertheless, it must not be discarded, for without liberalism Jews would have found no inner relationship to their faith.[32] Thus, while liberalism did not grow out of Judaism, it served to renew its spirit. Swarsensky's criticism was directed at the balance between rationalism and irrationalism, which had not been kept and must be restored. But this could only happen if the fateful mistake of joining religious to political liberalism were to be corrected.[33] Attempting to salvage religious liberalism meant in this context saving the tradition of liberal thought that was interwoven with Jewish religiosity: indeed, as we saw, liberal religion had absorbed and protected the humanistic liberal tradition.

The Jüdische Reformgemeinde joined this argument. The reaction of that congregation in 1936 to the closing of the *Jüdische Allgemeine Zeitung,* a newspaper representing a more moderate liberalism, was typical. We have attempted, so the *Mitteilungen* wrote, during the last twenty years to separate religious from political liberalism, ". . . and what we were not able to do the passage of time has accomplished."[34] This is surely an astonishing statement given the involvement of so many members and leaders of the congregation with liberal political parties. Perhaps this was wishful thinking projected onto the past, or an acknowledgment that theory had always had precedence over practice. Such a reaction on the part of the most dogmatically liberal of all German-Jewish congregations demonstrates that even here reality had to be faced, leading to a repudiation of liberal politics and a retreat into culture as the bastion of besieged liberal values.

The Jewish Kulturbund fulfilled a central function in the preservation and transmission of these values. To be sure, many cultural events sponsored by that organization reflected the light entertainment found in many German theater and concert programs as well; but it seems—in the absence of a detailed stocktaking—that a major part of its program was devoted to that theater and music which had traditionally provided the sign of a humanistic *Bildung*. We have attempted to outline elsewhere how the Kulturbund functioned in transmitting the liberal heritage.[35] Of course, here also this heritage was under pressure, not just from Nazi censorship but also from the perceived necessity of defining its "Jewish" content. This quest was never successful, once plays with a specific, generally East European Jewish note had proved unpopular, and it seemed easier to introduce a specifically Jewish content (such as the compositions of Ernst Bloch) into the musical program. For example, in order to make *Nathan der Weise* more "Jewish," he was made in one performance to hum a Hasidic tune in the first act (one wonders how many in the audience might have recognized it), and a menorah as well as a prayer stool graced with the Star of David were placed in his house. Subsequently it seemed sufficient that the actor himself would portray Jewish dignity through his comportment, whatever the play.[36] The liberal heritage dominated the specifically Jewish in most of the Kulturbund's performances, and the Kulturbund played an important role in preserving the alliance between Jews and liberal thought in dark times.

The amputation of liberal culture from liberalism as a political, social, or economic movement did lead to a certain vagueness in the definition of ideas like freedom and humanity. But while in Germany itself liberal ideals had threatened to degenerate into the transmission of liberal slogans through popular journals like the *Gartenlaube* at the end of the nineteenth century, Jews remained deadly serious in their commitment to liberal thought. It stood for the positive in the German-Jewish experience, the hopes aroused by the process of emancipation. Nevertheless, these noble ideals tended to become a utopia unless they were tied to a concept of politics that accorded to some extent with the political realities of the times. But after the First World War this was less and less the case, as we have pointed out, and under the Nazis, while contemplating this liberal tradition, one is projected into a world of dreams. Yet these liberal ideas were models for a better and healthier world, and their preservation in Nazi times was a historic deed. Whether non-Jews were also attracted to that German tradition within which so many plays of the Kulturbund had their place (or just by the quality of the performances), whether they also bought the books it recommended—many openly praising ideals of tolerance and the Enlightenment—is still unknown. And yet, such possible interaction during the Third Reich between Germans and German Jews largely on the basis of a shared liberalism would be an important part of the history of liberalism in Germany.

There is scattered evidence that this interaction may have been attempted. The often-repeated warnings and threats against so-called Aryans attending Kulturbund performances might lead to such a conclusion. A correspondent of *The Manchester Guardian* wrote in 1937 that not even foreigners could attend the Kulturbund unless they could prove that they were Jews. These restrictions, he continued, may have been a necessary precaution by the authorities, for if the Jewish theater were open to the general public it might prove too attractive.[37] German Jews were now, as in the past, one of the chief conveyors of the Enlightenment liberal tradition; they had, as we saw briefly above, attempted to infuse it into nonliberal movements such as Marxism or nationalism with indifferent success, and at the end of their history in Germany they stood as its sole guardians. Surely there were many non-Jewish Germans who shared these ideals, and liberal Jews had always found liberal partners in Gentile society. But here, under the Nazis, only the Jews were for some years permitted to advocate this liberalism through their cultural activities. Just as surely not all Jews were wedded to this heritage; some were religiously Orthodox, others orthodox Marxists, and a very few even political conservatives. But to a greater or lesser extent most of them were influenced by that system of ideas that had stood at the beginning of their history as Germans. We still lack research on the diffusion of liberalism through all branches of German Jewry, but it seems safe to say that the majority were, or aspired to be, *Bildungsbürger* in the classical sense of this term.

Liberal thought made a decisive contribution to Jewish emancipation and its influence upon German Jews is easily understood, but this liberalism may also have contributed to clouding their understanding of modern politics. The mass politics that began its triumphal march in postwar Germany was largely based upon a militant nationalism and a concept of the Volk that embraced all Germans except the Jews. German-Jewish *Bildungsbürger,* like some of their Christian counterparts, could find no relationship to such a nationalism or to this kind of politics; they were perplexed or attempted to trivialize a phenomenon so foreign to their cast of mind. Joseph Lehmann, the best known rabbi of the Reformgemeinde, did not have this postwar nationalism in mind when he wrote in 1933 that the feeling of belonging to Germany was the source of Jewish religiosity.[38] He had made clear what he meant by such national feeling earlier, in response to the first wave of antisemitism and racism that swept postwar Germany. His conclusions were not much different from those of his archenemies, the German Zionists. The opponents of emancipation, he wrote, had discovered their national soul, as if all the world were rooted in unchanging national sentiment. But the Jews were destined to stir up cultural ferment for all mankind.[39] These sentiments were reminiscent of a phrase from Leo Baeck's *The Essence of Judaism,* that the Jews were the leavening of history.[40]

Just as, on the one hand, the symbiosis between liberalism and the Jews made it possible for Jews in the Third Reich to preserve this liberal heritage, so, on the other, it blocked off political alternatives and the comprehension of political realities. Ideals such as Baeck's, or those of the other rabbis we have cited, did not encourage the joining of mass movements. Indeed, in the last years of the Weimar Republic, the Democratic party, a remnant of the once influential Liberal parties, attempted to regenerate itself and acquire a mass base by joining with the Jungdeutscher Orden, a former German youth movement, which, though volkish in attitude, had quarreled with the German political right. The new party was to be a synthesis of national and liberal traditions.[41] The very name of the new party, *Staatspartei,* shows how much liberal substance had vanished in what turned out to be an unsuccessful attempt to compete with existing mass political parties. Liberal thought with its roots in the Enlightenment found it difficult, if not impossible, to accommodate itself to the political right. But, as we have seen, until shortly before Hitler's accession to power, social democracy was also under suspicion; its class rhetoric disguised the reality of its liberal stance.

These observations are a critique of a liberalism that, after 1918, increasingly bypassed political realities it did not or could not understand. Yet a better grasp of political reality by such liberals would not have stopped the German catastrophe. Jewish emancipation and assimilation, with all their consequences, seemed time-bound after 1918, an emancipation and assimilation no longer in step with the times which apparently called for the formation of a true community as the center of the civic religion of nationalism. Conformity, and not a pluralistic and tolerant state, was in demand in a society that felt itself increasingly threatened.

But despite all the criticism that might be directed in retrospect against the alliance between Jews and liberalism, it seems to have been most fruitful precisely where it was most vulnerable: in its intellectualism and in its unrealistic timelessness. It did more than its share to preserve the values of the Enlightenment, the emphasis upon the individual, and the unity of all mankind. While in Germany the alliance between liberalism and the Enlightenment was constantly weakened, among most German Jews it held firm. The extent to which the German-Jewish liberal bourgeoisie contributed to the survival of the liberal heritage into postwar Germany still needs investigation. But that they attempted to transmit it is certain. It was nothing less than the tearing apart of theory and practice, so alarming before 1933, that made the survival of this heritage possible. Seen from this perspective the alliance of Jews and liberalism defied its critics and justified itself.

Even many Jews committed to Jewish nationalism did not repudiate their liberal heritage, and I have mentioned such Zionists already. Max Nordau and Gershom Scholem were influential thinkers in their own right, and both, through their ideas and attitudes, provide case studies in the evolution of liberalism in its relationship to modern national consciousness.

CHAPTER ELEVEN

Max Nordau: Liberalism and the New Jew

Max Nordau, liberal and Zionist, is today mainly remembered as the author of *Degeneration*. That famous book provides a key to his liberalism and to his nationalism as well. Therefore this book has to stand at the center of an analysis of the thought of that Zionist leader who at the beginning of the movement was second to (and much more famous than) Theodor Herzl. However, Max Nordau is important, not only because of the book's fame and its popularization of a concept that has lasted so long, but also because of what he himself stood for—the beliefs and hopes that characterized so many of his class, profession, and generation. His view of the dangers society faced, and his proposed cure, synthesized a series of convictions and preconceptions that made their mark even as the liberalism for which they stood threatened to collapse in the inferno of the First World War.

Max Nordau was a child of his times. *Degeneration,* published in 1892, addressed an age in which the ever-present challenges to established society were intensified, and we have referred to them often in the previous chapters: rapid urbanization, labor unrest, socialism and anarchism, and the rise of organized political mass movements—all these seemed to endanger the settled order of things. Moreover, for a good many people current epidemics like syphilis and tuberculosis indicated a diseased society. What Nordau in his *Degeneration* called "the end of an established order"[1] was symbolized by a new speed of time, that restlessness of modernity which threatened to shatter men's nerves. Here Nordau was part of a consensus among many bourgeois of his age and, just as important, among most of his fellow physicians as well. For Nordau was a doctor and looked at the challenges to contemporary society through a physician's eyes. The emphasis upon the shattering of man's nerves that runs throughout *Degeneration* was a reflection of the preoccupation with nervousness and hysteria that he shared with contemporary physicians like Cesare Lombroso or Jean-Martin Charcot, who unlike Max Nordau enjoyed fame and prestige within the medical profession itself. And it is telling that Nordau believed that the "affections of the nervous system" were a direct result of the new speed of time, of "railway spine and railway brain," as he saw it, the constant vibrations of modern travel.[2] Just so, Nordau voiced a majority opinion when he saw degeneration exemplified by the cities and their industrial proletariat in contrast to the peasants, who, so he thought, showed no signs of exhaustion.[3]

The conflict between society and such challenges at the *fin de siècle* was conceived as a struggle to preserve society's norms and thus to protect the normal against abnormality. This emphasis was reflected by the increasing attention given to the abnormal by physicians in general, and specifically by the new profession of sexology concerned with basic human behavior. The term degeneration had been coined in 1857 in order to characterize those whose nerves had been shattered by poison like alcohol and opium, through inherited bodily malfunctions, but also by their social milieu and moral debility.[4] Degeneration caused by such a mixture of clinical, social, and moral factors was defined as a certain life-style rather than simply as a bodily disease—a life-style that by the 1890s had become visible, practiced by men and women who were not afraid to call themselves decadent. Such men and women by their very visibility exemplified the challenges faced by society; they seemed to have taken Nietzsche's saying to heart that ordered society puts the passions to sleep. Nordau, unlike other critics of the decadence, was not directly concerned with those who actually lived a life-style that emphasized the abnormal as over against respectability. He does not, for example, mention the newfound visibility of homosexuals or lesbians that exercised sexologists and legislators. Instead, he was concerned with art and literature as symbolic of the decadence, for they seemed to challenge not just the division between genders but the entire liberal universe based upon scientific truth, "rational convictions arrived at by the sound labor of the intellect."[5] Nordau was, in fact, a convinced positivist.

Here, in the new world that artists and writers of the avant-garde sought to present, the very foundations of society seemed at risk. Their shattered nerves, diseased bodies, and love of the artificial, as Nordau saw it, climaxed the challenges to ordered society I have mentioned above. The artist, Nordau writes, should not create his work for its own sake, but in order to free his nervous system from tension.[6]

The so-called degenerates with whom Nordau dealt in his book were the counter-types to the image society liked to have of itself. Indeed, as one reads the description of his enemies, one is reminded of the stereotypes of others whom society considered outsiders: Jews, gypsies, criminals, the insane, or the permanently sick. All of them were considered nervous, incapable of clear thoughts, they were devious and turned their back upon nature. The asymmetry of face and cranium, as Nordau put it, reflects the degenerate's mental faculties as well.[7] His so-called "scientific classification" of decadent literature into categories of deviancy, insanity, and criminality,[8] roughly follows the categories of those considered "outsiders" by society and stereotyped accordingly. The Jews are, of course, omitted from his list, and yet it is significant, if ironical, that Nordau worked with stereotypes that had traditionally been turned against the Jews as well. But the very fact that, as we shall see, he had internalized the Jewish stereotype, that he shared society's view of the outsiders as abnormal and sick, formed an important link between Nordau, the author of *Degeneration,* and Nordau the Zionist. We will be concerned with Max Nordau in the Zionist phase of his life, for here the political role for which he is best remembered fuses with his fear of degeneration. There was no real division in his thought between his Zionism and the liberal world view he outlined in his non-Zionist and earlier writings.

Nordau saw the decadence as a challenge to Jews, just as it might destroy the established order itself if left unchecked. He eventually projected upon the East European Jews of the Diaspora the physical and mental sickness that characterized the modern in the arts—the stereotype of the degenerate (though he himself was born in Budapest but lived in Paris). Jews were, after all, for the most part city dwellers, overrefined, disputatious intellectuals who, as he saw it, had lost their taste for productive work. Like the artists and writers in *Degeneration* they fed on their overworked nerves, and here Nordau once more took up a Jewish stereotype, for Jews were regarded by physicians as especially subject to nervous and neurological disorders. For many Gentiles, but also for many Jews, the Jewish anatomical structure was inherently different from the norm and it had to be reshaped if Jews were to escape from their stereotype and recapture their dignity.[9]

Nordau constantly used the phrase "recapturing the dignity of the Jew" in his Zionist writings. This meant creating, as Nordau put it, deep-chested, powerfully built and keen-eyed men.[10] A new type of Jew must be created who could end the threat of decadence among the Jews. The new Jew who would emerge from the wreckage of the Diaspora symbolized the regeneration of the Jewish people. This new Jew was central to Nordau's Zionism.

Women were not the issue here. While they played no active role in his strategy to fight degeneration, Nordau in liberal fashion did support women's right to the vote even while he condemned the violence of the suffragette movement. Apart from advocating the political participation of women—advanced for his time—he was conventional in his view of woman's social role and her leadership potential. Manliness, dignity, and self-respect were linked in Nordau's mind, as in that of society as a whole. The Jew must be transformed from one who shared many characteristics of the degenerates to an ideal of manhood that exemplified society's standards of looks, comportment, and behavior. The new Jew must display all the social virtues enumerated so often in *Degeneration,* such as duty and discipline. Nordau summed up this manly ideal, and, in doing so, gave a perfect example of middle-class standards of masculinity as a response to degeneration; the egoists and those who lack willpower had separated themselves from the imperatives of society, as we read in *Degeneration,* for how could men like Huysmans's effete and overrefined Des Esseintes or Nietzsche compete with ". . . men who rise early and are not weary before sunset, who have clear heads, solid stomachs and hard muscles . . ."[11]

The description of the human body is important here; it emphasizes the constant juxtaposition of weak bodies and weak minds that runs throughout *Degeneration.* The Jew must acquire solid stomachs and hard muscles, not just to overcome his stereotype—though this was important for Nordau—but also to compete, to find his place in the world. Nordau built upon the widespread assumption that the healthiness and vigor of the body determined that of the mind as well. He used a medical and educational theory that, ever since the end of the eighteenth century, was supposed to rescue Europeans from some of the debilitating effects of modernity—especially city life—and to make them fit for the competition of an industrial age. Men who were robust and stalwart would embrace the work ethic in contrast to those whose weak bodies, lack of will or lack of energy made them shy away from work or activity in all its forms.[12] Already at the turn of the eighteenth to the nineteenth centuries physical education had been considered not only as a bodily but also as a moral necessity. Guths Muths's *Gymnastik für Jugend* ("Gymnastics for Youth," 1793), published in Germany, had set the tone: spirit, soul, and intellect depend upon the development of the body.[13] Gymnastics, so we hear by mid-nineteenth century, encompasses the body as it looks and moves and is the true expression of our very being.[14]

The *Jüdische Turnerzeitung* (Journal of Jewish Gymnastics), founded under the inspiration of Max Nordau, emphasized the idea that strength of mind was dependent upon the strength of the body; the Jews lacked willpower acquired through the vigorous activity of the spirit based upon muscular strength. Spiritual strength that benefits others besides ourselves, so we read in an article written by a physician in 1908, is only obtained when nerves put muscles in motion.[15] Here the fundamental importance assigned to the possession of healthy nerves was evident, together with the equation of bodily with spiritual strength. Nordau followed this line of thought, except where he found himself compelled to explain that Jews despite their stunted bodies had an inherent aptitude for gymnastics, an important point if the transformation of the Jew was to become a reality. Writing an article addressed to Jewish gymnasts he stated that the body was the servant of the spirit, and that the Jews with their spiritual alertness were well qualified to become excellent gymnasts.[16] Still, even here, mind and body were closely linked, while in *Degeneration* man was considered a human motor fueled by his physical condition.

Gymnastics, not sport, was important in the creation of the new Jew, just as in Europe as a whole (with the exception of Britain) gymnastics and not sport was considered essential for the construction of a masculine identity that could represent society and the nation. Sport was not considered as useful as gymnastics by those concerned with physical education because it was not specifically designed to perfect the human body.[17] Nordau himself referred to gymnastics, not sport, which, in the tradition we have mentioned, was supposed to aim at the harmonious formation of the human body, firm control over muscles, the steeling of the will, and increasing self-confidence.[18] He condemned football as "rough and devoid of spiritual substance."[19] A resuscitated Jewish body was the mark of the new Jew. Such an emphasis upon the human body was accompanied by the weight given to men's looks. They symbolized a healthy body and mind.

If Nordau's scattered remarks about how the new Jew should look are examined we are back with the ideal of masculinity advocated by middle-class society. Tall was better than small, and he speculated whether Jews have always been small in the past or if this was part of their degeneration.[20] The proper exercise will correct the Jews' bad posture.[21] The conditions under which Jews were forced to live in the Diaspora were to blame for their stunted bodies, for in biblical times they had produced strong men who could compete on equal terms with Greek athletes or nordic barbarians.[22] However, in reality, the body and looks so essential in the making of the new Jew were a product not of biblical times but of the Greek revival of the late eighteenth century, which, through the works of J. J. Winckelmann on male sculpture, had largely determined nineteenth-century standards of male strength and beauty. When one of Nordau's disciples, advocating gymnastics, wrote about the "manly beauty" of Samson, Saul, and Bar-Kochba,[23] he was projecting Winckelmann's Greek ideal of manliness upon these biblical heroes—an ideal of manly looks and comportment that had become commonplace by Nordau's time. The new Jew was a symbol of that normalization of Jewish life which Nordau desired. He stood, not for the assimilation of Jews into the cultured and intellectual circles that many in the Diaspora desired, but instead for their integration into middle-class tastes and ideals. Perhaps this was, in the end, a more thorough assimilation than that pursued by many of those Diaspora Jews he rejected.

The new Jew was identical with the stereotype of masculinity that had accompanied the rise of modern industrial society as the outward expression of true manliness. The new Jew's body was in every detail the reverse of the body the Jew possessed as an outsider—the diseased and deformed body that Sander Gilman has analyzed in his book on *The Jew's Body*. However, Nordau's call for a "muscle Jew" was not merely a reaction to the manner in which Gentiles saw Jews, but a matter of Jewish survival. Nordau was greatly concerned with the economic plight of the Jews. He saw the masses of Jewry living in Eastern Europe as "Luftmenschen" who lived from hand to mouth, and who through their way of life had acquired a distaste for honest work. The physical regeneration of the Jews was supposed to overcome this distaste by healing their nerves and strengthening their bodies. But even beyond this, the continued degeneration of the Jews would itself endanger the very existence of the Jewish people, for degeneration inevitably led to extinction. Concern with the Jew's body was an integral part of Jewish regeneration, just as concern with the body and manliness was uppermost in the minds of other men and movements concerned with steadying society in the modern age.

The ideal of manliness for which the new Jew stood was present in *Degeneration,* but it came to the fore with Nordau's turn to Zionism three years after that book was published. Here was a chance to use the weapons he had directed against degeneracy in order to bring about a transformation that lay at the root of the Zionist enterprise. The Jew was to be regenerated by work on the land. During a speech to the Zionist Congress of 1901 in Basel, a delegate, after picturing the supposed physical weakness and nervous condition of present-day Jews, blamed this state of affairs upon the absence of Jewish peasants or soldiers, precisely those occupations that were said to create healthy bodies.[24] All national movements at the time would have agreed that work on the land—and soldiering as well—created men who formed the backbone of the nation. But physical exercise such as gymnastics remained important: in a modern nation not all people could be peasants or soldiers, moreover gymnastics trained the body and made it beautiful. The physical ideal was entailed by the Zionist ideal, as Shmuel Almog has written, to the point where it was impossible to separate the two. This held true for all national movements, whether German, Czech, or Jewish, but for Zionists, he continues, physical qualities merge with mental qualities in the rejection of intellectualism and the spirit of the ghetto.[25] Nordau's concept of the new Jew was an important contribution to the Zionist movement. The bodily improvement of the Jews was to remain a constant topic of Zionist literature.

The image of the new Jew seems a militant one, and at times Nordau even praised a certain brutality. Indeed, for most European nationalisms the image of a new man, such as the "new German," did entail the praise of force, a soldierly ideal, a fighting spirit directed against internal and external enemies. But Nordau, after all, considered himself a liberal, a champion of individual rights and liberties. While here his liberalism and Zionism seem in conflict, in reality his ideal of the new Jew as well as his Jewish nationalism were adapted to liberal ends.

There is no need to go into a detailed discussion of Nordau's liberal credentials, which included as a matter of course belief in parliamentary government. His rationalism led to his belief in science, emphasis upon exact observation, and Darwinian ideas of evolution—in short, what he called "rational convictions arrived at by the sound labor of the intellect."[26] As Paul Wendling has written, science integrated the economic, social, and intellectual aspirations of the bourgeoisie.[27] Here again, there was no real difference between Nordau's ideology as set forth in *Degeneration* and his Zionism. Zionism, as Nordau saw it, was largely a pragmatic movement, a means for Jews to achieve freedom from persecution and to recapture their dignity. Those Jews who felt comfortable in their Diaspora environment could remain in their respective fatherlands. Only those Jews should come to Palestine for whom their present nation provided no home.[28] Here, surely, his pragmatism and his liberalism—that people should not be forced into action against their will—were in conflict with his fear of Jewish degeneration. This conflict was never resolved; perhaps the new Jew could be created in the Diaspora provided the requisite will and means were present. Nordau had, in fact, founded the Zionist gymnastic society Bar-Kochba, with its branches in most Jewish communities. He gives the impression that, in spite of the importance attached to the curative function of work on the land, Palestine was, above all, important as a place of refuge. Thus immediately after the proclamation of the Balfour Declaration he called for the transference of half a million Jews from "the antisemitic zone" of Eastern Europe to Palestine.

Nordau was more sober than Theodor Herzl; no romanticism clouded his vision, no concern with Jewish myths or symbols. Nordau did believe in organic evolution and was opposed to sharp breaks with the past. But, unlike others concerned with the regeneration of nations, his belief in organic evolution did not involve a deep concern for the nation's past. History cannot give answers to eternal questions; those are inherent in reality itself.[29] Nordau was fond of contrasting the subjectivity of history with the reality of nature. To be sure, Nordau talked about biblical Jewish heroes as providing models for the new Jew, but they were projected into the present as almost living examples, rather than standing in any historical continuity. He denied that a sense of history could have an impact upon those who actually make history: "the determining factor is the necessity of the present, not the experience of the past."[30]

Such an attitude toward history put still greater emphasis upon the new Jew as a man of action, as the savior here and now of the Jews from their degeneration. Nordau was interested in the creation of a new Jew through the regeneration of his body and willpower, rather than by way of a revival of Jewish culture in the Holy Land. Yet, when he thought about the survival of the Jewish people, he tried to explain their immortality through the existence of an undefined "secret."[31] As he rejected all mystics or mysticism, one has the impression that he had no great interest in solving this problem, one that his science could not address. Small wonder that a younger generation of Zionists led by Martin Buber confessed their disappointment in Max Nordau, who, as Buber wrote, had hurt their deepest feelings in his curt dismissal of a spiritual renaissance that must inform Zionism.[32] Nordau resisted the founding of the Hebrew University and was sceptical about the revival of the Hebrew language: "could there ever be a Hebrew word for a light bulb," he asked the philosopher Hugo Bergmann, who was close to the Buber circle.[33]

Nordau as a so-called political Zionist was not only opposed by young rebels around Buber, but also by Ahad Ha-am, the influential founder of a spiritual Zionism. He criticized Nordau's play *Dr. Kohn* (*A Question of Honour*, 1907), in which Dr. Kohn, a young Jew, was killed in a duel with a German officer who had insulted him and through him the honor of the Jewish people. Dr. Kohn felt that he had to fight the duel, otherwise all Jews would be called cowards. Perhaps here we can see Nordau's devotion to manly behavior once again, at a time when manly honor was still an important concept in certain influential bourgeois circles, one that had to be defended by a duel if necessary.[34] To this defense of manly honor Ahad Ha-am replied that it would have been better for the honor of the Jewish people if Dr. Kohn had not fought the duel. Jewish nationalists should be less concerned about such ethics and more with the national language. From this point of view Dr. Kohn's duel was assimilationist, a mere reaction to the Gentile's prejudices against the Jews.[35] However, duels were not just mimicking Gentile society but were the only resort left to Jews to defend their dignity against the rising tide of antisemitism in the 1890s, which had only begun to ebb when Nordau wrote his play. Indeed, there were those in France who kept a balance sheet of these encounters between Gentile and Jew.[36]

Nordau's belief in science, which made him reject both Ahad Ha-am's and Buber's Zionism, was part of his liberalism, leading him to accept the concept of manly honor and to link his Zionism to his preoccupation with the challenges to existing society. The regeneration of the Jews meant saving them from the dangers all of society faced, and not the construction of a romantic nationalism. Buber also believed in a healthy and perfect body but only as part of experiencing life as a totality. The result would be a burst of Jewish creativity based upon the freely found unity of the Jewish soul with the Jewish people.[37] What Buber called the priority of the "inner renewal" of the Jew was foreign to Max Nordau, in whose scheme of things the irrational had little place.

Here Buber was closer to the mainstream of European national movements than to Nordau's liberalism, though he also saw the nation as rooted in humanity as a whole.[38] Yet Nordau, like all nationalists, wanted the Jewish people to be rooted, if not in history, then on the land. Rootedness was, in fact, important to Nordau's concept of Zionism. The possession of Jewish land by the Jewish people was a prerequisite for the dignity and normalization of those who were treated like enemies in most of the nations where they now lived. Lack of settledness, an unsteady life, was for him a sign of degeneration, and it was this consideration, rather than any mystique attached to the Holy Land, that determined Nordau's attitude toward Jewish settlement in Palestine. He had, in fact, supported the alternative of Uganda as a place of settlement when it had been offered to the Zionists. Thus the priority assigned to Palestine as a land of refuge, mentioned earlier, was combined with Jewish regeneration through a steady, settled life. Nordau criticized undue travel, the hunger for luxury, movements without a set goal.[39]

Here Nordau was castigating that nervousness which was thought to ruin body and mind, and which, as mentioned earlier, he, in common with many physicians of his time, believed to be widespread among the Jews. But he was at the same time criticizing uncontrolled progress that lacked direction. His fears about society in general, which had found expression in *Degeneration,* were once again part of his Zionism. The Diaspora Jews, through their nervousness and their life-style, symbolized the degeneration of society as a whole. As in *Degeneration,* the corrupting influence of the big city was largely responsible. Echoing Nordau, an article in the *Jewish Journal of Gymnastics,* called "Coffeehouse Judaism" (1910), put it graphically: the small turnout for gymnastic exercises must be blamed on those nightly sessions in coffeehouses from which pale figures are seen slinking home at dawn.[40]

Return to the land will steady those who now live in the dark and dank streets of the ghettos of Eastern Europe, as Max Nordau described them. He did not join in the glorification of the masses of East European Jewry as the embodiment of Jewish authenticity, which had gripped many Zionist youth. These masses of Jewry, according to Nordau, were uneducated, tradition-bound, and preoccupied with the daily struggle to scratch out a living. Their attachment to Zionism was by instinct rather than reasoned reflection,[41] an attitude that Nordau, who based his Zionism on what seemed to him a rational solution to the Jewish problem, roundly condemned. While, as we have pointed out, romanticism held no attraction for him, in his description of the state of western as opposed to eastern Jewry he resorted to concepts like sentiment and emotion. Those who wanted the emancipation of East European Jewry to follow the course which that of West European Jewry had taken, he told the First Zionist Congress in 1897, were mistaken. Here in the West legal emancipation had not been preceded by the conviction that a great injury had been done to Jews in the past. Emotion and sentiment were lacking; instead emancipation had been the creation of pure intellect, rationalism operating in the world of reality based only upon logic.[42]

While his attitude toward East European Jewry seems to fit in with the demythologizing tendencies that inform his thought, his opposition to emancipation does bring irrational factors into play, just as his referring to the "secret" at the base of Jewish survival had been in apparent contradiction to his general attitude toward life. However, it was a mechanical application of rationalistic logic, which he likened to mathematics, that had brought emancipation to the Jews; a moral imperative was lacking. Morality itself had to be based upon Kantian and utilitarian principles.[43] The altruism by which he set such store was involved here, translated into a feeling of fraternity, absent among those who had emancipated the Jews.[44] His ideal of solidarity was based on moral, not economic or social, factors; it tempered his liberalism.

There could be no proper moral comportment without putting down roots, symbolized by the "quiet strength" and harmonious appearance of the new Jew. This new Jew, though nominally linked to the heroes of old, in reality exemplified a liberal utopia that sought to combine order with progress. Such ordered progress was supposed to cure the social ills that degeneracy symbolized in an age of industrialization and urbanization— an ideal that had informed the bourgeoisie ever since the beginning of the nineteenth century, and that had been crucial in the formation of the ideal of modern masculinity that the new Jew so accurately reflected.

The emphasis upon physical education, indeed the whole concept of a new Jew, could easily support right-wing ideals and a more chauvinistic nationalism. The Revisionist movement, ancestor of the present Likud, founded by Vladimir Jabotinsky in 1925, adopted the ideal of the new Jew and made it a crucial part of its own militancy. To be sure, Nordau's new Jew was a fighting Jew, but his achievement lay not on the field of battle but in his physical development and in putting down roots, thus recapturing his dignity. Jabotinsky's and the Revisionists' new Jew was similar to Max Nordau's in appearance and comportment, except for his glorification of military values. But this distinction was important, for the Revisionists were apt to raise physical force in the service of the Jewish nation to a value in and of itself.[45] Nordau's liberalism mitigated any aggressiveness on the part of the new Jew, who was, after all, also a man of action. Here liberalism meant regard for the individual, even though this individual voluntarily identified himself with a group. Man needs a *heimat* (native soil), a community he can call his own; otherwise, so Nordau told the Zionist Congress of 1897, he becomes unbalanced (*haltlos*), with all the consequences for body and mind this entails.[46]

Nordau also believed in the struggle for existence; however, surviving this struggle was not dependent upon a militant posture, but upon a fit body and mind and upon the self-discipline and the quiet strength of the new Jew. The ever-present enemy was not a people or even a particular person, but the danger of degeneration and an environment that deprived man of his dignity and honor. Victory was not attained by fighting battles but through a life lived according to scientific law. Nordau's attitude toward the nation state was determined by his individualism, and he castigated the narrow-minded and tyrannical nature of a nation that swallowed up the individual.[47] He was a liberal inasmuch as he did not reject the heritage of the Enlightenment and French Revolution as such; he condemned them specifically for not helping the Jews and for tightening their chains. The Enlightenment, in the larger view, overcame religious fanaticism, while the French Revolution in his view destroyed despotism, proclaimed the rights of man, and gave freedom to the world.[48] But accepting this heritage that had gone into the making of European liberalism, in spite of its attitude toward the Jews—as he saw it—meant a rejection of the romantic and integral nationalism that was even then racing toward victory.

Nordau had to balance his commitment to the regeneration and survival of the Jewish people with his concern for the rights of the individual. Thus in his novel *The Right to Love,* which appeared in the same year as *De-*

generation, the rights of individuals are suspended only when the survival of the species is at stake. A husband and wife must live in an empty marriage rather than endanger the adaptability of their children. However, while this position seems to reflect a concern with the falling birthrate of his time, it did not touch his then already old-fashioned patriotism. Nordau was in agreement with the kind of tolerant and broad-minded patriotism found in Theodor Herzl's liberal and Zionist utopia *Altneuland* (1902), discussed in chapter 8 of this book. The new Jew for all his masculinity and physical robustness was integrated into a liberal universe, and not into that modern nationalism that had by Nordau's time coopted this masculine stereotype. His was a rather unique combination of the old and the new.

And yet, even here the balance between the national imperative and individual rights was endangered. The new Jew was to be symbolic of the Jewish national character as it had existed in ancient times and must exist again in the future. The idea of a national character in itself presented a certain challenge to liberal individualism. Even Nordau's new Jew demanded a certain conformity inherent in a national stereotype whose body and mind were dedicated to recapturing the lost dignity and honor of his people. The settlers' need for self-defense eventually strengthened this image in the reality of life lived in Palestine, even though the majority of settlers—like Nordau himself—would have rejected the contention, put forward even before Jabotinsky's time, that every Jewish soldier was fulfilling a messianic dream, that the creation of a Hebrew fighting force would erase the Exile.[49] Nevertheless, such ideas, explicit, for example, in the figure of the new German, were implicit in the new Jew even if Nordau tried to balance this image with his liberal heritage.

After the First World War, Max Nordau did strike a more militant note, calling for the establishment of a Jewish majority in Palestine. Under the pressure of the postwar pogroms in Eastern Europe he seemed to draw closer to Vladimir Jabotinsky, who now called him "perhaps the most revolutionary thinker of the *fin de siècle* generation."[50] Yet it would never have occurred to Nordau, as it did to so many Revisionists, to work out how Jews could rule over an Arab population; instead he hoped for an understanding with "our future Moslem neighbours and compatriots" before their minds were poisoned by Syrian agitators.[51]

Nationalism always meant a certain conformity, however widely the boundaries of the acceptable were drawn. Rather than the latent danger to liberalism inherent in the national stereotype of the new Jew, it was the allegiance to bourgeois norms that actually restricted individual freedom and demanded conformity, and in this case Nordau's liberalism, once more in step with liberalism in general, was not tolerant but commanded obedience. Here middle-class norms took the place of the historical myths and symbols that were the staple of all nationalism. These norms of behavior and comportment were supposedly based upon scientific laws that had to be observed if the species were going to survive. Nordau measured the degenerates against such standards: the ideal of ordered progress, which has been mentioned already, but also those manners and morals that can be summarized under the heading of respectability.

Nordau ascribed to degenerates a wide variety of neuroses, and yet he hardly mentioned their sexual habits, and this in spite of the fact that, in the general discussions about degeneration, sexuality had become the test of sickness or health. The link between sexuality and degeneration was mentioned only on rare occasions. Thus the criminal instincts of a degenerate woman, according to Nordau, were said to express themselves through prostitution, reflecting the conventional attitudes toward women as sexual and instinctual, the opposite of the masculine ideal, and this in spite of his support for women's suffrage. Nordau's attitude toward nudity was more telling: public exposure was taken as a sign of degeneration. He wrote about bodily freedom, which he saw as being out of control. Theater censorship had been abolished in France, and as a result nude women populated the stage in what Nordau ironically called "a new triumph for democracy."[52] Now ancient times were said to have returned, those spectacles that had characterized Rome at its fall.[53] Here police action would do no good, nor the threats of philistines;[54] presumably only true personal regeneration would help.

Like most of his contemporaries Max Nordau had internalized the ideal of respectability, and in all probability saw no contradiction between it and his liberal individualism. Indeed, he may have thought that such standards were necessary to reinforce that principle of order which alone could keep progress from sliding into chaos. Nordau would never have approved left-wing kibbutz morality; chasteness was as much an attribute of the new Jew as of the new German, of equal importance with courage and energy. Indeed, it was the presumption not only of Nordau, but of all advocates of physical exercise, that manly chastity was characteristic of a steeled and well-formed body.

The new Jew was a symbol of regeneration but, at the same time, of conformity equated with bodily and mental health. There is, then, an obvious parallel between the new Jew and the middle-class manly ideal that dominated European nationalism as a whole. The true hero, Nordau tells us, did not chase after the Golden Vliess or rescue maidens in distress; he is unselfish and unpretentious, averse to posturing.[55] His greatness did not lie in the realm of thought, feeling, or fantasy, but instead was due to his power of will and his actions. This was a middle-class hero in national dress. Nordau's pragmatism, his suspicion of the imagination, so obvious in *Degeneration*, is present here as well—an attitude that made him see Palestine not as a "Holy Land" but as a place of settlement and a refuge. There is a sobriety about Nordau's thought and his writings that, though it makes him a very bad novelist, conformed to a middle-class ethos.

Yet Nordau's nationalism rose above the conventional nationalism of his time. Nationalism was part of a process that led from barbarism to altruism—that is, to a love of all humanity—and struck a balance between individual rights as over against the state on the one hand, and national solidarity on the other. While Nordau's version of the new man observed the conventions of bourgeois life, he lacked most of the historical sense of exclusiveness required of nationalists, as well as the inborn hostility toward other countries and peoples that characterizes modern nationalism.[56]

Degeneration has been called an infamous or a comical book, not to be taken seriously on either account. The moderns Nordau hated have triumphed. As it has turned out, they were not a destructive challenge and instead could be accommodated within the framework of a settled society. The new Jew has had a more successful life as part of Zionist thought, though his fate, now that the state of Israel has been born, has yet to be determined. The argument put forward in *Degeneration* is linked in Nordau's thought to the new Jew, just as his Zionism is linked to his liberalism. Above all, *Degeneration* is a document of its time: Nordau's fears, his strategy in fighting the challenge to society, his liberalism in its tolerance and conformity, reflected conventional wisdom. That his nationalism and his ideal of the new Jew, in respect of their militancy and aggressiveness, departed from the norm—were different, that is, from what one might be led to expect—gives Nordau's thought its special cast. He not only exemplified the hopes and fears of the bourgeoisie of his time, but also through his liberalism attempted to humanize both nationalism and modern masculinity.

CHAPTER TWELVE

Gershom Scholem as a German Jew

Analysis of Gershom Scholem's thought has focused upon his revitalization of long neglected sources of Jewish thought, upon his scholarly investigations of Jewish mysticisms. Within this framework of the Jews and the Nation, I intend to use a different approach. I will ask how his preoccupation with Jewish thought was related to the intellectual environment in which he grew up and spent much of his life, in order to gauge the influence of the liberal German and German-Jewish environment on the formation of his attitudes toward Judaism and upon his Zionist commitment. To inquire about Scholem as a German Jew may seem unjustified in view of his violent rejection of a German-Jewish symbiosis, especially before and after the Second World War. Nevertheless, background and intellectual environment count, especially in the case of Scholem's profound and lasting involvement with German culture. Moreover, many of his close acquaintances in Jerusalem, such as the chief collaborators in his short-lived political venture, came from the same background, one of German culture, even if some of them were born or educated in the Austrian Empire rather than in Germany. Finally, the situation of German-Jewish immigrants to Palestine, even if they were passionate Zionists, was such that there was no group, no cohesive culture, to which they could assimilate—as they could in England or America—and therefore their life-style continued much as before. Though not decisive, this fact nevertheless played a role in their development of a certain approach to Jewish concerns that would have been quite different if, for example, their minds had been formed in England or America.

That development in German thought and culture which must concern us also had the greatest influence upon Scholem's own generation: the German Youth Movement, the ideals of nationalism, and the concept of *Bildung*. The concept of *Bildung* will be of special importance, as we shall see, not just as a general phenomenon, but, as we saw in an earlier chapter, because of its special attraction for German Jews when the Germans themselves had long subverted that concept. Even so, all we can do is to raise the question of influence, to give food for further thought rather than come to any definitive conclusions, if only because so much in this chapter must be hypothetical and circumstantial. However, to raise the question of Scholem as a German Jew is important in order to complete the picture of Scholem's thought as well as for assessing the depth and force of the German-Jewish heritage; but it is especially relevant for the history of Zionism whose many-sided alternatives to the normative European nationalism are in danger of being forgotten.

The question that stood at the beginning of Scholem's rediscovery of his Jewishness could have been asked by any young Jew of his generation and class after years of comfortable assimilation: "I tried to understand what kept Judaism alive."[1] The approach he took to this question and to his Zionism—which constituted the core of his answer—can best illustrate some of the characteristics of Scholem as a German Jew. Yet it must be added at once that what he discovered in his commentary upon Jewish sources was crucial, and so was his firm belief in the autonomy of these sources, indeed, of the Jewish tradition. The German-Jewish influence appears, as we shall see, not only in his approach to some of the questions asked, but also in how he related his scholarship to contemporary Zionist concerns. Scholem's belief in the autonomy of the Jewish sources was an article of faith, and here we have followed his own belief. However, the recent work of Moshe Idel seems to indicate that German influence penetrated deeply into Scholem's reading of the Kabbalah as well.[2] Such a contention would not change but extend my argument.

If for Scholem the Jewish tradition and history were autonomous, self-contained, scholarship was not; it had didactic purpose, an aim closely tied to the question of what kept Judaism alive. Scholarship must lay bare Jewish history and Jewish sources that would lead to national regeneration and therefore to the survival of the Jewish people. The scholar, he wrote, must

have a definite commitment to his subject even while keeping his independence of mind.³ On another occasion he wrote how much he envied the
older German historians who at all times, ". . . strove for an active comprehension of their own history in the sense of a positive, nationally oriented perspective and future."⁴ Scholem enlisted his scholarship in the
service of a national ideal, but, quite unlike the German historians he professed to admire, this did not stand in the way of honest scholarship. Indeed, while the historical writings of German nationalist historians are
long forgotten, most of Scholem's scholarship has stood the test of time.
Given the aims of that scholarship, this is, as far as I know, a unique
accomplishment.

It is intriguing to speculate why he should have kept this balance between
scholarship and commitment when, as a rule, ideals of national regeneration had the opposite effect. Here, it seems to me, both his habitual posture
as the outsider and the German tradition of *Bildung* are important: the
former made it easier to keep the kind of distance he saw as necessary for
scholarly accomplishment, the latter helped give his nationalism a quite
different thrust than that of the German historians. Indeed, his concept of
peoplehood differed not only from traditional German ideas of nationhood
but from those of most Zionists as well. His was to be a Zionism against
the times. Basic to his Zionism, as to all of his thought, was a concept of
Jewish history as open-ended, without any predetermined direction, and
full of surprises—a view closely tied to his interpretation of the Kabbalah,
which did not permit a secure and settled Jewish identity.

The revolt against the establishment, against closed and settled forms,
is a constant in Scholem's thought. He considered himself in revolt much
of his life, someone whose duty as a scholar was to challenge accepted
truths and existing establishments. Judaism, so he wrote to Walter Benjamin in 1934, was a very unbourgeois phenomenon.⁵ What did he mean
by such a phrase, what sort of a revolt, what distancing was involved in
this posture? Here, we must look at Scholem's youth, at that movement
which, before and during the First World War, engaged his interest and
with which he was involved for a time: the German Youth Movement, or
rather the Jewish Youth Movement, built on its foundations. This revolt
. of youth against their elders was directed against the bourgeoisie, who
were, as they saw it, stifling, fossilized, and tyrannical. The bourgeoisie
itself was defined through its life-style and not as a social and political class.
Scholem did not align himself with the attack on bourgeois manners and

morals, for, like all Jews after their emancipation—as we saw earlier—he had internalized respectability. Instead he concentrated upon the accusation that the bourgeoisie was static, its horizons narrow and opposed to action of any kind. He was to push this condemnation to its logical conclusion in his controversies with the Jewish Youth Movement.

Quite correctly Scholem saw in the romanticism of the Youth Movement the reason for its taming: that "inwardness" which prevented decisive action and self-discipline.[6] The Jewish Youth Movement, so it seemed to him, refused to commit itself to Judaism through the self-discipline necessary for a study of the sources and the deed of emigrating to Palestine. He joined the Orthodox youth movement, Young Judäa, for a short time, hoping to find combined there a devotion to the study of Jewish sources and an opposition to bourgeois complacency. He was disappointed once more: as he will write later, accommodation with the bourgeoisie had fateful consequences for Jewish Orthodoxy, leading to a "denigration of the Jewish substance."[7] Judaism for Scholem, even at this time of his life, stood opposed to a settled and self-satisfied society that could only encourage Jewish assimilation. He couched his opposition in the language of the Youth Movement: ". . . we want to enjoy the strength and beauty of our youth and not the melancholy of exile."[8] Words such as vitality and spontaneity occurred throughout the discussion of his own work, and he never tired of pointing out that it was precisely the vitality of the Kabbalah, its potency, that enabled Judaism to survive dark times.[9] Zionism was, where it counted for him, always a movement of youth.

Scholem's criticism of the Youth Movement, it seems, was not directed at its general thrust, which he shared, but at its having stopped halfway. Moreover, he charged, it lacked intellectual substance and lacked a sense of history, which was a prerequisite for the Jewish renaissance and for which a vague inward feeling or romantic experiences were no substitute. The Youth Movement put into a larger framework a state of mind that had its origin in Gershom Scholem's revolt against his assimilationist and bourgeois family, and that centered upon the question of Jewish survival always uppermost in his thought. Scholem could not escape the influence of the Youth Movement any more than most articulate and educated members of his generation, and his definition of the term "bourgeois," as identical with all that was abominable (as he put it in 1917),[10] is only one symptom of this influence. A certain approach to life and to Zionism itself was involved—an oppositional posture, a distancing, which encouraged a certain analysis of Jewish history. It honed the critical spirit in which Scholem believed, and the dynamic, the open-endedness, of his system of thought.

Yet the romanticism he rejected so violently was difficult to avoid when it came to constructing a national identity. Here the fact that Scholem was a German Jew was certainly more significant than any influence the Youth Movement may have had upon his approach to the nature of the Jewish revival. Several scholars like Alexander Altmann have pointed to Scholem's debt to the German tradition of romantic nationalism.[11] To be sure, this was the nationalism that Central and East Europeans knew, including the Jews of Central and Eastern Europe. Here that very inwardness for which Scholem had criticized the German Youth Movement was important, as romanticism and nationalism were closely linked. The emphasis upon history and language revealed the roots of the nation, and history was the process by which those roots developed: it did not have to be chauvinistic, but in any case it evolved organically from past to present.

History and language were central ingredients of Scholem's Zionism as well. And so was a "mystical totality," which the recapturing of history and language symbolized. The esoteric, the interest in mysticism, could best grow on German soil, where both were closely connected to the revival of nationalism during the last decades of the nineteenth century. Had Scholem been born and worked in England or France, for example, such approaches to Judaism would not have lain so readily at hand. The identity of personal and national regeneration which Scholem assumed—and which was not only common to modern nationalism but one of its principle characteristics—must be mentioned as well. It had evolved over the span of the nineteenth century and was typical both of the German Youth Movement and of all cultural or integral nationalism at the *fin de siècle*. The identity of personal and national became fixed, in the end, as the nationalism that had focused upon territory and borders was superseded by a nationalism that took in all aspects of life.

Cultural Zionists shared the belief in the identity of personal and national regeneration, but they gave it a more humanistic content and a more universally valid emphasis. As we shall see, it was precisely the cultural Zionists who, out of their definition of Jewish culture, attempted to halt the fateful course of Zionism before and after the Second World War. Scholem was a cultural Zionist, but the thrust of his cultural Zionism was different. In this lies his original contribution to Jewish nationalism, in contrast to most Zionists who, in one way or another, followed a precedent set by a variety of previous nationalisms.

Scholem tried to deromanticize Jewish history by putting it on a sound scholarly foundation, the kind of distancing about which he spoke. The very nature of his interpretation of Jewish history challenged the foundation of traditional nationalism. Jewish history, he held, defines the living body of the Jewish people, and only if the Jew entered into his history could the Jewish Renaissance take place.[12] Defining a people through the constant flow of its history was not new; it was part and parcel of traditional nationalism—and German idealism had put forward a similar concept. But Scholem's view of history lacked the all-important ideal of progress, of organic, steady development. Moreover, it missed the kind of solid core that characterized both nationalist history and German idealism: there was no unfolding of a Hegelian Idea, no idealized past projected into the future as in nationalist histories. Nor were there ancient or medieval examples valid for all time. Instead of the kind of predetermined structure and goal the German nationalist historians admired, Scholem's history was a continuous process. There was no "essence of Judaism" such as that with which Jewish thinkers like Leo Baeck had tried to counter Adolf Harnack's "essence of Christianity."[13]

Yet historical relativism, which started to become fashionable when Scholem himself began writing, was furthest from his mind. He believed in a mystical totality of truth which, as he wrote to Salman Schocken, can only become visible through historical commentary and philological criticism.[14] I am not an expert on the history of Jewish mysticism and it is not my intention to try to penetrate further into this totality. But it is important for my argument to point to the religious substance within this totality, the moral impetus which it contains and to which I will return. But here, once again, "such hidden sources of new life"[15] cannot be codified in laws and regulations; this would, in Scholem's words, contradict the infinite meanings of the word of God.[16] There is truth behind the flow of history, and historical or philological scholarship alone can make it visible. This scholarship Scholem elaborated against the ever-present background of the *Wissenschaft des Judentums* (Science of Judaism): a group of nineteenth-century scholars who modeled themselves upon the tradition of impartial scholarship as an end in itself. He condemned such scholars as assimilationist because they failed to read the message of the Jewish texts.

For all that, the German element enters once more: he held a constant dialogue with the work of Heinrich Grätz and other German-Jewish historians who followed the example set by the *Wissenschaft,* and while the East European tradition of *Hochmat Yisrael* (the study of Judaism in Hebrew) provided precedents for the examination of texts, it was not central to that scholarship, against which he constantly measured himself.

Scholem's deromanticizing of nationalism was accompanied by a deromanticizing of mysticism. Here, too, the study of mysticism must be based upon historical scholarship in order to fathom its intent and meaning. Moreover, precisely that mysticism which foreclosed German national history, making it a matter of faith that could be grasped only by the soul, now kept history open and provided a Jewish tradition that permitted no foreclosure or set goals. The traditional function mysticism had performed within German nationalism was turned upon its head.

Scholem's controversy with Martin Buber concerned above all Buber's rejection of history. The impact of Buber's Hasidim upon so many readers was precisely that they provided a valid and immediate Jewish tradition that needed no commentary or mediation. Buber did not ignore the historical dimension; he, too, rattled at times what one of his admirers called the "dry bones of history,"[17] but this took second place to experiencing one's Jewishness. Buber rather than Scholem was close to a certain German nationalism: he had, at one time, entered into this nationalism, its thought and its vocabulary. The German mystics had fascinated him as they had never fascinated Scholem, and his own portrait of the Hasidim never lost the romanticism with which those mystics had been endowed as part of their national function. Yet, even when Buber used the vocabulary of blood and Volk, he attempted to give his own Jewish nationalism a human face; for Buber the nation was only a necessary stepping-stone to the embrace of all humankind.[18] While Scholem believed in the autonomy of the Jewish tradition, viewing Jewish mysticism as having nothing in common with that of other nations, he also attempted to give his own Jewish nationalism a humanist dimension. Moreover, Scholem and Buber both believed in a Judaism that was not institutionalized but dynamic, driven by a love for the Jewish people. Both, as we shall see, will work together in Jerusalem in order to bring about a shared vision of Zionism. But for Scholem, as we have seen, Judaism was based upon the deromanticization of Jewish history and Jewish mysticism, and also upon historical scholarship. Their common vision was similar, in retrospect, and yet through his unique combination of commitment and scholarship Scholem gave a foundation to his Zionism that was at once more daring and more firmly based.

Scholem broke out of the confines of traditional nationalism, transforming into a wager a movement that was supposed to provide certainty. Yet some of the basic approaches remained intact: the centrality of history, however defined, as well as the emphasis on language, which, being at once divine and human, can symbolize hidden meanings and thereby make transparent the nature of Judaism; without the knowledge of Hebrew, Scholem believed, no Jewish regeneration is possible.[19] The identity of personal and national regeneration has been mentioned already. Once again, Scholem's approach is influenced by the fact that he was a German Jew, but his content derives from his scholarly reading of the Jewish sources, which he supposed to be self-contained in their Jewishness.

The modern nation expressed itself through myths and symbols. Ultimately, it would be difficult to disentangle, in Scholem's own symbolic mode of expression, what he took from the esoteric sources of Judaism or what he received from his own culture, which treasured symbolic expression. Symbols, he wrote, taking over the normative definition, crystallize a world view; they have great emotional power. Thus, in keeping with the modern understanding and use of symbols, and in imitation of the symbols so long used by Christianity, the Jews had adopted the Star of David as their symbol.[20] As a national Jewish symbol, Scholem felt, it was empty and hollow, typical of the decadence of Jewish life in the period of assimilation.[21] He did not, however, reject the use of symbols, for through them, he claimed, hitherto repressed materials find their way into the open, including the historical tradition that defines Judaism. Scholem's sources themselves, like the Kabbalah, required the reading of myths and symbols, as did all history that was thought to be basic to the definition of national identity: for example, Grimm's fairy tales, which recaptured the national past through symbolic language, or national monuments, which preserved and symbolized national memories.

If the way in which Scholem confronted such contemporary phenomena as the Youth Movement and modern nationalism is important to an understanding of his thought and its unique qualities, then a fundamental concept closely related to the self-identity of German Jews had still greater weight. The ideal of *Bildung,* as we saw earlier in this book, had facilitated Jewish emancipation in Germany at the beginning of the nineteenth century, and Jews clung to its original definition to the very end. No one can doubt that Scholem was *gebildet,* knowledgeable in every aspect of German culture, but there was much more to the concept than knowledge or learning; it encompassed character and morality as well.

The true purpose of man, according to Wilhelm von Humboldt—who sought to define *Bildung*—is to cultivate his intellectual powers until they form a harmonious unity. This self-cultivation in the thought of Goethe or Wilhelm von Humboldt was based on a continuous quest for knowledge that activated the moral imperative. Self-cultivation was not meant to be chaotic but rather controlled, through a study of the ancients—that is, the Greeks whose language itself was supposed to discipline and energize the mind. Thus informed, reason must secure its domination over the senses and activate man's ethical nature.[22] The eighteenth-century Enlightenment created the ideal of *Bildung* with its belief in reason and its optimism about the potential of men and women. *Bildung* transcended all differences of nationality and religion. Tolerance was one of its hallmarks, a consequence of its rationalism and view of human nature. This was a uniquely Germany ideal and it cannot be found as a concept in any other nation.

At first glance, it seems highly unlikely that the ideal of *Bildung* could have influenced Gershom Scholem. It was not ready-made for modern nationalism, but instead provided the foundation for Jewish assimilation. In this aspect Scholem explicitly condemned *Bildung* through one of its founders, Wilhelm von Humboldt, who, as he put it, did not desire the disappearance of Jews but their complete transformation. He respected men like Schiller and Humboldt as spokesmen for "pure humanity," but saw them as enemies who frustrated the survival of the Jewish people.[23] In short, he opposed those Enlightenment ideas that were an integral part of the concept of *Bildung,* with its exaltation of reason and its belief in Jewish assimilation. Moreover, Enlightenment rationalism as a whole was opposed to the religious ethic of Judaism as he saw it. However, for all that, he wholeheartedly accepted *Bildung*'s emphasis upon critical reason. Reason, so he told an interviewer, is an instrument of destruction rather than construction; even the use of critical reason, which he advocated, had its limits. Morality as a constructive force could not exist without religion, without some power beyond pure reason.[24] Similarly, Scholem did not share the optimism implied in the ideal of *Bildung,* though, inasmuch as it was an ingredient of humanism, and stripped of its notion of inevitable progress, he tolerated it.

During its German itinerary, the concept of *Bildung* itself was soon assimilated to the spirit of German Protestantism, and, as Greek was cut back as a subject in school in favor of religious instruction, the idea of freedom as expressed in Greek texts was no longer fit for discussion.[25] Such a perversion of the original concept of *Bildung* facilitated its cooptation by the Prussian state; obedience and loyalty soon took the place of open-endedness. Prussian schools, which prided themselves on producing men of *Bildung,* now turned out a finished product: students who could make good civil servants.

Scholem never followed this path; there was to be no finished product, no ideal Jewish type to match the German. German Jews clung to the original ideal of *Bildung* to the bitter end, but few followed the Prussian annexation of *Bildung.* The process of *Bildung* as one in which all could join on equal terms was essential to their assimilation; it was crucial to the integration of Jews into the educated classes that ruled Germany. Scholem, of course, used *Bildung* to the opposite effect, projecting such of its ideals as self-cultivation, life as a process, and the importance of ancient sources as a training in ethics, upon the quest for Jewish nationhood.

We must single out certain crucial ingredients of *Bildung* in order to see the connection with Scholem's thought: its ideal of totality, its moral, humanist posture—never at ease with normative nationalism—and, last but not least, its regard for life as a process rather than a finished product. Scholem joined in the quest to embrace the totality of life, which had been a part of the concept of *Bildung* with its ideal of the harmonious personality, but which was also present in the ideals of the Youth Movement. Indeed, a longing for totality informed Scholem's whole generation in the midst of modernity's drive toward fragmentation. Scholem in a rather typical statement wrote early on in his life that the new Jew should be "not just muscle Jew, not just philosopher, but one who at one and the same time is an assailant and knowledgeable."[26]

The ideal of totality was inherent in the concept that personal and national regeneration were one and the same, for all such nationalist movements were meant to end the alienation of man. Though Scholem did not think in such cosmic terms—for him it was the survival of Judaism that was always at issue—the general quest for totality, without which the ideal of *Bildung* would collapse, must have been deeply ingrained in his mind as he examined his sources. All parts of life are interrelated, and the individual must be immersed in the open-ended stream of Jewish history. The complex connection between Scholem and *Bildung* is best illustrated in practice, through his vision of Zionism, in which all the influences I have mentioned had their place.

Making aliyah, emigrating to Palestine, Scholem wrote, was a moral and not a political decision, directed against dishonesty and playing hide-and-seek with one's Jewishness.[27] This meant joining the stream of Jewish history where it was purest and least subject to foreign influence. "I really thought that a Jew has to go to Eretz Israel," he once said in retrospect; "... if there was any prospect of a substantive regeneration of Judaism revealing its latent potential—this could only happen here, through the Jewish person's encounter with himself, with his people, with his roots."[28] Solely in Eretz Israel could one encounter the stream of Jewish history clear and not muddied by the dishonesty of Jewish assimilation. The accusation of dishonesty and concealment was generally directed against Diaspora Jews by the Zionists. Perhaps, however, one can find here echoes of Scholem's accusations against the bourgeoisie discussed earlier; a self-consciously nonbourgeois preoccupation with clarity and honesty in all relationships had, after all, been an article of faith of the Youth Movement as well.

Scholem once described the conflict between continuity and rebellion as a determining factor in the history of Zionism. However, in reality, he continued, there was no conflict, for continuity and rebellion were part of the living manifestation of a Judaism that had arrived at no particular synthesis at the moment, though it might do so at a future time.[29] Zionism was neither the bedrock of history, giving it aim and order, nor the culmination of Jewish history—only the future can tell. Moreover, Zionism was neither a dogma nor a matter of political necessity, but an ethical imperative and guide to comportment: "... if the dream of Zionism is numbers and borders and if it can't exist without them," he wrote in 1931, "... then Zionism will fail, or, more precisely, has already failed."[30] The regeneration of the nation, then, does not take place on the political scene but through ethics and morals, which entail a commitment to Judaism, not as a secure haven, but as an open-ended process instead. Zionism was a calculated risk, arising out of destruction in the time of exile and a subsequent immersion in a Judaism freed of dogma. Zionism for Scholem meant a constant renewal, everlasting youth, without the promise of a final goal. The thrust of this argument was the same as that which *Bildung* had advocated and which had penetrated deeply into German-Jewish consciousness: that culture not politics is important in shaping man's character and ethical posture. Jewish history did not call for any particular political configuration, but understanding its nature did lead to certain moral qualities which were anchored in the Divine.

This emphasis upon culture as expressing the totality of life from which politics was all but excluded led to lasting attitudes toward the political process among most educated German Jews: they faced the aggressive mass politics of the left and the right without a compass. Scholem's objection to Walter Benjamin's Marxism was not just its assimilationism or philosophical materialism, but that it was centered upon political power and its own method rather than on an unambiguous moral commitment.[31]

The moral posture and the idealism inherent in *Bildung* are reflected, then, not in the details of Scholem's thought, but in his overall posture and view of life. As such *Bildung* affected his interpretation of Zionism, not in its Jewish essence, but, once again, in his approach to the movement. Here Scholem, for a very brief time, attempted to put theory into practice, as he took part in Zionist politics. This seems to contradict the ideal of *culture d'abord,* but in reality it exemplified the application of *Bildung* to an effort to keep, in his view, the Zionist movement true to itself.

The Brit-Shalom (Covenant of Peace), in which he participated from roughly 1929 to 1933, believed that Palestine should be neither a Jewish nor an Arab State, but a binational state in which Jews and Arabs would enjoy equal political, civil, and social rights.[32] Within such a Palestinian state, Jews and Arabs should remain culturally autonomous peoples. Brit-Shalom also advocated mixed Arab-Jewish institutions like trade unions.[33] Theirs was not the only group advocating a binational state in Palestine at the expense of Jewish sovereignty. Many in the Zionist-socialist labor movement also supported such a project out of their socialist tradition, which was different from the theoretical framework of Brit-Shalom. For Brit-Shalom, in accordance with the tradition of *Bildung*, the Jewishness of the Jewish national home was safeguarded through its cultural autonomy, not through politics or institutions. Such a program corresponded to Scholem's view of Zionism: Jews needed the land; to be a Jew meant living in Palestine, but the regenerative function of Eretz Israel was not tied to particular political boundaries or institutions. As he wrote to Walter Benjamin a few years after Brit-Shalom had ceased to exist, ". . . it would not be so terrible if Jerusalem remained an English mandate even in a Jewish homeland as long as Hebrew was not abolished as an official language."[34] There was, in other words, no emphasis upon a Jewish state with all the attributes of sovereignty to which any modern state would think itself entitled.

Hans Kohn, himself a prominent member of Brit-Shalom, emphasized the primacy of culture at its most extreme when he wrote in 1929 that the Zionism he championed was in no way political: "I and a group of my friends regarded Zionism as a moral cum spiritual movement within which we could realize our most fundamental humane convictions, our pacifism, liberalism and humanism."[35] Schmuel Hugo Bergmann, the philosopher, one of the animating spirits of Brit-Shalom, wrote much later that Brit-Shalom was the last flicker of the humanist nationalist flame at a time when antihumanism was triumphant all over the world.[36] Scholem and the members of Brit-Shalom agreed that primarily a cultural, but also a moral and ethical, posture must inform the Zionist enterprise. They attempted, quite consciously, to give nationalism a human face, an attempt against the times, as Hugo Bergmann realized.

Brit-Shalom was a very small group consisting of a core of Hebrew University professors whose intellectual formation had taken place in the German-speaking Jewish world where Bildung in its original Enlightenment meaning had remained alive. The enemies of Brit-Shalom were quite aware of this cohesive background. For example, Berl Katznelson, a powerful figure among socialist Zionists intent on building a Jewish nation state, referred to them as "uprooted people" of Central European background without roots in Jewish popular culture.[37] Bergmann, at any rate, countered such accusations by maintaining that Brit-Shalom was the yeast that would leaven the Zionist movement; that here quality and not quantity counted.[38] And Scholem believed that the organization provided a cadre for the future, while Martin Buber, another member of the group, saw in Brit-Shalom a chance to individualize the masses.[39] What united these men were common ideals they had brought from their education and environment; all were gebildet and many, according to Robert Weltsch, another member of the group, may as Zionist youth have come under the influence of the German Youth Movement as well.[40]

Scholem shared a common background with such German Jews, and for a few years, according to Bergmann, he took a leading part in their discussions. Here he put into practice the beliefs mentioned above: his oppositional posture, his Bildung, and his concept of Jewish history. But his differences with many important members of Brit-Shalom highlight Scholem's own alternative Zionism, as mentioned at the beginning of this chapter. His disagreement with Martin Buber has also been discussed; nor did he agree with many of the other approaches to Zionism, for example those of Hans Kohn or Robert Weltsch. If he rejected the antihistoricism of Martin Buber he also repudiated the liberalism and universalism which, as part of the ideal of *Bildung*, were shared by most of the members of Brit-Shalom: the belief that membership in the Jewish nation was a step toward embracing all mankind. That all these men could nevertheless agree upon the program of Brit-Shalom demonstrates the relative strength of their German-Jewish intellectual heritage.

Disappointment in the course Zionism had taken led many of the leading men of this group eventually to leave Palestine. Hans Kohn left as early as 1934. His commitment to Enlightenment ideals and his concept of *Bildung* could not be reconciled with a Jewish nationalism that insisted on its own state in a way that would lead inevitably to a Jewish-Arab confrontation. Indeed, it was the founding of the state of Israel that created a crisis among such men of mostly German-Jewish background. By that time a political party made up of Central European immigrants, the Aliyah Hadasha, had taken up most of Brit-Shalom's program.[41] Georg Landauer, once the leader of that party, later formulated why he and other important figures like Max Kreuzberger and Robert Weltsch went into a second exile after 1948 and Martin Buber into an inner emigration: "given our ambition to break out of ghetto and galuth through the Jewish Renaissance," Landauer wrote, "it is a tragedy that it should end in normalization through taking refuge in a state . . ."[42] The ideals of the Enlightenment, which were also those of *Bildung,* shine through here; so do universal, humanist concerns, as Landauer deplored that Zionism should fulfill its goal by erecting one state on the ruins of another, the Jewish state at the expense of the Arab.[43]

Throughout modern European history new states had always been created at the expense of already existing nations: Germany on part of French territory, Italy at the expense of territory claimed by Austria. These men were not so wrong in their view of what a Jewish state would mean, and they were not ready to face the consequences that would result in their eyes from having set the wrong priorities. Zionism was a spiritual and cultural renewal without regard for national sovereignty. Zalman Shazar— later Israel's president—a sympathetic observer and good friend of many of this group, summed up in 1959 what he thought had happened and was still happening at the time: Zionism was being deprived as intellectual circles became alienated from the movement by the overestimation of sovereignty in Israel and the *Galut*.[44]

While some figures of note refused to be part of the new state, others like Hugo Bergmann welcomed the state warmly once it had come into being, believing that now was the time to stand up for one's ideals even if the only action possible was that of small improvements, to do what one could in daily life and in the university.[45] Among all these men, those who left and many who stayed, the basic link between *Bildung* and the Enlightenment was not broken. Buber is the exception here; his ideals had other roots even if the results were the same.

Scholem, too, differed: it would never have occurred to him to emigrate; he considered this treason. Sharing the cultural nationalism of these men and their humanistic outlook, and even sharing many of the most basic presuppositions of *Bildung,* the difference between the ideal of *Bildung* to which they clung and his own Jewish ideals is obvious. Scholem was saved from some of his former friends' negative attitudes toward the new state by his open-ended concept of Jewish history and by his insistence on the Hebrew language and living on Jewish soil as preconditions for the Jewish revival. Scholem's ideal of Jewish autonomy, his attempt to disentangle Judaism from foreign influence, is always to the fore. The reasons for this we have seen earlier; neither Jewish history nor the Hebrew language can yield their secrets in the Diaspora.

The difference between Scholem and the men in Brit-Shalom was not their common goal or the priority of culture over politics, but his rejection of cosmopolitanism, which viewed Judaism as primarily an opening to general humanistic concerns. However, he was divided from these men by a general attitude toward life as well: by his antibourgeois stance, mentioned earlier, and by his love for vitality and for Zionism as a wager. Scholem once confessed that he had been attracted to anarchism even though it filled him with terror.[46] Nevertheless, it seems that he always walked a fine line between, on the one hand, his fascination with the unconventional, even bizarre—toward the end of his life he collected books written by professors who were later institutionalized in insane asylums, and he was attracted by a spontaneous, uncertain dynamic, almost a Nietzschean life-force— and, on the other hand, his need for self-discipline as a scholar. To be sure, the antibourgeois, in the meaning he gave it, was focused upon historical and philosophical concerns and did not spill over into his daily life, where he had little use for the unconventionality of the Youth Movement.

Scholem never broke with Zionism, as has been wrongly claimed, if Zionism is defined as he defined it: the Jewish Renaissance in the Jewish homeland.[47] This does not mean that he approved the direction Israeli nationhood was taking; he did not like the traditional Israeli political parties and especially the right wing and its conventional concept of Jewish nationhood. Scholem, after first voting for Labor in Israel's elections, subsequently supported the left-liberal Citizens' Rights Movement. His Jewish-centeredness and his approach to Jewish power contained much that was part of *Bildung* without its original ambivalence toward nationality: the ethical and humanist elements, the devaluation of the political, remained.

Scholem found most of the themes that informed his thought in the Kabbalah. But why he turned to the Kabbalah in the first place and the way in which he approached his themes and what he made of them must be analyzed against the background in which he wrote: the constant preoccupation with the problems and controversies of German culture that, for example, informs his correspondence with Walter Benjamin. I have made the connection between the German and the specifically Jewish in Scholem's thought only in a tentative manner; it needs someone with equal knowledge of German culture and the Kabbalah to penetrate more deeply into how the two influences shaped his mind.

The fact that Scholem was above all a German Jew had an effect upon his Zionist ideal as over against Zionist reality, though here, once more, it was a matter of approach rather than essence. The Zionism of Gershom Scholem was a process filled with a youthful vitality that does not allow for the trappings of a normative nationhood. To be sure, Scholem accepted and fully participated in the Jewish state once it had come into being, but it had not been necessary in order to bring about the Jewish revival, while Zionism as a cultural movement was indispensable for the encounter of the Jew with himself. Zionism is inner-directed, centered upon the total regeneration of the Jew as a part of his people, similar in form to more traditional nationalism, and yet it is an integral part of an open-ended dynamic of history. This history made transparent the moral and ethical imperative that must be at the core of Zionism, integral to the living body of the Jewish people. Here, too, the effect of his *Bildung* is visible, as it is in his approach to scholarship as building character, indeed as central to the Jewish revival. There were, of course, many other influences at work quite apart from his Jewish sources: he himself acknowledged, for example, that of the anarchist-socialist Gustav Landauer and, above all, of Ahad Ha-am, whose adherent he once called himself in his youth.[48] All cultural Zionism was indebted to Ahad Ha-am, and yet Scholem's concept was different in its thrust and cultural ideal. Like every scholar aware of the currents of his time, Scholem was subject to many influences out of which we have attempted to isolate the important German-Jewish connection.

The ideal of a Zionism without a state, without the security of historical precedent, and without a set goal that has to be reached, and the belief that only by accepting this wager could Jewish survival be assured, is a striking if perhaps unrealistic alternative to the present. In the last resort, Scholem did what every educator should do, but most do not: attempt to break open petrified structures, to challenge accepted truths on behalf of an ethical ideal within which men and women can be honest and true to themselves. And if his nationalism seems perhaps further removed from reality today than even in Scholem's own time, it must be remembered that people must hope before they can act.

Notes

INTRODUCTION (PP. 1–10)

1. See G. L. Mosse, *The Nationalization of the Masses* (New York, 1975).

2. Thomas Nipperdey, *The Rise of the Arts in Modern Society,* The 1989 Annual Lecture, German Historical Institute, London (London, 1990), 8, 12.

3. Gustave Le Bon, *The Crowd* (New York, 1960), 41.

4. Friedrich Ehrenberg, *Der Charakter und die Bestimmung des Mannes, Cabinets Bibliothek der Deutschen Klassiker* (Hildburghausen and New York, 1934), 72.

5. Alexander Stille, *Uno su mille* (Milan, 1991).

6. Suzanne Citron, *Le Mythe National* (Paris, 1989), 85, 95.

7. Pierre Birnbaum, *Anti-Semitism in France* (Oxford, 1992), 49.

8. Mona Ozouf, *L'homme régénéré, Essais sur la Révolution française* (Paris, 1989), 125.

9. See G. L. Mosse, *Nationalism and Sexuality* (New York, 1985; reprint, Madison, 1988).

10. See David Sorkin, *The Transformation of German Jewry, 1780–1840* (Oxford, 1987).

CHAPTER 1. NATIONAL ANTHEMS (PP. 13–26)

1. "Das Streiflicht," *Süddeutsche Zeitung,* 29 April 1955 ("Nationalhymne," Archiv, Institut für Zeitgeschichte, Munich).

2. Fritz Sandmann, "Das Deutschlandlied und der Nationalismus," *Geschichte in Wissenschaft und Unterricht* 13 (1962): 653; for the cooption of the song by the Nazis, see Ernst Hauck, *Das Deutschlandlied* (Dortmund, 1941).

3. *Verhandlungen des Deutschen Bundestages,* 1. Wahlperiode, 1949. Stenographische Berichte, Band I; p. 12. Sitzung, 20. Oktober 1949, pp. 263, 266.

4. *Süddeutsche Zeitung,* 31 August 1955 ("Nationalhymne," Archiv, Institut für Zeitgeschichte, Munich).

5. *Die Abendzeitung,* 3 September 1949 ("Nationalhymne," Archiv, Institut für Zeitgeschichte, Munich).

6. For the poll, see "Die Hymne der Deutschen," broadcast by the *ZDF,* 19 Mai 1986, 17:15 p.m.; for teaching the anthem, see "Nationalhymne," *Der Spiegel* 40 (21 July 1986): 153–54.

7. Cf. G. L. Mosse, *The Nationalization of the Masses* (New York, 1975; reprint, Ithaca, 1991), where, however, almost nothing is said about national anthems; citations and analyses of national anthems are taken from Martin Shaw and Henry Coleman, eds., *National Anthems of the World* (London and New York, 1960), and the much less complete *Nationalhymnen: Texte und Melodien* (Stuttgart, 1982).

8. John A. Lynn, *The Bayonets of the Republic* (Urbana and Chicago, 1984), 174. For the changed status of the soldier, see Geoffrey Best, *War and Society in Revolutionary Europe, 1770–1870* (London, 1982), 76ff., and Mona Ozouf, *La fête révolutionnaire* (Paris, 1976), passim.

9. G. L. Mosse, *Fallen Soldiers: Reshaping the Memory of the World Wars* (New York, 1990), ch. 2 and passim for the history of the volunteers in war.

10. G. L. Mosse, *Nationalism and Sexuality: Respectability and Abnormal Sexuality in Modern Europe* (New York, 1985; reprint, Madison, 1988), ch. 4.

11. Quoted in Christoph Prignitz, *Vaterlandsliebe und Freiheit* (Wiesbaden, 1981), 121.

12. Werner Kohlschmidt, *Das deutsche Soldatenlied* (Berlin, 1935), 47.

13. Lynn, *Bayonets,* 147.

14. C. Cambry, *Rapport sur les Sépulcres* (Paris, 1792), 65–66. See also Mosse, *Fallen Soldiers,* ch. 5.

15. Meinhold Lurtz, *Kriegerdenkmäler in Deutschland,* vol. 1, *Befreiungskriege* (Heidelberg, 1985), 275.

16. Eugen Wildenow, ed., *Theodor Körners Sämtliche Werke in zwei Teilen* (Leipzig, n.d.), 1:130.

17. Ibid., 126, "Bundeslied vor der Schlacht."

18. Ibid., 120, "Aufruf (1813)."

19. Hoffmann von Fallersleben, "Auf der Wanderung"; quoted in Heinrich Gerstenberg, *Deutschland, Deutschland über alles: Ein Lebensbild des Dichters Hoffmann von Fallersleben* (Munich, 1916), 50.

20. Prignitz, *Vaterlandsliebe und Freiheit,* 133; Mosse, *Nationalization,* 82–87.

21. *Deutschland, Deutschland über alles! Aufsätze und Reden aus zehn Jahrgängen "Akademische Blätter"* (Leipzig, 1896), 255.

22. Text of bulletin taken from Hans Dollinger, ed., *Der Erste Weltkrieg in Bildern und Dokumenten* (Munich, 1965), 90; cf. also Karl Unruh, *Langemarck* (Koblenz, 1986), 14.

23. Josef Magnus Wehner, *Langemarck: Ein Vermächtnis* (Munich, 1932), 6; Michael Gollbach, *Die Wiederkehr des Weltkrieges in der Literatur* (Kronberg, 1978), 187.

24. Emil Terson, *L'Internationale. Edité par la Commemoration du 30ᵉᵐᵉ Anniversaire de la Mort de Pierre de Geyter* (Paris, 1962), 12.

25. Frantisek Gel, *Internationale und Marseillaise* (Prague, 1954), 178.

26. Fiamma Nicolodi, *Musica e Musicisti nel Ventennio Fascista* (Fiesole, 1984), 318, 382.

27. Asvero Gravelli, *I Canti della Revoluzione* (Rome, 1928), 66–67.
28. Ibid., 77.
29. Ibid., 112.
30. Julien Tiersot, *Histoire de la Marseillaise* (Paris, 1915), 57.
31. Meinhold Lurtz, *Kriegerdenkmäler in Deutschland* (Heidelberg, 1986), vol. 5, *Drittes Reich*, 308.
32. "Ausserordentlicher Sängertag in Berlin," *Völkischer Beobachter* 24 April 1934 (London, Wiener Library, Clipping Collection).
33. Robert Michels, *Patriotismus* (Munich and Leipzig, 1929), 228–29.
34. Ulrich Ragozat, *Die Nationalhymnen der Welt* (Freiburg, 1982), 100. I have used this book extensively for the discussion of the derivation and nature of the music of national anthems.
35. Quoted in Robert Michels, "Elemente zu einer Soziologie des National-liedes," *Archiv für Sozialwissenschaft und Sozialpolitik* 55 (1926): 321.
36. Ibid., 355.
37. Ibid., 352; Paul Nettl, *National Anthems* (New York, 1952), 43.
38. Nettl, *National Anthems*, 38.
39. G. C. Macaulay, *James Thomson* (London, 1908), 190.
40. Vernon L. Lidke, *The Alternative Culture: Socialist Labour in Imperial Germany* (New York, 1985), 119.
41. See Mosse, *Fallen Soldiers*.

CHAPTER 2. NATIONAL SELF-REPRESENTATION (PP. 27–40)

1. Alfred Haworth Jones, *Roosevelt's Image Brokers* (Port Washington, New York, 1974), 60.
2. See G. L. Mosse, *The Nationalization of the Masses* (New York, 1975; reprint, Ithaca, 1991).
3. Philippe Burrin, *La Dérive Fasciste, Doriot, Déat, Bergery, 1933–1945* (Paris, 1986), 86.
4. Ibid., 88.
5. Dominique Desanti, *Drieu la Rochelle* (Paris, 1975), 315; Robert Brasillach, *Notre Avant Guerre* (Paris, 1941), 268–73.
6. Charles C. Alexander, *Nationalism in American Thought* (Chicago, 1969), 70.
7. James Dennis, *Grant Wood* (New York, 1975), 195.
8. G. L. Mosse, *The Crisis of German Ideology* (New York, 1964), 27, 112.
9. Dennis, *Grant Wood*, plate 33.
10. Jeffrey Herf, *Reactionary Modernism* (Cambridge, 1984), 15.
11. Leo Marx, *The Machine in the Garden: Technology and the Pastoral Ideal in America* (Oxford, 1964), passim.
12. Herf, *Reactionary Modernism*, 83.
13. Francesco Sapori, *L'Arte e il Duce* (Milan, 1932), 141.
14. Alexander, *Nationalism*, 71.
15. G. L. Mosse, *Masses and Man: Nationalist and Fascist Perceptions of Reality* (New York, 1980), ch. 12, 275.
16. Sapori, *L'Arte*, 141.
17. Pasquale Falco, *Letteratura popolare fascista* (Cosenza, 1984), 37.

18. John E. Bowlt, ed., *Russian Art of the Avant-Garde, Theory and Criticism* (New York, 1976), 293.

19. Ibid., 293.

20. Christel Lane, *The Rites of Rulers: Ritual in Industrial Society—The Soviet Case* (Cambridge, 1981), 26, 196, 208.

21. G. L. Mosse, *Nationalism and Sexuality* (New York, 1975; reprint, Madison, 1988), ch. 4.

22. Elmar Jansen, *Ernst Barlach Werke und Werkentwürfe aus fünf Jahrzehnten* (Berlin, 1981), 97, 98; Mosse, *Nationalization,* ch. 3.

23. William Stott, *Documentary Expression and Thirties America* (Chicago, 1986; first published 1973), 134.

24. Quoted in Alfred Kazin, *On Native Grounds* (Garden City, New York, 1956; first published 1942), 395.

25. This was the title of an exhibition in the Paris Museum of Modern Art, November 1986, documenting the manipulation of photographs for political ends.

26. Stott, *Documentary Expression,* 255.

27. Kazin, *On Native Grounds,* 379.

28. Stott, *Documentary Expression,* 93ff.

29. Kazin, *On Native Grounds,* 392.

30. Y. Arieli, "Individualism and National Consciousness in the United States," *Scripta Hierosolymitana* (Jerusalem, 1961), 7:297–98, 304.

31. For the background to this peculiar development of American national identity, see the by now classic, Yehoshua Arieli, *Individualism and Nationalism in American Ideology* (Cambridge, Mass., 1964).

32. G. L. Mosse, *Towards the Final Solution: A History of European Racism* (New York, 1978; reprint, Madison, 1985), ch. 2.

33. Burrin, *La Dérive Fasciste,* 86.

34. G. L. Mosse, *Fallen Soldiers: Reshaping the Memory of the World Wars* (New York, 1990).

35. Carroll Smith-Rosenberg, "Davey Crockett as Trickster: Pornography, Liminality and Symbolic Inversion in Victorian America," *Journal of Contemporary History* 17 (1982): 327.

36. John W. Ward, "The Meaning of Lindbergh's Flight," *Studies in American Culture, Dominant Ideas and Images* (Minneapolis, 1960), 30, 31, 33.

37. Sander L. Gilman, *Differences and Pathology* (Ithaca, 1985), ch. 4.

CHAPTER 4. POLITICAL STYLE AND POLITICAL THEORY (PP. 60–69)

1. J. L. Talmon, *The Rise of Totalitarian Democracy* (Boston, 1952), 253.

2. Ibid., 1.

3. See S. L. Gilman, *Seeing the Insane* (New York, 1982), x–xii.

4. J. L. Talmon, *The Unique and the Universal* (London, 1965), 308.

5. S. J. Whitfield, *Into the Dark: Hannah Arendt and Totalitarianism* (Philadelphia, 1980), 99.

6. Talmon, *Rise,* 95.

7. G. L. Mosse, *Nationalism and Sexuality* (New York, 1985; reprint, Madison, 1988), ch. 1.

8. Quoted in G. L. Mosse, *Masses and Man: Nationalist and Fascist Perceptions of Reality* (New York, 1980), 40.

9. Talmon, Rise, 95.

10. Mona Ozouf, *La fête révolutionnaire 1789–1799* (Paris, 1976), 300.

11. Ibid., 294.

12. A. Aulard, *Christianity and the French Revolution* (New York, 1966), 106.

13. Jean-Jacques Rousseau, *The Government of Poland* (Indianapolis, 1926), 8, 15.

14. Ozouf, *La fête*, 338.

15. J. L. Talmon, *Political Messianism* (London, 1960), 513ff.

16. M. Agulhon, *Marianne into Battle* (Cambridge, 1981), 16ff.

17. Cited in Z. Sternhell, *La Droite Révolutionnaire* (Paris, 1978), 81.

18. P. H. Hutton, "Popular Boulangism and the Advent of Mass Politics in France," *Journal of Contemporary History* 11 (1976): 85–106; idem, *The Cult of the Revolutionary Tradition: The Blanquists in French Politics 1864–1893* (Berkeley, 1981).

19. Adolf Hitler, *Mein Kampf* (Munich, 1934), 369.

20. W. R. Tucker, "Politics and Aesthetics—The Fascism of Robert Brasillach," *Western Political Quarterly* 15 (1962): 605–6.

21. Ibid., 609.

22. A. Gerard, *La Révolution française: Mythes et interpretations 1789–1970* (Paris, 1970), 76–77.

23. G. L. Mosse, *The Nationalization of the Masses* (New York, 1975; reprint, Ithaca, 1991), ch. 7.

24. C. Rearick, "Festivals in Modern France: The Experience of the Third Republic," *Journal of Contemporary History* 12 (1977): 438.

25. D. J. Boorstin, *The Genius of American Politics* (Chicago, 1953), 2.

26. Ibid., 94.

27. Ibid., 2.

28. G. L. Mosse, *The Crisis of German Ideology* (New York, 1964), ch. 13.

CHAPTER 5. FASCISM AND THE FRENCH REVOLUTION
(PP. 70–90)

1. *Oeuvres complètes de J. J. Rousseau*, vol. 5 (Paris, 1907), 43.

2. Mona Ozouf, *La fête révolutionnaire 1789–1799* (Paris, 1976), 55ff; G. L. Mosse, *The Nationalization of the Masses* (New York, 1975; reprint, Ithaca, 1991), ch. 4.

3. Albert Mathiez, *La Theophilantropie et le Culte Décadaire* (Paris, 1904), 36.

4. Michel Vovelle, *Die Französische Revolution* (Frankfurt am Main, 1985), 115.

5. Friedrich Heer, *Der Glaube des Adolf Hitler* (Munich, 1968), 56.

6. Ernst Moritz Arndt, *Entwurf einer Teutschen Gesellschaft* (Frankfurt, 1814), 36.

7. Victor Klemperer, *LTI* (Frankfurt am Main, 1985), 118–19.

8. A. Aulard, *Christianity and the French Revolution* (New York, 1966), 106.

9. Mosse, *Nationalization*, 200.

10. Christoph Prignitz, *Vaterlandsliebe und Freiheit* (Wiesbaden, 1981), 138.

11. I.e., Hitler's Proclamation at the Nuremberg Party Day, 1934.

12. G. L. Mosse, *Nationalism and Sexuality: Respectability and Abnormal Sexuality in Modern Europe* (New York, 1985; reprint, Madison, 1991), ch. 4.

13. Ozouf, *La fête*, ch. 9.

14. Mona Ozouf, "Le Panthéon. L'École des Morts," in Pierre Nora, ed., *Les Lieux de Memoire* (Paris, 1984), vol. 1, *La Republique*, 155ff.

15. Adolf Hitler, *Mein Kampf* (Munich, 1934), 286; Ranier Zitelmann has given the best account of Hitler's attitude to the French Revolution, even if it seems too positive. See his *Hitler. Selbstverständnis eines Revolutionärs* (Hamburg, 1987), 44–49.

16. Hitler, *Mein Kampf*, 269.

17. Alfred Rosenberg, *Der Mythos des 20. Jahrhunderts* (Munich, 1935), 500–501.

18. I.e., Hermann Wendel, *Danton* (Königstein/Ts., 1978), 362.

19. Ibid., 344.

20. Hitler, *Mein Kampf*, 371.

21. Jean-Jacques Rousseau, *The Government of Poland* (Indianapolis, 1972), 11, 14.

22. Jean Starobinski, *1789: The Emblems of Reason* (Charlottesville, Va., 1982), 118.

23. Vovelle, *Die Französische*, 124.

24. Alfred Stein, "Adolf Hitler and Gustav le Bon," *Geschichte in Wissenschaft und Unterricht* (1955), 367; Renzo de Felice, *Mussolini il rivoluzionario* (Turin, 1965), 467, n.1.

25. Robert A. Nye, *The Origins of Crowd Psychology* (London and Beverly Hills, 1975), 73.

26. Gustav Le Bon, *The Crowd* (New York, 1960), 68.

27. Ibid., 118–19.

28. Emilio Gentile, *Il Culto del Littorio. La Sacralizzazione della Politica nell'Italia Fascista* (Rome, 1993), 93, 151.

29. Piero Melograni, "The Cult of the Duce in Mussolini's Italy," *Journal of Contemporary History* 11 (October 1976): 228.

30. Ibid., 223.

31. Mosse, *Nationalization*, 200.

32. Emilio Gentile, *Le Origini dell'Ideologia Fascista* (Rome-Bari, 1975), 184.

33. G. L. Mosse, *Masses and Man: Nationalist and Fascist Perceptions of Reality* (New York, 1980), 97.

34. Gentile, *Le origini*, 184.

35. Ozouf, *La fête*, 97.

36. G. L. Mosse, *Fallen Soldiers: Reshaping the Memory of the World Wars* (New York, 1990), ch. 3.

37. Sergio Panunzio, *Italo Balbo* (Milan, 1923), 36–37.

38. Hans-Peter Gorgen, *Düsseldorf und der Nationalsozialismus* (Düsseldorf, 1969), 98. See also Jay W. Baird, *To Die for Germany: Heroes in the Nazi Pantheon* (Bloomington and Indianapolis, 1990).

39. Emil Ludwig and Peter O. Chotjewitz, *Der Mord in Davos* (Herbstein, 1986), 139.

40. Avner Ben-Amos, "Les Funerailles de Victor Hugo," in Pierre Nora, ed., *Les Lieux de Mémoire* (Paris, 1984), vol. 1, *La République*, 474, 487ff.

41. As, for example, in the "L'Apoteosi del Caduto" in the "Sala dedicata alle Medaglie d'Oro," *Redipuglia*, ed. Ministero della Difesa, Commissariato Generale Onoranze Caduti in Guerra (Rome, 1972), 18.

42. Ozouf, "Le Panthéon," 145ff.

43. G. L. Mosse, "National Cemeteries and National Revival: The Cult of the Fallen Soldiers in Germany," *Journal of Contemporary History* 14 (January 1979): 1–20.

44. John McManners, *Death and the Enlightenment* (New York, 1981), 359–60.

45. Mosse, *Masses and Man*, ch. 4.

46. Vovelle, *Die Französische Revolution*, 117.

47. Renzo de Felice, *Intervista sul fascismo*, ed. Michael A. Ledeen (Rome-Bari, 1975), 53–54.

48. Gentile, *Le Origini*, 328; Felice, *Intervista*, 53.

49. Emilio Gentile, *Il Mito dello State Nuovo dall'Antigiolittismo al Fascismo* (Rome-Bari, 1982). I should like to thank Professor Gentile for his valuable suggestions.

50. Alberto Maria Ghisalbert, "Giacobini," *Encyclopedia Italiana* (1932), 16:934.

51. Ibid., 934.

52. Zeev Sternhell, *Neither Right nor Left: Fascist Ideology in France* (Berkeley, 1986), 106.

53. *Je Suis Partout*, Numéro Speciale sur la Révolution, no. 449 (30 June 1939), 1.

54. Ibid., 1.

55. Robert Brasillach, "Jacobins et Thermidoriens," *Oeuvres complètes de Robert Brasillach* (Paris, 1964), 12:604.

56. Roger Joseph, "Alcibiade et Socrate," *Cahiers des Amis de Robert Brasillach*, no. 13 (6 February 1968), 63–64.

57. Brasillach, "Jacobins," 605.

58. Joseph, "Alcibiade," 64.

59. Robert Soucy, *Fascist Intellectual: Drieu La Rochelle* (Berkeley, 1979), 214.

60. Brasillach, "Jacobins," 605.

61. *Je Suis Partout*, 1.

62. Philippe Burrin, *La Dérive Fasciste* (Paris, 1986), 404.

63. Hitler, *Mein Kampf*, 536.

CHAPTER 6: THE POLITICAL CULTURE OF ITALIAN FUTURISM (PP. 91–105)

1. See Emilio Gentile, "La politica di Marinetti," *Storia Contemporanea* 7 (September 1974): 415.

2. G. L. Mosse, "Rushing to the Colors: The History of Volunteers in War," *Religion, Ideology and Nationalism in Europe and America, Essays in Honour of Yehoshua Arieli* (Jerusalem, 1986), 173–84. G. L. Mosse, *Fallen Soldiers: Reshaping the Memory of the World Wars* (New York, 1990), ch. 2.

3. Gentile, "La Politica," 426; the program is reprinted in Renzo de Felice, *Mussolini il revoluzionario* (Turin, 1965), see esp. 741.

4. Stephen Kern, *The Culture of Time and Space 1880–1918* (Cambridge, Mass., 1983), esp. ch. 9.

5. Ibid., 64–88.

6. L. Baudrier de Saunier, *Histoire Générale de la Velocipédie* (Paris, 1891), 107.

7. Kern, *Culture,* 68–69.

8. This is one of the theses of Arnim Mohler in his stimulating "Der Faschistische Stil," *Von rechts gesehen* (Stuttgart, 1974), 179–221.

9. Gottfried Benn, "Rede auf Marinetti," *Kunst und Macht* (Stuttgart, 1934), 106.

10. Ibid., 106. For a stimulating criticism of the link I have made between futurism and fascism, stressing instead the influence of the Florentine radical nationalists around *La Voce,* see Walter L. Adamson, "Fascism and Culture: Avant-Gardes and Secular Religion in the Italian Case," *Journal of Contemporary History* 24 (July 1989): 411–35.

11. G. L. Mosse, "Fascism and the Intellectuals," in S. J. Woolf, ed., *The Nature of Fascism* (New York, 1968), 205–25.

12. Degrelle cited specifically Hitler, Mussolini, and Codreanu; Robert Brasillach, *Léon Degrelle* (Paris, 1936), 78.

13. Fanette Roche-Pezard, *L'Aventure Futuriste 1909–1916* (Rome, 1983), 155, 157.

14. F. T. Marinetti, *Teoria e Invenzione Futurista* (Milan, 1968), 424.

15. Mario Isnenghi, *Il mito della grande guerra* (Rome-Bari, 1973), 169.

16. G. L. Mosse, "National Cemeteries and National Revival: The Cult of the Fallen Soldiers in Germany," *Journal of Contemporary History* 14 (January 1979): 1–20.

17. Marinetti, *Teoria,* 287.

18. Ibid., 209.

19. Henri Massis and R. Brasillach, *Le Siège de L'Alcazar* (Paris, 1939), vii.

20. Robert Brasillach, *Histoire de la Guerre d'Espagne* (Paris, 1969; first published, 1939), 174; for Nazi Germany, see Peter Monteath, "Die Legion Condor im Spiegel der Literatur," in Helmut Kreuzer, ed., *Spanienkriegsliteratur,* vol. 60, *Zeitschrift für Literaturwissenschaft und Linguistiks* (1986), 95–96.

21. Horst Überhorst, *Elite für die Diktatur. Die National-politischen Erziehungsanstalten 1933–1945* (Düsseldorf, 1968), 400; Goebbels put the death of Horst Wessel in this context as well; Helmut Heiber, ed., *Goebbels-Reden* (Düsseldorf, 1971), vol. 1, 1932–1939, 128.

22. *Redipuglia Oslavia,* Sacrari Militari della Prima Guerra Mondiale, Commissariato Generale Onoranze Caduti in Guerra (Rome, 1972), 18. On National Socialist views of death, see Jay W. Baird, *To Die For Germany: Heroes in the Nazi Pantheon* (Bloomington and Indianapolis, 1990).

23. Jose Pierre, *Futurism and Dadaism* (London, 1969), 11.

24. G. L. Mosse, *Nationalism and Sexuality* (New York, 1985; reprint, Madison, 1988), esp. ch. 1.

25. Alberto Cavaglion, *Otto Weininger in Italia* (Rome, 1982), 17, 58ff.

26. Mosse, "Fascism and the Intellectuals," 212.

27. Mosse, *Nationalism and Sexuality,* ch. 5.

28. The most complete book on futurism is still Rosa Trillo Clough, *Futurism* (New York, 1961), from which these descriptions are taken.

29. Ernst Jünger, quoted in G. L. Mosse, *Masses and Man: Nationalist and Fascist Perceptions of Reality* (New York, 1980), 187.

30. Ernst Jünger, *The Storm of Steel* (New York, 1975), 235.

31. Ibid., 263; 110.

32. Ernst Jünger, *Der Arbeiter. Herschaft und Gestalt* (Hamburg, 1932), 105–7.

33. Ibid., 107–8.

34. Ibid., 114.

35. As reported in *L'Oeuvre*, 24 August 1937.

36. Wyndham Lewis, *Blast*, Review of the Great English Vortex (War Number, July 1915), 6.

37. *Mostra della rivoluzione fascista* (Rome, 1933), 123.

38. Ibid., 229. For the dominance of futurism over this exhibition, see Guido Armelini, *Le Imagini del Fascismo Nelle Arti Figurative* (Milan, 1980), 86–93; Emilio Gentile, *Il culto del littorio. La sacralizzazione della politica nell' Italia fascista* (Rome, 1993), 200, n.79.

39. Jeffrey Herf, *Reactionary Modernism: Technology, Culture and Politics in Weimar and the Third Reich* (Cambridge, 1984), 209–10.

40. Ibid., 32.

41. From a speech given at the Party Day of Unity, 1934; Hamilton T. Burden, *The Nuremberg Party Rallies: 1923–1939* (New York, 1937), 81.

42. G. L. Mosse, "The Genesis of Fascism," *Journal of Contemporary History*, 1 (1966): 14–27.

43. Mohler, "Der Faschistische Stil," 203; G. L. Mosse, *Fallen Soldiers: Reshaping the Memory of the World Wars* (New York, 1990), ch. 8.

44. H. W. Koch, *Der Deutsche Bürgerkrieg* (Berlin, 1978), 145.

45. Quoted in G. L. Mosse, *The Culture of Western Europe* (Chicago, 1961; reprint, Boulder City, Col., 1988), 299.

46. Marc Augier, *Götterdämmerung, Wende und Ende einer Zeit* (Buenos Aires, 1950), 79. Marc Augier, writing later under the pseudonym of Saint Loup, became the principal mythmaker of the French SS batallions.

47. Koch, *Der Deutsche Bürgerkreig*, 53; Jean Mabire, *La Brigade Frankreich* (Paris, 1973), 146, 179.

CHAPTER 7. BOOKBURNING AND BETRAYAL BY THE GERMAN INTELLECTUALS (PP. 106–117)

1. See the *Deutsch-Israelitische Zeitung*, Hamburg (12 May 1933).

2. Hans Naumann and Eugen Lüthgens, *Kampf wider den undeutschen Geist* (Bonn: Bonner Universitäts-Buchdruckerei, 1933), 5.

3. Ibid.

4. Ibid., 5, 10.

5. Walter Flex, *Der Wanderer zwischen beiden Welten* (Munich, n.d.), 37, 46.

6. The poem is entitled "Peace," which is not meant ironically: "Now, God be thanked Who has matched us with His hour, / And caught our youth, and wakened us from sleeping, / With hand made sure, clear eye, and sharpened power,

/ To turn as swimmers into cleanness leaping." *The Collected Poems of Rupert Brooke* (London, 1981; first published, 1918), 298.

7. Klaus Peter Philipi, *Volk des Zornes* (Munich, 1979), 99.

8. G. L. Mosse, "War and the Appropriation of Nature," in Volker R. Berghahn and Martin Kitchen, eds., *Germany in the Age of Total War* (London, 1981), 102–23.

9. G. L. Mosse, "Tod, Zeit und Geschichte. Die völkische Utopie der Überwindung," in Reinhold Grimm and Jost Hermand, eds., *Deutsches utopisches Denken im 20. Jahrhundert* (Stuttgart, 1974), 50–70; Ernst Bloch, *Thomas Münzer als Theologe der Revolution* (Munich, 1921), 293.

10. See Martin Gregor-Dellin, *Richard Wagner* (Munich, 1980), 640.

11. Paul Clements, *Gedenkrede auf Stefan George. Bonner Akademie-Reden* (Bonn, 1934), 21.

12. See Naumann and Lüthgens, *Kampf,* 9.

13. Clements, *Gedenkrede,* 21, 23.

14. Ernst Weymar, *Das Selbstverständnis der Deutschen* (Stuttgart, 1961), 65; Robert Minder, "Das Bild des Pfarrhauses in der deutschen Literatur von Jean Paul bis Gottfried Benn," *Kultur und Literatur in Deutschland und Frankreich* (Frankfurt am Main, 1962), 44–73.

15. Quoted in W. Schwipps, *Die Garnisonskirchen von Berlin und Potsdam* (Berlin, 1964), 92.

16. Quoted in Gerhard Sauder, ed., *Die Bücherverbrennung* (Munich, 1983), 248.

17. See G. L. Mosse, "Fascism and the Intellectuals," *Germans and Jews* (New York, 1970), 144–71.

18. G. L. Mosse, "The Poet and the Exercise of Political Power: Gabriele D'Annunzio," *Masses and Men: Nationalist and Fascist Perceptions of Reality* (New York, 1980), 87–104.

19. G. L. Mosse, "Nationalism and Respectability: Normal and Abnormal Sexuality in the 19th Century," *Journal of Contemporary History* 17 (April 1982): 221–37; G. L. Mosse, *Nationalism and Sexuality: Respectability and Abnormal Sexuality in Modern Europe* (New York, 1985).

20. Sander L. Gilman, *Difference and Pathology: Stereotypes of Sexuality, Race, and Madness* (Ithaca, 1985), 150–62.

21. See Sander L. Gilman, *Seeing the Insane* (New York, 1982).

22. See Mosse, *Nationalism and Sexuality,* esp. ch. 7.

23. Reprinted in *"Das war ein Vorspiel nur . . ." Bücherverbrennung Deutschland 1933* (Berlin/Wien, 1983).

24. Rudolph Vierhaus, "Umrisse einer Sozialgeschichte der Gebildeten in Deutschland," *Quellen und Forschungen* 60 (1980): 403.

25. Quoted in David Sorkin, "Von Humboldt on Self-Formation," *Journal of the History of Ideas* (January-March 1983): 67.

26. Wilhelm von Humboldt, "Wesen der Schönheit," *Gesammelte Werke* (Berlin, 1943), 4:344.

27. Sorkin, "Von Humboldt," 68.

28. Christoph Prignitz, *Valerlandsliebe und Freiheit. Deutscher Patriotismus von 1790 bis 1850* (Wiesbaden, 1981), 133–34.

29. Naumann and Lüthgens, *Kampf,* 7.

30. See R. J. V. Lenman, "Art and the Law in Wilhelmine Germany: The Lex Heinze," *Oxford German Studies* 8 (1973–74): 86–113.

31. Rüdiger vom Bruch, *Wissenschaft, Politik und Öffentliche Meinung* (Husum, 1980), 419ff., 68–70.

32. Theodor Fontane, *Frau Jenny Treibel* (New York, 1976), 161.

33. Hans Weil, *Die Entstehung des Deutschen Bildungsprinzips* (Bonn, 1930), 147, 149.

34. Vierhaus, "Umrisse," 403.

35. Anson Rabinbach, "L'age de la fatigue, Energie et Fatigue a la fin du 19ᵉᵐᵉ Siècle," *Vrbi* 2 (December 1979): 33–48.

36. See G. L. Mosse, *German Jews Beyond Judaism* (Bloomington, 1985).

CHAPTER 8. THE JEWS AND THE CIVIC RELIGION
OF NATIONALISM (PP. 121–130)

1. Thomas Nipperdey, *Deutsche Geschichte 1800–1866* (München, 1983), 300.

2. Thomas Nipperdey, *Nachdenken über Deutsche Geschichte* (München, 1986), 140.

3. G. L. Mosse, *Nationalism and Sexuality: Respectability and Abnormal Sexuality in Modern Europe* (New York, 1985; reprinted Madison, 1988), chs. 1 and 4.

4. G. L. Mosse, *The Nationalization of the Masses* (New York, 1975; reprinted Ithaca, 1991), passim.

5. G. L. Mosse, *Fallen Soldiers: Reshaping the Memory of the World Wars* (New York, 1990), chs. 3 and 5.

6. For Herzl and the problem of Jewish-Arab relations, see Walter Laqueur, *A History of Zionism* (New York, 1972), ch. 5.

7. Theodor Herzl, *Der Judenstaat* (Leipzig-Wien, 1896), 76. For a good discussion of Theodor Herzl and the civic religion of nationalism, see Amos Elon, *Herzl* (New York, 1975). The best discussion of the creation of a Zionist liturgy is Michael Berkowitz, *Zionist Culture and West European Jewry Before the First World War* (Cambridge, 1993).

8. Paul Mendes-Flohr, *Divided Passion: Jewish Intellectuals and the Experience of Modernity* (Detroit, 1991), 189.

9. Vladimir Jabotinsky, *Samson the Nazarite* (London, 1930; first published in Russian in 1927), 80.

10. Yaacov Shavit, *Jabotinski and the Revisionist Movement, 1925–1948* (London, 1988), 67, 123.

11. Charles S. Liebman and Eliezer Don-Yehia, *Civic Religion in Israel* (Berkeley and Los Angeles, 1983), 74.

12. Erich Burin, "Das Kaffeehaus Judentum," *Jüdische Turnerzeitung* 9 (1908): 33ff.

13. Shmuel Almog, *Zionism and History* (New York, 1987), 109.

14. See John Maurice Efron, *Defining the Jewish Race: The Self-Perceptions and Responses of Jewish Scientists to Scientific Racism in Europe 1882–1993* (New Haven, 1993).

15. The Israeli Ministry of Defense published *Gal-Ed, Memorials to the Fallen* (1990, in Hebrew) where these monuments are reproduced. I am grateful to Tom Segev, who visited some of them with me and then published my analyses in "What

do the Monuments do at night? A Travel Report" (in Hebrew), *Ha-Aretz,* 27 April 1990.

16. Emmanuel Sivan has written an important analysis of the *Yizkor* Books to be published shortly.

17. Vicki Caron's interesting essay, "The Ambivalent Legacy: The Impact of the Enlightenment and Emancipation on Zionism," *Judaism* 38 (Fall 1989), centers upon the idea of regeneration but says nothing about nationalism.

CHAPTER 9. JEWISH EMANCIPATION (PP. 131–145)

1. David Sorkin, "Wilhelm von Humboldt: The Theory and Practice of Self-Formation (*Bildung*), 1791–1810," *Journal of the History of Ideas* 44 (1983): 55–73.

2. Hans Weil, *Die Entstehung des deutschen Bildungsprinzips* (Bonn, 1930), 47.

3. Johann Wolfgang von Goethe, *Wilhelm Meister's Apprenticeship,* trans. Thomas Carlyle (New York, 1962), 274.

4. Berthold Auerbach, *Schrift und Volk* (Leipzig, 1846), 323.

5. *Sulamith* 5 (1818–19): 301–2.

6. Jacob Grimm and Wilhelm Grimm, *Deutsches Wörterbuch* (Leipzig, 1905), 1266–72.

7. "Betrachtungen in verschiedenen Hinsichten, über die Israeliten in Frankfurt am Main," *Sulamith* 1 (1807): 153.

8. For the history of respectability, see G. L. Mosse, *Nationalism and Sexuality: Respectability and Abnormal Sexuality in Modern Europe* (New York, 1985; reprint, Madison, 1988), ch. 1.

9. I. Wolf, "Inhalt, Zweck, und Titel dieser Zeitschrift," *Sulamith* 1 (1806): 1.

10. Ibid., 5 (1818–19): 47.

11. Mosse, *Nationalism and Sexuality,* 96.

12. *Sulamith* 2 (1807): 153.

13. Gotthold Salomon, *Twelve Sermons Delivered in the New Temple of the Israelites at Hamburg,* trans. Anna Maria Goldsmid (London, 1839), 90, 92.

14. *Sulamith* 6 (1822–24): 328.

15. Eduard Kley, *Predigten in dem neuen Israelitischen Tempel* (Hamburg, 1826) 2:69, 184.

16. Salomon, *Twelve Sermons,* 92–93.

17. See J. H. Campe's popular *Wörterbuch der deutschen Sprache* (Braunschweig, 1808), 2:852.

18. Leopold Zunz, *Die gottesdienstlichen Vorträge der Juden, historisch entwickelt* (Berlin, 1832), 479. For other examples, see G. L. Mosse, "The Secularization of Jewish Theology," in *Masses and Man: Nationalist and Fascist Perceptions of Reality* (New York, 1980), 249–63.

19. Cited in "Theologie," *Allgemeine Zeitung des Judentums* 1 (2 July 1837): 101–3.

20. "Theologie," *Allgemeine Zeitung des Judentums* 1 (16 May 1837): 26–27.

21. "Zum dritten August," *Allgemeine Zeitung des Judentums* 1 (3 August 1837): 177.

22. Marriage sermon of the district rabbi of Bamberg, reprinted in *Sulamith* 7 (1833): 390.

23. Marion A. Kaplan, *The Making of the Jewish Middle Class* (New York, 1991), 10, 76.

24. Ismar Schorsch, "Art as Social History: Oppenheim and the German Jewish Vision of Emancipation," in *Moritz Oppenheim: The First Jewish Painter* (Jerusalem: Israel Museum, 1983), 44, 51.

25. Shulamit Volkov, "Erfolgreiche Assimilation oder Erfolg und Assimilation: Die deutsch-jüdische Familie im Kaiserreich," *Jahrbuch, Wissenschaftskolleg zu Berlin* (1982–83), 373–87.

26. Mosse, *Nationalism and Sexuality,* 142.

27. Paul Lawrence Rose, "The Noble Anti-Semitism of Richard Wagner," *Historical Journal* 25 (1982): 751–63.

28. Georg Hermann, *Jettchen Gebert* (Berlin, 1906), 350; 259–61.

29. Account of lecture by Dr. Walter Perl, 11 June 1935, in Jüdischer Kulturbund, box 3, Wiener Library, University of Tel Aviv.

30. G. L. Mosse, *German Jews Beyond Judaism* (Bloomington, Ind., 1985), ch. 1.

31. See Sander L. Gilman, *Seeing the Insane* (New York, 1982). For more on the medicalization of outsiders, see Mosse, *Nationalism and Sexuality,* esp. ch. 6.

32. Sander L. Gilman, "Jews and Mental Illness: Medical Metaphors, Anti-Semitism and the Jewish Response," *Journal of the History of the Behavioral Sciences* 20 (1984): 153. See also Sander Gilman, *The Jew's Body* (New York and London, 1991).

33. Mosse, *Nationalism and Sexuality,* 139, 140.

34. Max Nordau, *Zionistische Schriften* (Cologne and Leipzig, 1909), 379. The Second Zionist Congress met in Basel in 1898.

35. "Das Kaffeehaus-Judentum," *Jüdische Turnerzeitung* 2 (May–June 1910): 74.

36. Gilman, "Jews and Mental Illness," 154.

37. Helmut Jenzsch, *Jüdische Figuren in deutschen Bühnentexten des 18. Jahrhunderts* (Hamburg, 1971), 151.

38. Ernst Michael Jovy, "Deutsche Jugendbewegung und Nationalsozialismus" (Inaugural dissertation, University of Cologne, 1952), 223.

39. Eberhard Jäckel and Alex Kuhn, eds., *Hitler: Sämtliche Aufzeichnungen, 1905–1924* (Stuttgart, 1980), 195–96.

40. Mosse, *Nationalism and Sexuality,* ch. 5.

41. For these and other examples, see Mosse, *German Jews Beyond Judaism,* esp. ch. 3.

42. Berthold Litzmann, speech of 26 November 1914, in *Ernst von Wildenbruch und der nationale Gedanke* (Berlin, 1914), 10.

43. Mosse, *German Jews Beyond Judaism,* ch. 3.

44. James J. Sheehan, *German Liberalism in the Nineteenth Century* (Chicago, 1978), 107; Jacob Auerbach, "Lessing und Mendelssohn," in Sigismund Stern, *Einladungsschrift zu der öffentlichen Prüfung der Bürger und Real-Schule der Israelitischen Gemeinde* (Frankfurt am Main, 1867), 57.

CHAPTER 10. GERMAN JEWS AND LIBERALISM
IN RETROSPECT (PP. 146–160)

1. See G. L. Mosse, *German Jews Beyond Judaism* (Bloomington, Ind., 1985).

2. Werner E. Mosse, *Liberal Europe* (London, 1974), ch. 5.

3. Theodor Schieder, *Das Deutsche Kaiserreich als Nationalstaat* (Köln-Opladen, 1961), 61.

4. Jacob Toury, *Die politischen Orientierungen der Juden in Deutschland. Von Jena bis Weimar*, Schriftenreihe wissenschaftlicher Abhandlungen des Leo Baeck Instituts 15 (Tübingen, 1966), 17, 19.

5. G. L. Mosse, *Masses and Man: Nationalist and Fascist Perceptions of Reality* (New York, 1980), ch. 13.

6. Leo Baeck, *Das Wesen des Judentums* (Frankfurt am Main, 1926), 90, 228, 232–33.

7. G. L. Mosse, *German Jews Beyond Judaism*, 56ff.

8. Ernst Bloch, *Auswahl aus seinen Schriften* (Frankfurt am Main, 1967), 158; Emilio Lussu, *Sul Partito d'Azione e gli altri* (Milan, 1968), 40.

9. See Georg Landauer, *Der Zionismus im Wandel dreier Jahrzehnte* (Tel-Aviv, 1957).

10. Ernest Hamburger, *Juden im öffentlichen Leben Deutschlands. Regierungsmitglieder, Beamte und Parlamentarier in der monarchischen Zeit 1848–1918*, Schriftenreihe wissenschaftlicher Abhandlungen des Leo Baeck Instituts 19 (Tübingen, 1968), 163.

11. Marjorie Lamberti, *Jewish Activism in Imperial Germany* (New Haven, 1978), 25, 37.

12. James J. Sheehan, *German Liberalism in the Nineteenth Century* (Chicago, 1978), 266; Lamberti, *Jewish Activism*, 118.

13. Kurt Sontheimer, *Thomas Mann und die Deutschen* (Frankfurt am Main, 1961), 77.

14. Arnold Paucker, *Der jüdische Abwehrkampf gegen Antisemitismus und Nationalsozialismus in den letzten Jahren der Weimarer Republik*, 2d ed., Hamburger Beiträge zur Zeitgeschichte Band IV (Hamburg, 1969), 91ff.; Ernest Hamburger and Peter Pulzer, "Jews as Voters in the Weimar Republic," *LBI Year Book* XXX (1985), 52ff.; Arnold Paucker, "Jewish Self-Defence," *Die Juden im Nationalsozialistischen Deutschland/The Jews in Nazi Germany 1933–1943*, ed. Arnold Paucker with Sylvia Gilchrist and Barbara Suchy, Schriftenreihe wissenschaftlicher Abhandlungen des Leo Baeck Instituts 45 (Tübingen, 1986), 58–60.

15. Wolfgang Hamburger, "The Reactions of Reform Jews to Nazi Rule," in Herbert A. Strauss and Kurt R. Grossmann, eds., *Gegenwart im Rückblick. Festgabe für die Jüdische Gemeinde zu Berlin 25 Jahr nach dem Neubeginn* (Heidelberg, 1970), 150–52, treats their commitment to Germany in excellent fashion, but does not address the problem of liberalism; Klaus J. Herrmann, "Weltanschauliche Aspekte der *Jüdischen Reformgemeinde* in Berlin," *Emuna* 9 (March-April 1974): 83–92, is the best and most thorough discussion of the post-First World War congregation to date.

16. Herrmann, "Weltanschauliche," 91.

17. On the *Reichsbund* as a forum for right-wing Jewish *Bünde* after 1933,

see G. L. Mosse, *Germans and Jews: The Right, the Left, and the Search for a "Third Force" in Pre-Nazi Germany* (New York, 1970), 105. There is need for an examination of the liberal potential that might exist here in contrast to German veterans' organizations.

18. Julius Jelsky, "Konfirmationspredigt," *Mitteilungen der Jüdischen Reformgemeinde* (hereafter *Mitteilungen*), 1 May 1931, 9.

19. Benno Gottschalk, "Religion und Politik," *Mitteilungen*, 1 July 1932, 11.

20. Karl Rosenthal, "Ernst Machen!," *Mitteilungen*, 15 February 1935, 23.

21. Kurt Loewenstein, "Die innerjüdische Reaktion auf die Krise der deutschen Demokratie," in *Entscheidungsjahr 1932. Zur Judenfrage in der Endphase der Weimarer Republik,* Schriftenreihe wissenschaftlicher Abhandlungen des Leo Baeck Instituts 13, ed. Werner E. Mosse with Arnold Paucker (Tübingen, 1966), 371.

22. *Zum Gedächtnis an Dr. Moritz Levin,* 13 December 1914, 9.

23. Rosenthal, "Ernst Machen!," 23.

24. *Mitteilungen,* 15 January 1935, 12.

25. Ibid., 15 January 1934, 10; Ibid., 15 September 1934, 11; on the importance of the Jewish Youth Movement for the hard-pressed Jewish youth in the Third Reich, see Werner T. Angress, *Generation zwischen Furcht und Hoffnung. Jüdische Jugend im Dritten Reich* (Hamburg, 1985).

26. Karl Rosenthal, "Im neuen Reich," *Mitteilungen,* 1 September 1933, 3.

27. Wilhelm Michel, "Was heisst: Ende des Liberalismus?" *Der Morgen* 8 (June 1932): 83.

28. Joseph Lehmann, "Judentum und Deutschtum," *Mitteilungen,* 1 July 1920.

29. Baeck, *Das Wesen,* 165; Leonard Baker, *Days of Sorrow and Pain: Leo Baeck and the Berlin Jews* (New York, 1978), 131.

30. Lutz Weltmann, "Zur Antigone-Aufführung des Kulturbundes," *Mitteilungen,* 14 April 1936, 36.

31. Hans Margolius, "Der Kulturbund Deutscher Juden," *Mitteilungen,* 15 August 1934, 6–7; Paul Rothkugel, "Zur geistigen Situation der Jüdischen Jugend," *Mitteilungen,* 10 May 1937, 56.

32. Manfred Swarsensky, "Liberale Bestimmung," *Die Gemeinschaft,* ed. by Liberale Synagoge Norden in Berlin, no. 21–22 (24 November 1934), 3–4.

33. Ibid., 4–5.

34. Heinrich Stern, "Abschied vom Neu-Aufbau," *Mitteilungen,* 10 September 1936, 96.

35. G. L. Mosse, *German Jews Beyond Judaism,* 78ff. See Herbert Freeden, "Kultur 'nur für Juden': 'Kulturkampf' in der jüdischen Presse in Nazideutschland," in *Juden im Nationalsozialistischen Deutschland,* 259–71.

36. G. L. Mosse, *German Jews Beyond Judaism,* 16, 80.

37. "Jüdischer Kulturbund: Intellectual Life of German Jewry," *The Manchester Guardian,* 15 October 1937, 316 (Wiener Library, London, clipping collection).

38. Joseph Lehmann, "Unsere Stellung," *Mitteilungen,* 1 May 1933, 2.

39. Joseph Lehmann, "Judentum und Deutschtum," *Mitteilungen,* 1 July 1920, 11.

40. Baeck, *Das Wesen,* 281.

41. Klaus Hornung, *Der Jungdeutsche Orden* (Düsseldorf, 1958), 99.

CHAPTER II. MAX NORDAU, LIBERALISM, AND
THE NEW JEW (PP. 161–175)

1. Max Nordau, *Degeneration* (New York, 1968), 5.
2. Ibid., 41.
3. Max Nordau, *Menschen und Menschliches von heute* (Berlin, 1915), 329.
4. Erwin H. Ackerknecht, *Kurze Geschichte der Psychiatrie* (Stuttgart, 1957), 52.
5. Hans-Peter Söder, "A Tale of Dr. Jekyll and Mr. Hyde? Max Nordau and the Problem of Degeneracy," in Rudolf Käser and Vera Pohland, eds., *Disease and Medicine in Modern German Cultures* (Ithaca, 1990), 61, 62.
6. Nordau, *Degeneration*, 324.
7. Ibid., 18.
8. Hans-Peter Söder, "Disease and Health as Contexts of Modernity: Max Nordau as a Critic of Fin de Siècle Modernism," *German Studies Review* (Fall 1991), 476.
9. Sander Gilman, *The Jew's Body* (New York, 1991), 52. I am greatly indebted to Sander Gilman's pioneering work.
10. *Max Nordau's Zionistische Schriften*, ed. Zionistisches Aktionskomitee (Köln, 1909), 380.
11. Max Nordau, *Degeneration*, 541.
12. Anson Rabinbach, *The Human Motor: Energy, Fatigue and the Origins of Modernity* (New York, 1990), 167.
13. Jacques Ulmann, *De La Gymnastique aux Sports Modernes* (Paris, 1965), 220.
14. Horst Überhorst, *Geschichte der Leibesübungen* (Berlin, 1980), 3:341.
15. M. Jastrowitz, "Muskeljuden und Nervenjuden," *Jüdische Turnerzeitung* (1908), 35.
16. *Max Nordau's Zionistische Schriften*, 386.
17. Ulmann, *De la Gymnastique*, 336.
18. Nordau, *Menschen und Menschliches*, 13.
19. *Max Nordau's Zionistische Schriften*, 386.
20. Ibid., 384.
21. Ibid., 383.
22. Ibid., 380–81.
23. Gustav Kohn, "Die Turnerbewegung und der Jüdische Student," *Jüdische Turnerzeitung* 12 (1911): 151.
24. *Stenographisches Protocoll über die Verhandlungen des V. Zionisten Kongresses in Basel* (Wien, 1901), 126.
25. Shmuel Almog, *Zionism and History* (New York, 1987), 109.
26. G. L. Mosse, "Introduction" to Nordau, *Degeneration*, xxiii; see also the discussion of Nordau's liberalism, xvii–xxi.
27. Paul Wendling, *Health, Race and German Politics Between National Unification and Nazism, 1870–1945* (Cambridge, 1989), 31.
28. *Max Nordau's Zionistische Schriften*, 218.
29. Max Nordau, *Der Sinn der Geschichte* (Berlin, 1908), 465.
30. Almog, *Zionism*, 56.
31. G. L. Mosse, "Introduction," xxvi.
32. Hans Kohn, *Martin Buber* (Köln, 1961), 41.

33. Schmuel Hugo Bergmann, *Tagebücher und Briefe,* ed. Miriam Samburski (Königstein/Ts., 1985), vol. 1, 1909–1948, 132.

34. Ute Frevert, *Ehrenmänner, Das Duell in der bürgerlichen Gesellschaft* (Munich, 1991), passim.

35. Leon Simon, *Ahad Ha-Am, Asher Ginsberg* (Philadelphia, 1960), 167.

36. Pierre Birnbaum, *Anti-Semitism in France* (Oxford, 1992), 165–66.

37. Martin Buber, *Die Jüdische Bewegung* (Berlin, 1920), 14.

38. Martin Buber, "Unser Nationalismus," *Der Jude* 2 (April–May 1917): 3.

39. Nordau, *Menschen und Menschliches,* 282.

40. Erich Burin, "Das Kaffeehaus Judentum," *Jüdische Turnerzeitung* 11 (May–June 1910): 75.

41. See Steven E. Aschheim, *Brothers and Strangers* (Madison, 1982), 87.

42. Arthur Herzberg, *The Zionist Idea* (New York, 1969), 236.

43. Nordau, *Degeneration,* 321.

44. Herzberg, *The Zionist Idea,* 236.

45. Anita Shapira, "Reality and Ethos: Attitudes towards Power in Zionism," in Ruth Kozodoy, David Sidorsky, Kalman Sultanik, eds., *Vision Confronts Reality* (Rutherford, N.J., 1989), 99.

46. *Max Nordau's Zionistische Schriften,* 51.

47. Ibid., 298.

48. Ibid., 269.

49. Anita Shapira, "Reality and Ethos," 72.

50. Vladimir Jabotinsky, *The War and the Jews* (New York, 1942), 190.

51. Max Nordau, *Zionism: Conditions of Success and Causes of Failure* (London: New Zionist Organization of Britain, 1923), 9.

52. Nordau, *Menschen und Menschliches,* 60.

53. Ibid., 64.

54. Ibid., 53.

55. Nordau, *Menschen und Menschliches,* 82.

56. *Max Nordau's Zionistische Schriften,* 292.

CHAPTER 12. GERSHOM SCHOLEM AS A GERMAN JEW
(PP. 176–192)

1. "With Gershom Scholem: An Interview" (Spring 1975), in Werner J. Dannhäuser, ed., *On Jews and Judaism in Crisis* (New York, 1976), 20. I want to thank in particular David Sorkin for sharing his thoughts on Scholem and the German tradition with me.

2. For Scholem's supposedly Goethean definition of symbolism, see Moshe Idel, *Kabbalah, New Perspectives* (New Haven, 1986), 218.

3. Gershom Scholem, "Identifizierung und Distanz. Ein Rückblick," *Eranos Jahrbuch* 48 (1979): 466.

4. Gershom Scholem, "Leo Baeck Lecture, 1959," quoted in Henry Pachter, "Gershom Scholem: Towards a Mastermyth," *Salmagundi* 13 (Winter 1978): 17.

5. Gershom Scholem, *Walter Benjamin—die Geschichte einer Freundschaft* (Frankfurt am Main, 1975), 140.

6. "With Gershom Scholem: An Interview," 12, 13.

7. Gershom Scholem, "Politik der Mystik," *Jüdische Rundschau* (17 July

1934): 1; Hannah Weiner, "Gershom Scholem and the Young Judäa Youth Group in Berlin. 1913–1918," *Studies in Zionism* 4 (Spring 1984): 29–42.

8. Gershom Scholem, "Laienpredigt," *Die Blau-Weiss Brille* (1915): n.p.

9. "With Gershom Scholem: An Interview," *Jews and Judaism in Crisis* 19; Gershom Scholem, *Von Berlin nach Jerusalem* (Frankfurt am Main, 1977), 259.

10. Gershom Scholem, *Briefe an Werner Kraft* (Frankfurt am Main, 1986), 31.

11. Alexander Altmann, "Gershom Scholem (1897–1982)," *Proceedings of the American Academy of Jewish Research* 51 (1984): 4–5.

12. Arthur Herzberg, "Gershom Scholem as a Zionist and Believer," in Harold Bloom, ed., *Gershom Scholem* (New York, 1987), 197. Here also his supposedly romantic nationalism is once more emphasized.

13. David Myers, "The Scholem-Kurzweil Debate and Modern Jewish Historiography," *Modern Judaism* 6 (October 1986): 266.

14. David Biale, *Gershom Scholem, Kabbalah and Counter-History* (Cambridge, Mass., 1979), 75ff.

15. Gershom Scholem, *Major Trends in Jewish Mysticism* (New York, 1941), 24.

16. Gershom Scholem, *Über einige Grundbegriffe des Judentums* (Frankfurt am Main, 1970), 109.

17. Maurice Friedman, "Interpreting Hasidim: The Buber-Scholem Controversy," *Yearbook of the Leo Baeck Institute* (1988), 33: 449–67.

18. G. L. Mosse, "The Influence of the Völkish Idea on German Jewry," *Germans and Jews* (New York, 1970), 85ff.

19. Biale, *Gershom Scholem*, 91.

20. Gershom Scholem, "Zum Verständnis der messianischen Idee im Judentum," *Judaica* (Frankfurt am Main, 1963), 1:114.

21. Ibid., 117.

22. David Sorkin, *The Transformation of German Jewry 1780–1840* (New York and Oxford, 1987), 16, 17; Klaus Vondung, *Die Apokalypse in Deutschland* (Munich, 1988), 167ff.

23. Gershom Scholem, "Jews and Germans," *Commentary* 36 (November 1966): 34.

24. "With Gershom Scholem: An Interview," 32.

25. Margret Kraul, *Das deutsche Gymnasium* (Frankfurt am Main, 1984), 54, 56ff.

26. *Blau-Weiss Brille* (1915): n.p.

27. Gershom Scholem, *Von Berlin nach Jerusalem* (Frankfurt am Main, 1977), 191.

28. "With Gershom Scholem: An Interview," 23.

29. Gershom Scholem, "Zionism—Dialectic of Continuity and Rebellion," in Ehud Ben Ezer, ed., *Unease in Zion* (New York, 1974), 275.

30. Quoted in Biale, *Gershom Scholem*, 181.

31. *Walter Benjamin, Gershom Scholem, Briefswechsel*, ed. Gershom Scholem (Frankfurt am Main, 1980), 87.

32. Walter Laqueur, *A History of Zionism* (New York, 1972), 251.

33. "The Statutes of Brit-Shalom," *Jewish-Arab Affairs*, occasional papers published by the Brit-Shalom Society (June 1931), 59. Elkana Margalit, "Binationalism: An Interpretation of Zionism 1941–1947," *Studies in Zionism* 1 (Autumn 1981): 275–312.

34. *Walter Benjamin Gershom Scholem Briefwechsel,* 243.

35. Quoted in Paul R. Mendes-Flohr, ed., *A Land of Two Peoples: Martin Buber on Jews and Arabs* (New York, 1983), 97.

36. Laqueur, *History,* 252.

37. Anita Shapira, *Berl: The Biography of a Socialist Zionist* (Cambridge, 1984), 171.

38. Schmuel Hugo Bergmann, *Tagebücher und Briefe,* ed. Miriam Sambursky (Frankfurt am Main, 1985), 1:394.

39. Ibid., 392.

40. Robert Weltsch, *An der Wende des Modernen Judentums* (Tübingen, 1972), 264; Hillel Kieval, *The Making of Czech Jewry* (New York, 1988), 149–53, 163–64.

41. *Aliyah Hadasha Statement of Policy* (Tel Aviv, 1946), n.p.

42. Georg Landauer, *Der Zionismus im Wandel der Zeiten* (Tel Aviv, 1957), 451.

43. Ibid., 241.

44. Bergmann, *Tagebücher,* 2:322.

45. Ibid., 409.

46. "With Gershom Scholem: An Interview," 32–33.

47. Henry Pachter, "Gershom Scholem," 15.

48. Gershom Scholem, *Von Berlin nach Jerusalem,* 72; Gershom Scholem, "Israel and the Diaspora," in Dannhäuser, ed., *On Jews and Judaism in Crisis,* 249.

Acknowledgments

"National Anthems: The Nation Militant," from *From Ode to Anthem,* ed. Grimm and Hermand, copyright 1989, reprinted by permission of the University of Wisconsin Press, Madison, pp. 86–99.

"National Self-Representation during the 1930s in Europe and the United States," from *L'Estetica Della Politica Europa e America Negli Anni Trenta,* ed. Maurizio Vaudagna, 1989, reprinted by permission of Gius. Laterza & Figli, Rome, pp. 3–23.

"Community in the Thought of Nationalism, Fascism, and the Radical Right," from *Community as a Social Ideal,* ed. Eugene Kamenka, 1982, reprinted by permission of Hodder and Stoughton Ltd., Sevenoaks, Kent, pp. 27–42.

"Political Style and Political Theory: Totalitarian Democracy Revisited," from *Totalitarian Democracy and After,* 1984, reprinted by permission of The Israel Academy of Sciences and Humanities and the Magnes Press, Jerusalem, pp. 167–176.

"Fascism and the French Revolution," reprinted by permission of *The Journal of Contemporary History,* Vol. 24 (January 1989), © 1989 Sage Publications Ltd., London, pp. 5–26.

"The Political Culture of Futurism," reprinted by permission of *The Journal of Contemporary History,* Vol. 25 (July 1990), © 1990 Sage Publications Ltd., London, pp. 253–268.

"Book Burning and the Betrayal of German Intellectuals," reprinted by permission of *New German Critique,* Vol. 31 (Winter 1984), pp. 143–155.

"The Jews and the Civic Religion of Nationalism," reprinted by permission from *The Impact of Western Nationalisms,* ed. Jehuda Reinharz and George L. Mosse, © 1992 Sage Publications Ltd., London, pp. 319–329.

"Jewish Emancipation: Between *Bildung* and Respectability," from *The Jewish Response to German Culture,* ed. Jehuda Reinharz and Walter Schatzberg, © 1985, reprinted by permission of University Press of New England, Hanover, N.H., pp. 1–16.

"Jews and Liberalism in Retrospect," reprinted by permission from the *Year Book XXXII* (1987) of the Leo Baeck Institute, ed. Arnold Paucker, pp. xiii–xxv.

"Max Nordau: Liberalism and the New Jew," reprinted by permission from *The Journal of Contemporary History,* Vol. 27 (October 1992), © 1992 Sage Publications Ltd., London, pp. 565–581.

"Gershom Scholem as a German Jew," reprinted by permission from *Modern Judaism,* Vol. 10, No. 2 (May 1990), pp. 117–133.

Index

Printed in the United States
6700

9 780874 516364